Supply Chain - Recent Advances and New Perspectives in the Industry 4.0 Era

Edited by Tamás Bányai, Ágota Bányai and Ireneusz Kaczmar

Published in London, United Kingdom

Supply Chain - Recent Advances and New Perspectives in the Industry 4.0 Era
http://dx.doi.org/10.5772/intechopen.98060
Edited by Tamás Bányai, Ágota Bányai and Ireneusz Kaczmar

Contributors
Ping-Kuo Chen, Qiu-Rui He, Xiang Huang, Mohammad Akhtar, Thuso Mphela, Christopher J. Savage, Alejandro Gutierrez, Andre T. Mayounga, FathyElsayed Youssef Abdelmajied, Erica Varese, Maria Chiara Cesarani, Magdalena Wojnarowska, Shahrin Nasir, Paul-Eric Dossou, Valentin Verdier, Alan Ogor, Enna Hirata, Daisuke Watanabe, Maria Lambrou, Ágota Bányai, Arthur Mzwandile Gonyora, Pfano Mashau

First published in London, United Kingdom, 2022 by IntechOpen
IntechOpen is the global imprint of INTECHOPEN LIMITED, registered in England and Wales, registration number: 11086078, 5 Princes Gate Court, London, SW7 2QJ, United Kingdom

British Library Cataloguing-in-Publication Data
A catalogue record for this book is available from the British Library

Additional hard and PDF copies can be obtained from orders@intechopen.com

Supply Chain - Recent Advances and New Perspectives in the Industry 4.0 Era
Edited by Tamás Bányai, Ágota Bányai and Ireneusz Kaczmar
p. cm.
Print ISBN 978-1-80355-372-6
Online ISBN 978-1-80355-373-3
eBook (PDF) ISBN 978-1-80355-374-0

For EU product safety concerns:
IN TECH d.o.o., Prolaz Marije Krucifikse Kozulić 3, 51000 Rijeka, Croatia,
info@intechopen.com or visit our website at intechopen.com.

Meet the editors

Tamás Bányai received a master's degree in 1993 and a Ph.D. in 1999 from the University of Miskolc, Hungary, where he is currently an associate professor. He has more than twenty-five years of teaching and research experience in the design and control of materials handling systems and supply chain management, with special emphasis on heuristic optimization of large-scale systems. He has published more than 150 research papers, book chapters, and conference proceedings. He has been a member and manager of more than fifty national and international R&D projects. Away from academia, Dr. Bányai's other interests include playing the piano and taking photographs.

Ágota Bányai was awarded an MSc in Mechanical Engineering from the University of Miskolc, Hungary, in 1993, and a Ph.D. in Engineering Sciences from the same institution in 1999. She is currently an associate professor at the Institute of Logistics, University of Miskolc. She has more than twenty years of teaching and research experience in the design and control of logistic systems and supply chain management, with a special emphasis on purchasing and distribution. She has worked in academia for nearly twenty-five years and has published more than 100 research papers, book chapters, and conference proceedings.

Ireneusz Kaczmar is an IT engineer with a master's degree in Economics. In 2011, he obtained a Ph.D. in Economics at the Faculty of Management and Social Communication, Jagiellonian University, Poland. He is currently an associate professor, teaching classes in economics and management at the Institute of Technical Sciences, East European State University, Poland. He is interested in quantitative research in management and the application of computer simulations in the industry. He has about twenty years of teaching and research experience in the design of simulation models and multi-criteria decision-making systems. He is the author of many international scientific articles.

Contents

Preface IX

Chapter 1 1
Industry 4.0 and Its Implications: Concept, Opportunities, and Future Directions
by FathyElsayed Youssef Abdelmajied

Chapter 2 25
Enabling Sustainable Supply Chains in the Industrial 4.0 Era
by Thuso Mphela, Christopher J. Savage and Alejandro Gutierrez

Chapter 3 41
Industry 4.0: The Tenets of the Next Generation of Supply Chain Management
by Andre T. Mayounga

Chapter 4 53
Application of Internet of Things in the Movement of Goods at Customs Level during Covid-19 Pandemic
by Erica Varese, Maria Chiara Cesarani and Magdalena Wojnarowska

Chapter 5 67
Industry 4.0 Technologies Impact on Supply Chain Sustainability
by Mohammad Akhtar

Chapter 6 85
Open Innovation Strategies on New Product and Process Development Prospects: A Case of the Automotive Component Manufacturers in South Africa
by Arthur Mzwandile Gonyora and Pfano Mashau

Chapter 7 107
Shipping Digitalization and Automation for the Smart Port
by Enna Hirata, Daisuke Watanabe and Maria Lambrou

Chapter 8 129
Enhancing the Resilience of Sustainable Supplier Management through Combination with Lean and Audit
by Ping-Kuo Chen, Qiu-Rui He and Xiang Huang

Chapter 9 **153**
Production Systems Performance Optimization through Human/Machine Collaboration
by Paul-Eric Dossou, Valentin Verdier and Alan Ogor

Chapter 10 **173**
Supply Chain: A Modeling-Based Approach for Cyber-Physical Systems
by Ágota Bányai

Chapter 11 **203**
Sustainable and Efficient City Logistics
by Shahrin Nasir

Preface

This book offers a selection of chapters in the field of supply chain management in the era of Industry 4.0, promoting new research results in the field. It is written by experts from Botswana, China, Egypt, Greece, Hungary, Ireland, Italy, Japan, Malaysia, Poland, South Africa, the United Kingdom, and the United States. The transformation of conventional manufacturing and service processes into cyber-physical systems using Industry 4.0 technologies influences the complexity of connected supply chain solutions. The book covers eleven topics determined by the theoretical and practical aspects of supply chain solutions based on Industry 4.0 technologies.

Chapter 1, "Industry 4.0 and Its Implications: Concept, Opportunities, and Future Directions", introduces the framework of Industry 4.0 and discusses the drivers, potential effects, and obstacles of the Industry 4.0 paradigm.

Chapter 2, "Enabling Sustainable Supply Chains in the Industrial 4.0 Era", focuses on the potential of Industry 4.0 technologies. As the chapter shows, these technologies offer solutions for environmentally and commercially sustainable processes.

Chapter 3, "Industry 4.0: The Tenets of the Next Generation of Supply Chain Management", describes the supply web concept and its distinctive tenets focusing on vertical, diagonal, and horizontal dimensions.

Chapter 4, "Application of Internet of Things in the Movement of Goods at Customs Level during Covid-19 Pandemic", identifies potential governmental solutions at the customs level for improving customs operations and enhancing their efficiency and effectiveness in a pandemic situation.

Chapter 5, "Industry 4.0 Technologies Impact on Supply Chain Sustainability", describes the most important Industry 4.0 technologies including big data analytics, artificial intelligence, machine learning, Internet of Things, sensors, blockchain technology, robotic systems, cloud computing, cyber-physical systems, additive manufacturing, virtual reality, augmented reality, and autonomous vehicles and drones and focuses on their impact on sustainability, efficiency, cost reduction, transparency, traceability, and collaboration.

Chapter 6, "Open Innovation Strategies on New Product and Process Development Prospects: A Case of the Automotive Component Manufacturers in South Africa", discusses potential open innovation practices and their impact on the processes of automotive component manufacturers focusing on sustainable new product development.

Chapter 7, "Shipping Digitalization and Automation for the Smart Port", describes a potential framework for shipping digitalization and port automation. It presents a case study to illustrate the advantages of blockchain technology applications.

Chapter 8, “Enhancing the Resilience of Sustainable Supplier Management through Combination with Lean and Audit”, shows how to pull production and employee involvement under lean practices to strengthen supplier management robustness and enhance the prevention ability of resilience in dealing with opportunistic behavior. It also highlights how the combination of lean practices with an audit mechanism strengthens the practice effect of pull production and employee involvement.

Chapter 9, “Production Systems Performance Optimization through Human/ Machine Collaboration”, chapter presents potential robotic displacement solutions in production systems. It also proposes solutions for human-machine interaction problems.

Chapter 10, “Supply Chain: A Modeling-Based Approach for Cyber-Physical Systems”, focuses on the optimization of green supply chain solutions using Industry 4.0 technologies. The mathematical model and the computational results validate that Industry 4.0 technologies can improve the performance of supply chain processes.

Finally, Chapter 11, “Sustainable and Efficient City Logistics”, describes the main trends, impacts, and challenges of city logistics solutions. It also discusses the importance of smart technologies, with a focus on last-mile delivery operations.

The aim of this book is to help students as well as managers and researchers to understand and appreciate the concept, design, and implementation of supply chain solutions in the Industry 4.0 era.

The editors thank the chapter authors for their scientific contributions. The chapters were edited and published following a rigorous selection process. We also wish to thank and acknowledge the many individuals who helped us throughout the editorial process that made this book possible.

Tamás Bányai and Ágota Bányai
Institute of Logistics,
University of Miskolc,
Miskolc, Hungary

Ireneusz Kaczmar
Institute of Technical Sciences,
East European State University in Przemyśl,
Przemyśl, Poland

Chapter 1

Industry 4.0 and Its Implications: Concept, Opportunities, and Future Directions

FathyElsayed Youssef Abdelmajied

Abstract

This chapter aims to analyze the Industry 4.0 framework, identify the definition and drivers of the Industry 4.0 paradigm, discuss its potential effect, and determine obstacles of the Industry 4.0. For the research methodology, a critical literature review is performed, we relied on the recent studies related to industry 4.0. Findings – This study concluded that Industry 4.0 describes a future production system's vision; it is an inevitable revolution and radical change, covering a wide range of innovative technologies, and all sectors. Industry 4.0 brings significant advantages to organizations, including real-time data analysis, increased visibility, autonomous monitoring, enhanced productivity, and competitiveness. The key features of Industry 4.0 are collaboration and integration of schemes, both horizontal and vertical. Innovation performs an essential role in organizations, sectors, countries. Industry 4.0 has enormous potential effect in many areas, and its application will have an impact across transforming the work environment. Industry 4.0 leads to potentials in three dimensions of sustainability. The KUKA corporation is an application for industry 4.0, for instance, smart factories, M-2-M, intelligent robots, etc., these technologies help industry 4.0 to separate rapidly. In contrast, there are some barriers, to implementing Industry 4.0 for example financial constraints, technical competency, organizational restraints.

Keywords: industrial revolutions, components of industry 4.0, impacts of industry 4.0, industry 4.0 drivers, barriers of industry 4.0

1. Introduction

Issues related to Industry 4.0 are constantly discussed among researchers, entrepreneurs, representatives of government agencies, and public organizations. Specifically, the impacts of the Industry 4.0 paradigm in the global and national economies, individual industries, employment, and capital markets are attracting more and more attention from economists. The global industrial environment has transformed dramatically in recent years as a result of technological advances and inventions. Industry 4.0 can be compared to three industrial revolutions that happened in the previous centuries and represent the most significant disruptive shifts in manufacturing as a result of technology advancements [1].

The advent of the steam engine accelerated the First Industrial Revolution, which began in Britain in the middle of the 18th century. The Second Industrial Revolution arose in Europe and the United States in the second mid-nineteenth century. This revolution had characterized by mass manufacturing and the substitution of chemical and electrical energy for steam. Many technologies and mechanization had been developed to meet the increased demand, allowing productivity to increase [2]. The Third Industrial Revolution was sparked by the creation of the Integrated Circuit (microchip). Using electronics and information technology to accomplish increased automation in manufacturing is a significant characteristic of this revolution, which arose in many industrialized countries around the world in the later years of the twentieth century [1].

Every industrial revolution centered around boosting productivity. The first three industrial revolutions had a significant impact on industrial operations, allowing for increased productivity and efficiency by utilizing innovative technological breakthroughs, such as steam engines, electricity, and digital technology [3]. Industry 4.0, which could ultimately be referred to as the fourth industrial revolution, is a highly complex framework that has been commonly debated and discovered. It has a significant impact on the industrial sector because it introduces relevant improvements related to smart and future factories. This developing Industry 4.0 concept is an umbrella term for a new industrial paradigm that includes Cyber-Physical Systems (CPS), the Internet of Things (IoT), the Internet of Services (IoS), Robotics, Big Data, Cloud Manufacturing, and Augmented Reality, etc. [4].

The adoption of these technologies, which will bring together the digital and physical worlds through embracing a set of future industrial developments, is essential in the development of further smart industrial processes. This adoption includes devices, machines, production modules, and products that can exchange information and control each other independently, resulting in a smart manufacturing environment [5]. This new approach will allow the improvement of productivity and efficiency, carrying enormous potential effects, and it will support a set of economic and social opportunities among the companies that are adopting this new manufacturing paradigm [1].

This chapter intends to provide clear insight into the current developments within Industry 4.0 phenomenon, due to the inconsistency within the existing literature, some stress positive effects of Industry 4.0, while others, negative ones. As a result, the purpose of our research is to provide a full explanation of the Industry 4.0 paradigm, as well as to determine whether or not it is appropriate for businesses, stockholders, and countries to adopt this new approach. This chapter gives a review of Industry 4.0 and definitions in the literature, as well as introduces a brief on Industry 4.0's main components. Additionally, this chapter's research methodology was based on papers related to Industry 4.0, which are the most recent and cited references. As well as this study differs from past studies in several aspects, as shown in 1) It conducts a comprehensive survey of all Fourth Industrial Revolution technologies or applications, whereas earlier literature focused on one or a few technologies. 2) It performs a case study of KUKA Corporation, a pioneer company in the manufacturing technologies and applications of the Fourth Industrial Revolution.

Thus, this chapter is structured in seven sections. After this introduction about the Industry 4.0 phenomenon. Section 2 answers the question "What is the industry

4.0?", presenting two points: an overview or background about Industry 4.0, and provides a comprehensive definition of this concept, its visions. The key Industry 4.0 technology enablers or components of Industry 4.0 characteristics are described in Section 3, which is divided into ten parts. The characteristics of Industry 4.0 state in Section 4. Section 5 provides an analysis of the impacts and influence of this new industrial paradigm: industrial sector, business models and markets, work environment, work skills, economy and sustainability, the value chains, and supply chains. While Section 6 presents the key drivers and obstacles or barriers of the Industry 4.0 concept; also, this part presents a pioneering experience in implementing the applications of the Fourth Industrial Revolution technology "KUKA corporation." Finally, Section 7 draws the main conclusions and findings of the Industry 4.0 vision and implications.

2. What is industry 4.0?

2.1 An overview of industry 4.0

There have been three earlier industrial revolutions that have resulted in a transformation in manufacturing patterns: mechanization via water and steam power, mass production in assembly lines, and automating through computer and information technology [6].

The first industrial revolution *(Industry 1.0)* was developed in the United Kingdom at the end of 18th century with the advent of water and steam power and mechanization of production. It was the most significant advancement in human productivity, which considerably aided mechanical production and greatly improved agriculture and trade. Where steam engines could be used for power. Developments such as the steamship or the steam-powered locomotive brought about further massive changes because humans and goods could move great distances in fewer hours [4]. Then, it was followed by the second one (*Industry 2.0*) at the beginning of 19th century which introduced the electrically powered machines and assembly line production, which is described as the period when mass manufacturing became the dominant style of production in general. The introduction of railways into the industrial system was assisted by steel mass manufacturing, which in turn assisted mass production [7]. The third industrial revolution (*Industry 3.0*) took a place in the 1970s by adopting electronics and devices within the machines, which led to developing automation and robots within the manufacturing process. Industry 3.0 developed with the introduction of the Digital Revolution, which is more well-known than Industry 1.0 and 2.0, since most people today are familiar with industries that rely on digital technology in production [4].

The *Fourth Industrial Revolution* is presently being implemented. This is also known as "Industry 4.0," and it is defined by the use of information and communication technology in the industry. It is based on the Third Industrial Revolution's advancements. Production systems using computer technology are enhanced by a network link and, in a sense, have a digital twin on the Internet. These enable communication with other systems as well as the production of data about themselves. This is the next phase in the automation of production [8].

All systems are connected, resulting in "cyber-physical production systems" and, as a result, smart factories, in which production systems, components, and people interact through a network and production is almost autonomous. When these enablers are combined, Industry 4.0 has the potential to offer some amazing improvements in manufacturing environments. Machines that can foresee faults and initiate maintenance operations on their own, for example, or self-organized logistics that adapt to unexpected changes in production are examples (**Figure 1**) [9].

It also has the ability to alter people's working habits. Individuals can be drawn into smarter networks by Industry 4.0, which might lead to more efficient working. The manufacturing environment's digitization provides for more flexible means of providing the appropriate information to the right person at the right time. Maintenance personnel may now receive equipment documentation and service history more quickly and at the point of use, thanks to the growing usage of digital devices inside factories and out in the field. Maintenance personnel prefer to spend their time addressing issues rather than waste time looking for technical knowledge [10].

In a summary, Industry 4.0 is a game-changer in the industrial world. Manufacturing will alter as a result of digitization, including how things are manufactured and delivered, as well as how products are maintained and enhanced. As a result, it may legitimately claim to be the start of the fourth industrial revolution. Industry 4.0 is presently taking shape and its supporting technologies, such as the Internet of Things (IoT) and Cloud Manufacturing (CM), are, nevertheless, poorly defined, and under-researched.

2.2 Definition industry 4.0

Industry 4.0 is better known as the fourth industrial revolution and describes a future production system's vision. The idea of Industry 4.0 was established by a group of professionals from several professions (such as business, politics, and academia) as part of an endeavor to integrate all manufacturing industries systems to achieve sustainability. The German government initially officially approved and implemented industry 4.0 for supporting automation in manufacturing, and for boosting German competitiveness in the manufacturing industry. Essentially, as a result of Industry 4.0, operations and manufactures will become further efficient and less expensive. These are accomplished through the simple interchange of information, integrated control of industrial goods and equipment, which work synchronously

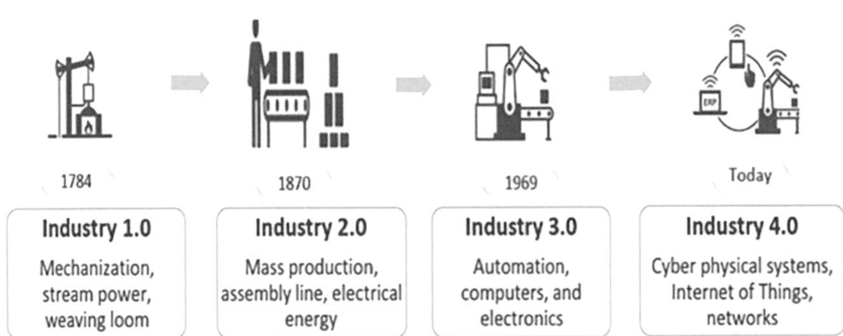

Figure 1.
Represents a graphic illustration of the industrial revolutions overall. Source: Constructed by the author.

and intelligently in interoperability [11]. However, several researchers have different perceptions of the meaning of industry 4.0.

Kagermann, et al. [12] stress that industry 4 utilizes the power of communications technology and innovative inventions to boost the development of the manufacturing industry. Corresponding to Kagermann et al., the primary features of the industry 4.0 idea are characterized by three aspects: (1) horizontal integration, (2) vertical integration, and (3) end-to-end digital integration of engineering. Qin, Liu, and Grosvenor [13] emphasize that industry 4.0 encourages manufacturing efficiency by collecting data, making correct decisions. By using the most advanced technologies, the procedures will be easier. The interoperability operating ability to ensure a stable manufacturing environment. This overall consciousness gives Industry 4.0 the most important aspect of artificial intelligent functions.

The Fourth Industrial Revolution, 4IR, or Industry 4.0 conceptualizes rapid change to technology, industries, and societal patterns and processes in the 21st century due to increasing interconnectivity and smart automation [14]. Schwab pointed out that Industry 4.0 is one of the most important concepts in the development of global industry and the world economy, he accentuates that, Industry 4.0 is differentiated by a few characteristics of new technologies, the improvement in technologies is bringing significant effects on industries, economies, and governments' development plans [15]. Industry 4.0 also denotes a social, political, and economic transformation from the digital age of the late 1990s and early 2000s to an era of embedded connection marked by widespread technological use (e.g., a metaverse). That, in comparison to humans' inherent senses and industrial ability alone, we have constructed and are entering an augmented social reality [16].

Wang et al., [17] defined the fourth industrial revolution as the modern and more sophisticated machines and tools with advanced software and networked sensors that can be used to plan, predict, adjust, and control the societal outcome and business models. Thus, Industry 4.0 is an advantage to stay competitive in any industry. Also, Industry 4.0 can be perceived as a strategy for being competitive in the future. It is focused on the optimization of value chains due to autonomously controlled and dynamic production [18]. Furthermore, industry 4.0 is possible to indicate three future-relevant themes related to it, such as: dealing with complexity, capacity for innovation, and flexibility [19].

According to the concepts above, the majority of the researchers considered Cyber-Physical Systems (CPS), Internet of Things (IoT), Industrial Internet, and other topics to be part of Industry 4.0. Numerous authors also emphasized Industry 4.0 on the cost and profitability of recently created high-tech information and intelligent services. According to previous research on Industry 4.0, the early focus was mostly on the industrial manufacturing sector, but many industries are now adopting Industry 4.0, including automotive, engineering, chemical, and electronics. As a result, Industry 4.0 is aggregating existing ideas into a different value chain that leads to an improvement in transforming entire value chains of goods life cycles while developing innovative products in manufacturing, involving the connection of systems and things that create self-organizing and dynamic control within the organization.

Industry 4.0, often referred to as the fourth industrial revolution, is the vision or scenario of a future production process characterized by new levels of controlling, organizing, and transforming the entire value chain with the life cycle of products through three types of effective integration: horizontal, vertical, and end-to-end engineering integration, resulting in increased productivity and flexibility, the industry 4.0 leads to cost optimization and reduction [11]. The Cyber-Physical Systems (CPS), Internet of Things (IoT), artificial intelligence (AI), additive manufacturing, cloud computing, and other technologies are then combined to construct dynamic, real-time optimized, and self-organizing cross-company value networks. All of these components are necessary and integral to the futuristic Industry 4.0 concept.

3. Components of industry 4.0 and the key enabling technologies

Industry 4.0 is a complicated technical pattern characterized primarily by connection, integration, and industrial digitalization, highlighting the possibilities for integrating all components in a value-adding system. Digital manufacturing technology, network communication technology, computer technology, and automation technology are all included in this approach. Industry 4.0 technology breakthroughs are blurring the lines between the digital and physical worlds by merging human and machine agents, materials, products, production systems, and processes [20]. Industry 4.0 enables rapid technological advancements in a variety of areas; however, the emerging fourth industrial revolution is being shaped largely by the technical integration of Cyber-Physical Systems into manufacturing processes, as well as the use of the Internet of Things and Services in industrial processes [1]. As a result, this section gives a brief overview of each significant technology driver for Industry 4.0. It also is providing information on the basic components of Industry 4.0 or key technologies enablers for Industry 4.0, which consists of 10 components.

3.1 Cyber-physical system (CPS)

Cyber-Physical Systems (CPS) is the combination of computational and physical processes, which are essential components of Industry 4.0 implementations. They integrate imaging and control capabilities into the relevant systems. The ability of these systems to respond to any input generated is a key feature. They provide rapid control and verification of process feedback in order to generate predicted outputs. Bergera et al. (2016) defined cyber-physical sensor systems as part of cyberspace, special types of embedded systems, based on powerful software systems, enable integration in digital networks, and generate whole new system features [21]. Generally speaking, the evolution of a CPS is characterized by three phases. Identification technologies are included in first-generation CPS. Second-generation CPS is equipped with some sensors and actuators with a limited number of functions. In the third-generation CPS, data is kept and analyzed in addition to setting up the equipment. The CPS has many sensors and actuators and is meant to be network compatible. CPSs offer various features [19].

The CPS has several sensors and actuators and is meant to operate with a network. CPSs have features including quicker information access, preventative maintenance, pre-defined decision-making, and optimization processes. Also, CPS can boost consumers awareness and consciousness. Conversely, the CPS has certain security issues, which means that further usage will definitely result in increased dangers. It was pointed out that CPS equipment might cause disruptive societal changes since intelligent assistive or autonomous environments can cause mental illnesses, which can lead to bias toward new technology adoption and usage [21]. Cyber-Physical Systems have consisted of two key components: i) A virtual environment built through computer simulation of items and actions in the actual world, and ii) a network of objects and systems interacting with each other over the internet with a designated address [4].

3.2 Cloud systems (CS)

The term "cloud" is utilized for applications, for instance, remote services, color management, and performance benchmarking applications. It has taken remarkable attention from the IT community, and its role in other business areas will continue to grow. Machines, data management, and functionality will continue to transition away from traditional ways and toward cloud-based solutions as technology improves. The cloud enables significantly faster distribution than standalone systems, as well as quick upgrades, current performance models, and other delivery possibilities [19].

The industry has found a significant shift toward cloud solutions, which will continue to develop and represent a substantial challenge to traditional data storage methods. Cloud technology is the most basic online storage service that gives operational comfort with web-based apps that do not require any installation. Cloud computing refers to the process of storing all applications, programs, and data on a virtual server. It improves efficiency by guaranteeing those input suppliers, employees, and consumers have access to the same information at the same time [22]. Cloud Systems lower costs, simplify infrastructure, expand work areas, safeguards data, and allow for instant access to information. There are four types of the system, mainly: i) Public Cloud; ii) Private Cloud; iii) Hybrid Cloud (combination of public and private cloud); 4) Community Cloud (this refers to the co-operation of any service on the cloud with a few companies) [9].

Cloud systems are an excellent source of Big Data (which might be organized or unstructured) management solutions. Because traditional computers may not be capable of managing large amounts of data, using a cloud system to do the necessary analysis, would be much easier and more efficient. As a result, data analysis and cloud systems should be inescapable components of Industry 4.0. The integration of cloud-connected robots into everyday life, as well as their impact, is considerable [4].

3.3 Machine to machine (M2M) communication

Machine to machine (M2M), refers to the technology that allows direct communication between devices using any channel, wired or wireless. Machine-to-machine communication can include industrial instrumentation and personal communications [23]. M2M is also considered to be an essential component of Industry 4.0. Machine to machine (M2M) is a technology that allows devices to communicate directly with one another over any channel, wired or wireless. Machine-to-Machine Communication can include industrial instrumentation and personal networks. M2M is also considered to be an essential component of Industry 4.0. The apps are geared toward adding value to the enterprises by introducing alternative revenue streams and reducing operational costs [24].

Ackermann (2013) clearly states that M2M operations have to enable aspects with different networked organizations including i) Remote Service and Asset Information Management delivering, which provide information federation and lifecycle support. ii) Connected Vehicles, which creates relationships and interactions. iii) Smart Vending, which includes retail, supply chain, and associated sub-elements [4]. The M2M vision has raised a number of issues, including establishing smart settings, smart architecture, and a smart grid with wireless sensors, as well as developing a communication language between machines and humans, as well as between humans in different locations [23].

3.4 Internet of things and internet of services

The Internet of Things (IoT) is an emerging concept that combines various technologies and techniques, based on the interaction between physical things and the Internet. The advancement of technology in recent decades has enabled the Internet to be expanded into a new level known as "smart objects," which is the foundation of an IoT vision, for this, the novel pattern consists in awarding ordinary things with intelligence, permitting them not only to accumulate information and cooperate with their surroundings, but also to be interrelated with other items, communicating information, and conducted a preliminary via the Internet. The growing interest in this field, which is widely regarded as one of the primary drivers of Industry 4.0, has produced the development of a number of visions and definitions for (IoT) [1].

The Internet of Things (IoT) refers to the interconnection of physical devices, cars, buildings, and other entities that are equipped with electronics, software, sensors, actuators, and network connections to gather and share data to create a smart manufacturing environment, also known as a smart factory [25]. Additionally, the concept of "The Internet of Services (IoS)" takes a similar approach to IoT but applies it to services rather than physical assets. The Internet of Services (IoS) idea will open up new prospects for the service sector by providing a commercial and technological foundation for the construction of business networks between service providers and clients [4].

The expansion of IoT in industrial contexts and value chains will give several opportunities for users, manufacturers, and businesses, having a significant influence in a variety of industries. The Internet of Things is breaking new ground, with a slew of new applications emerging around three key pillars: i) process optimization; ii) resource optimization, and iii) the building of sophisticated autonomous systems. IoT technology will continue to evolve and spread, allowing objects to become smarter, more dependable, and autonomous, allowing for the supply of higher-value products and services [1]. On the other hand, the effectiveness of Industry 4.0 depends upon existing network infrastructure, the intelligence, and human knowledge embedded into the system [22].

3.5 Smart factories or smart manufacturing

Smart factories or Smart manufacturing is a type of manufacturing that aims to improve concept creation, production, and product interactions by moving away from traditional methods toward automated and digitized systems. It aims to take advantage of advanced information and manufacturing technologies in order to operate and produce fully flexible production at the highest speed required [6].

"Dark factories," "lights off factories," and "unmanned factories" are all terms used to describe smart factories, this system is integrated with the small intervention of human beings. The individual is entering into these systems mainly in the problem-solving stages. The concept known as Lights out (dark) or unmanned factories nowadays is an automation and autonomy enhanced methodologies including equipment used in factories that actively operate the production [4, 26]. The most famous characteristic of dark factories is that they do need no human power. In unmanned factories, there is not enough time to enter the plant from the raw material to the exit from the factory. That is to say that in these factories, production is carried out entirely with robotic systems [18]. It is self-evident that smart factories will have the characteristics and procedures required by the Fourth Industrial Revolution. And these processes, which are of great importance to our future of production. Furthermore, the essential activity for generating a smart factory running under Industry 4.0 is integrating different other components together, such as big data, CPS, cloud, IoT, M2M, etc. [4].

There are many challenges that determine the formation of smart factories, such as the availability of energy and its supply, the efficiency of the labor, and the availability of the technological infrastructure necessary to shift toward smart factories. On the other hand, these factories will have a negative impact on existing employment and increase unemployment rates [7].

3.6 Big data and data mining

Big data is being generated continuously by everything in environments. Every digital process and social media exchange produce data. Systems, sensors, and mobile devices transmit those. Big data is arriving from multiple sources at an alarming velocity, volume, and variety. To extract meaningful value from big data, there is a need for optimal processing power, analytics capabilities, in addition to information management skills [4]. An abundance of heterogeneous data abounds in the world around us. Without properly applying data mining technology, it appears impossible to make this atmosphere keenly intelligent. With today's automation, data mining can be supervised, unsupervised, or reinforcement learning. When executed in numerous layers in a hierarchical way, computer-assisted learning becomes more exact. Machine Learning is the process of automatically extracting features through supervised or unsupervised learning in a hierarchical fashion (ML) [27].

3.7 Intelligent robotics

Every day, new goods and systems emerge as a result of technological advancements. Flying automobiles, holographic television, and hundreds of electrical devices to be implanted into the human body are all possibilities [26]. Humanoid robots will be a part of everyday life in the not-too-distant future. Recent innovations have brought about skills that empower robots to control their environment. Artificial intelligence will contribute to the development of having robot teams cooperating and collaborating in achieving certain tasks defined for a specific purpose [28].

Implementing a collaborative robot in a factory will provide several benefits for the company, including i) preventing humans from performing repetitive, non-ergonomic, and dangerous work; ii) producing high-quality products with favorable cost–benefit ratios while also increasing productivity; and iii) increasing competitiveness in comparison to countries with cheap labor [29]. When a robot is used in a productive process, the benefits of the robot utilization are combined with the effort of an operator. There is no teamwork between the man and the robot on the first level. The workplace is totally shared between the man and the robot at the final level [30].

3.8 Augmented reality and simulation

Simulation, the data obtained and processed from big data and cloud systems can be used as a feed to a virtual model to evaluate all possible scenarios related to the product design, development, and production. Simulation is used broadly in business models to leverage the available real-time data and simulate the actual working world in a virtual ecosystem. Process testing and optimization through simulation permit people to decrease business changeover, risk, setup time, and enhance quality control for future processes and services, even before the implementation of adjustments in the actual physical world [22].

Simulation and augmented reality (AR) is a type of enhanced reality in which live direct or indirect views of physical real-world environments are augmented with computer-generated visuals projected on top of them. Industry 4.0 applications rely heavily on this technology. This innovative technology, which is critical to the industrial revolution, was created by combining real operations and simulation industries [4]. These strategies have a lot of advantages, especially when it comes to creating products and manufacturing processes. One of the cutting-edge technologies included in the Industry 4.0 trend is augmented reality, which is particularly useful in producing smart manufacturing functions [28].

3.9 Enterprise resource planning (ERP) and business intelligence

Enterprise resource planning (ERP) refers to information systems that are designed to integrate and efficiently employ all of an organization's resources. An ERP software is a system that supports an organization in bringing together processes and data that are executed all over the processes (suppliers, production, stock, sales). ERP systems are able to provide an integrated approach to information use, to start forecasting and extracting information, which can use in various departments [4]. There is a connection between big data and Industry 4.0, Manufacturing Executive Systems (MES), cloud systems, and ERP are integrated. It is critical that all procedures in the design stage as well as the customer journey are compatible with the Industry 4.0 approach. The ERP process is also a vital component in this framework [28].

The idea of Industry 4.0 necessitates connection and collaboration criteria. End-user feedback is critical, as is providing immediate additional value to all interested parties. In order for personalization to be possible, network systems must be intelligent [22]. A telecom operator may be able to analyze network performance during fluctuations and use preventive scenarios to reduce client dissatisfaction. A well-structured ERP system can enable these characteristic features. ERP systems can help with Industry 4.0 implementations, especially as a result of the following advantages: i) Real-time data may be evaluated and allow for early detection; ii) ERP systems can provide sales and purchasing transparency; iii) ERP data may be used by mobile applications to communicate; iv) Optimum resource utilization may be achieved under varying job descriptions; v) Clients may be able to track their orders online and receive the necessary information quickly [4].

3.10 Smart virtual product development system (SVPD)

The Smart Virtual Product Development (SVPD) system is a product development decision support technology that saves, uses, and shares the experiential knowledge of previous decisional events in the form of SOEs. It was created to address the requirement for digital knowledge captured in smart manufacturing product design, production planning, and inspection planning. As a result, product quality and development time will be improved, as required by Industry 4.0 concepts [31].

4. Industry 4.0 characteristics

The core progress from traditional manufacturing toward Industry 4.0 concluded into four key features and characteristics [32]: (1) vertical networking of smart manufacture schemes; (2) horizontal integration through a new generation of global value chain networks; (3) through-life engineering across the entire value chain; and (4) the impact of exponential technologies.

4.1 Vertical networking of smart production

Industry 4.0′s first main characteristic is the vertical networking of smart manufacturing systems. Vertical integration in Industry 4.0 establishes a connection between the many levels of the industry, from the manufacturing floor up, via production monitoring, control, and supervision, quality management, operations, product management, processing, and so on. This interconnectedness across all corporate levels provides for a fluid, transparent data flow, allowing for data-driven strategic and tactical choices [20]. Hence, the main objective behind vertical networking is to utilize Cyber-Physical Production Systems (CPPSs), to enable industries to quickly respond to unexpected order changes resulting from demand fluctuations, equipment failure or stock shortage. Vertical networking improves an organization's capacity to adequately adapt to changes in market requirements and benefit from new possibilities [22].

Furthermore, it makes it easier to link resources to goods and find supplies and parts at any time. Similarly, processing data, anomalies, and defects from various processing stages of the manufacturing line are automatically captured and registered, allowing for quick responses to order changes, quality variations, and even machinery breakdowns. As a consequence, waste is decreased, and resource efficiency, notably in terms of material usage, energy consumption, and human resources is improved [28].

4.2 Horizontal integration through a new generation of global value chain networks

In the Industry 4.0 concept, horizontal integration refers to the network of diverse processes, companies, and services that make up a product's global value chain. This can be viewed at the production level as a total consolidation of all associated manufacturing processes. Vertical integration, on the other hand, refers to a high level of coordination between production and top management layers such as quality management, product management, and production control [33].

The horizontal integration in an Industry 4.0 enterprise occurs at different levels: production floor, multiple production facilities, and entire value chain. Each connected machine or production unit becomes a node with well-defined properties within the production network. These nodes continuously communicate their status to respond autonomously to dynamic production requirements cost-effectively and reduce system downtime through predictive maintenance . If an enterprise owns several production sites, the horizontal integration enables to share inventory levels and unexpected delays, and possibly redistribute work among owned facilities to respond to market demand fluctuations rapidly or increase the efficiency and speed of the production process. However, the most critical and global horizontal integration remains the integration across the entire value chain [12].

Industry 4.0 offers a highly automated and transparent collaboration across the complete value chain, using CPPSs, from the inbound assembly, packaging, storing, production, quality control, marketing, and sales, to outbound distribution, logistics, and retail services. The horizontal integration across all these activities creates a transparent value chain that is updated in real-time. Hence, this feature provides a high level of flexibility to respond more rapidly to changing market demands, shortcomings, and problems, facilitates the optimization of the production process, increases its efficiency, and reduces the generated waste [17]. Additionally, the fact that any part or product's history is logged and can be accessed at any time ensures constant traceability, also known as "product memory" [19].

4.3 Through-life engineering across the entire value chain

Among the characteristics of the Fourth Industrial Revolution is also the impact of the ten components of the 4th Industrial Revolution *"ten types of innovation,"* Efficient management of innovation, and finally, Efficient life cycle management. These are shown below.

The "ten types of innovation" (Components of Industry 4.0). Industry 4.0 will enable integrated and cross-disciplinary engineering throughout the value chain, as well as throughout product and customer life cycles. Industry 4.0 applications are intended to ensure the traditional domain of product innovation. Innovation is not limited, innovation has traditionally been related mainly to product offerings, but it also has significant potential in areas such as company structures, processes, networks, and profit models, as well as customer-facing functions [5].

Efficient management of innovation. The digital transformation to industry 4.0 will make it possible to improve further the efficiency of innovation management in all the Components of Industry 4.0. Interactive and designed curricula make individualized learning achievable, thereby, speeding up strategic implementation and organizational development [34]. Industry 4.0 solutions in project portfolio management make it easier to track not only the return on investment (ROI) in innovation, but also to identify risks by utilizing global comparative project data for monitoring and remediation. Information technology can be utilized to speed up R&D in the field of product development [5].

Efficient life cycle management. The digital transformation industry 4.0 will allow essential data for life cycle management to be provided at any time and from any location. These data will include not just information and reports, but also the outcomes of big data processing, which will be used to develop appropriate early indicators using artificial intelligence (Al). Al will employ global cross-checking to determine the plausibility of developing suitable bases for data-driven decision-making. It will allow businesses to better understand and address the needs of their customers, as well as customize product cycles [5].

4.4 The impact of exponential technologies

Exponential technologies solutions. Corporate venture capital firms have a strong chance of profiting from disruptive innovation and exponential technology by investing in new trends early on. Corporate venture capital Investing in start-ups allows businesses to participate in the development of new products and services while also ensuring their long-term competitiveness. This type of investment allows for early and convenient access to new technologies. Companies must be given more leeway to "see around the next corner." Only then can a new business region be formed, which will eventually become the company's new heart. Companies' survival may be jeopardized if such possibilities are neglected [2].

The learning organization. If companies are to fully use the promise of exponential technologies in making the digital transformation to industry 4.0, they must change into learning organizations. Exponential technology adoption and integration must be slow but continuous. Learning is essential for long-term organizational development. It is time to make a change that is not so counterproductive. New ideas, processes, and business sectors are most successful when they begin as a learning niche and eventually migrate to the center of the organization, establishing themselves as a new leading segment [5].

5. Effects of industry 4.0

Innovation and scientific advancements perform an essential role in businesses, sectors, and countries. However, the digital improvements and the increasing interconnectivity will bring additional challenges and upgrades to societies, since, Industry 4.0 (Ir 4.0) will significantly change the manufacturing systems in terms of design, processes, operations, and services. Industry 4.0 will lead to potential deep changes in a variety of fields outside of the industrial sector. Its influence and effect may be divided into six categories: (1) Industry sector, (2) Products and services, (3) Business models, entrepreneurship, and market competition, (4) Economies of nations, (5) Work environment, and (6) Skills development.

5.1 The impact of industry 4.0 on the industrial sector

The industry sector will be the first to feel the effects of Industry 4.0. This new industrial paradigm will usher in a vision of manufacturing that is decentralized and digitalized, with production elements that can autonomously govern themselves, trigger operations, and adapt to changes in their surroundings. Furthermore, the developing paradigm recommends fully integrating products and processes, altering industrial vision from mass production to mass customization, resulting in increased complexity [35]. Consequently, advanced technologies and the building of smart factories will have a significant impact on production processes and operations, providing for greater operational flexibility, and more efficient utilization of resources. Industry 4.0 will have a considerable effect on the production systems, supply chains, and industrial activities. This new paradigm is changing the current industrial landscape in three ways: (1) production digitization, (2) automation, and (3) integrating the manufacturing site to a larger supply chain. Industry 4.0, in this sense, entails complete network integration and real-time data sharing [1]. Productivity growth is at the core of each industrial revolution. The 4th industrial revolution, on the other hand, will influence the entire supply chain, from product creation and manufacturing to outbound logistics, in addition to enhancing productivity [36].

ROJKO, et al. (2020) used the vector autoregression model forecast for data from the manufacturing sector in the United States over the period (2008–2018) and concluded that, the share of manufacturing output and employment has declined, and that the manufacturing sector has reached a turning point, after which robotization can increase employment and labor productivity of workers while also stimulating further growth of their education levels. They concluded that the shift to Industry 4.0

has a significant impact on the growing demand for new knowledge and skills in order to boost productivity. As a result, anticipated growths of assessed manufacturing indicators imply that the negative effects of robotization in the recent past were only transient, as the Industry 4.0 age has begun. Nonetheless, further policies are needed to enable long-term industry development [37].

5.2 The impact of industry 4.0 on products and services

This new industrial paradigm has a significant impact on products and services. Rapid changes in the economic landscape and dynamic market demands have resulted in an increased demand for the development of more complicated and intelligent products in recent years [36]. Products will become increasingly modular and configurable, allowing for mass customization to match individual consumer needs [35]. As a result, Industry 4.0 is defined by the emergence of new products and services as embedded systems that can become attentive and interactive, be managed, and tracked in real-time, optimize the entire value chain, and provide pertinent information about their status throughout their lifecycle [37].

5.3 The impact of industry 4.0 on business models and market

In the previous few years, company models and markets have swiftly altered, and new inventive business models will emerge. In the context of Industry 4.0, the introduction of new disruptive technologies has altered the way products and services are sold and delivered, disrupting established enterprises, and introducing new business prospects and models [33]. As a result, value chains are becoming more responsive, as Industry 4.0 encourages integration between manufacturers and customers, allowing for closer customer connection and business model adaption to market demands. The rising digitalization of industrial production, combined with system integration and complexity, will result in the establishment of increasingly sophisticated and digital market models, boosting competitiveness by removing barriers between information and physical structures [1].

5.4 The impact of industry 4.0 on the work environment

Because of technological advancements, the workplace environment is changing fast, and Industrial revolution 4.0 is redefining jobs and key competencies. The most significant transition is the human-machine connection, which includes employee contact and a set of new collaborative work approaches [18]. The number of robots and intelligent technologies is growing, the real and virtual environments are merging, implying the existing work environment is undergoing a considerable transition [13].

The rising importance of human-machine interfaces will encourage interaction between production elements as well as the necessary communication between smart machines, smart products, and employees, which will be aided by CPS' vision of IoT and IoS. As a result, ergonomic concerns should be considered in the context of Industry 4.0, and future systems should emphasize the relevance of workers. Job profiles, as well as work management, organization, and planning will be affected by the integration of Industry 4.0 in industrial systems and the rising deployment of new technologies [12]. In this scenario, the major task is to avoid technological unemployment by reframing present jobs and taking steps to adapt the workforce to the new jobs that will be generated [28].

5.5 The impact of industry 4.0 on skills development

One of the most significant fundamental factors for a successful acceptance and implementation of the Industry 4.0 framework is skill development, which will lead to demographic and societal changes. New competencies will be required in the future work vision, and it will be vital to provide opportunities for the acquisition of these abilities through high-quality training. This new industrial paradigm will have a significant impact on the labor market and professional roles, and it will be critical to ensure that more jobs are generated than are lost [26].

Interdisciplinary thinking will be vital, and outstanding abilities in social and technological domains will be desired. The new required competency sectors must be included in schooling. As a result of Industry 4.0's rising automation of jobs, workers must be prepared to take on new responsibilities [28]. The same can be said for engineering education, which has a lot of promise in terms of training future professionals and informing them about new technical trends and opportunities, as well as managers who need to adapt their management strategies to meet changing market demands. Furthermore, in order to address Industry 4.0, more qualified personnel will be required in technological sectors [1].

In summary, Industry 4.0 has enormous potential in many areas, and its implementation will have an impact across the entire value chain, improving production and engineering processes, improving product and service quality, optimizing customer-organization relationships, bringing new business opportunities and economic benefits, changing educational requirements, and transforming the current work environment.

5.6 The impact of industry 4.0 on the economy

An economy can be inspired by the introduction of new models and emerging technological improvements. Digitization involves the convergence between physical and virtual worlds and will have a widespread impact in every economic sector [15]. This will be the primary driving force behind innovation, which will be crucial to productivity and costs of production, which is reflected in the competitiveness (companies, sectors, and nations) [17].

Industry 4.0 also, can transform existing relationships in the manufacturing process, allowing the manufacturing sector to join the information age by allowing communication at all stages of the manufacturing process. Some academics anticipate that Industry 4.0 would lead to new economic forms in the industry, agriculture, and services [3]. The majority of businesses expect a two-year payback on their Industry 4.0 investments, which leads to a considerable rise in investment in this area is likely, it's reflected in economic growth [37].

On the other hand, some experts believe that Industry 4.0 will result in increased inequality due to its threat of disrupting labor markets. It is argued that the continuous growth in automation, robots, and computers will take the jobs of workers in many industries with the most worrying factor being the increased danger of the disappearance of low-skill/low-pay jobs which will cause a lot of challenges for the poor, which will lead to a rise in social tensions [37]. The most concerning fact in Industry 4.0 is that it is not only the transfer of labor from one sector of the economy to another but also the availability of technology that will replace human capital, in other words, taking people's jobs. The technological revolution will also have an impact on topics such as material or ideological changes brought about by the introduction of new gadgets or systems, all of which will have an impact on redefining humanity's culture [3].

In general, digitization and interconnection of industrial processes, lead to potentials in all three dimensions of sustainability. However, achieving long-term benefits of sustainability is accompanied by several challenges respectively, especially in the implementation phase of Industry 4.0 [38].

Referring to the economic perspective of Industry 4.0, transparency and interconnection of processes enable process optimization, resulting in increased efficiency, flexibility, quality, and customization. Industry 4.0 allows load balancing between smart manufacturing technologies, innovative value propositions, and increasing demand orientation. All these are enabling smart products, which boost a company's competitiveness [39]. In the same regard, increasing process openness in intra- and inter-firm logistics can also be accomplished, lowering logistics costs. On the other hand, such procedures, as well as the adoption of Industry 4.0 in general, represent risks in terms of high investments and uncertain profitability [38]. Furthermore, manufacturers consider the transition to Industry 4.0 of their current business models to be difficult. Furthermore, Industry 4.0 necessitates the standardization of processes both within and between businesses. Due to their low degree of process standardization, more flexible but less automated manufacturing equipment, and resource limits, among other things, both undertakings, i.e., business model change and standardization, can become particularly problematic for SMEs [40].

Regarding the ecological dimension of sustainability, Industry 4.0 offers a number of advantages: transparency in demand and process enables for an intelligent task and process scheduling, resulting in lower energy use [38]. Furthermore, direct data linkage from product consumption back to design can improve manufacturing design, resulting in improved product lifecycle management, including recycling, as a result, Industry 4.0 aids in the identification and reduction of greenhouse gas emissions [40]. As a result, waste reduction and resource consumption can be improved. Reduced transportation operations and superfluous material flows can also be realized in logistics [25]. Furthermore, data openness across the entire supply chain can reduce the frequency of incorrect deliveries, wasteful waiting time, and damaged items. Decentralized production close to the point of consumption minimizes both logistics costs and environmental concerns [41]. Similarly, emerging manufacturing technologies such as additive manufacturing can aid in the reduction of waste in manufacturing and logistics processes, such as replacement parts [42].

Regarding the social dimension of Industry 4.0, several benefits for employees are named, such as improved human learning through intelligent assistance systems as well as human-machine interfaces that lead to increased employee satisfaction in industrial workplaces [8, 22]. However, current literature cannot provide a unified perspective on whether Industry 4.0 will cause an increase or decrease in employee numbers in the industry. In this regard, concrete numbers named differ to a large extent [3, 15]. In general, a further replacement of simple tasks is expected, whereas tasks such as monitoring, collaboration, and training will still be required [3]. Hereby, new job profiles with novel requirements for training and education are expected to emerge, mostly referring to decreasing importance of manual labor in contrast to IT skills. On the other hand, tasks that include planning and monitoring, as well as decision-making, could fall to autonomous systems, therefore, possibly replacing jobs in this area.

Regarding the social dimension of Industry 4.0, Several benefits for employees are mentioned, such as improved human learning through intelligent support systems and human-machine interfaces that lead to increased employee satisfaction in industrial environments [38]. However, the present research cannot agree on whether Industry 4.0 would result in an increase or decrease in the number of employees in the industry [25]. In general, easy jobs will be replaced further, while monitoring, collaboration, and training will continue to be required. It is possible that occupations in this field will be replaced [38]. As a result, implementing Industry 4.0 in an organization necessitates deliberate transformation activities, sometimes known as "digital transformation." It necessitates new attitudes for dealing with digital transformation difficulties as well as a unified approach for staff qualification and acceptance [43].

5.7 The impact of industry 4.0 on value chains and supply chains (SC)

The fourth industrial revolution has a significant impact on supply chain interactions, which is mainly due to the exponential growth of sensible data and the widespread of digitalized processes [40]. To understand the impact of the adoption and exploitation of Industry 4.0 technologies on the value chains and supply chains (SC). Based on the review, the effect of Industry 4.0 implementation on the supply chains (SC) are identified as follows:

Agility and Customization. Industry 4.0 implementation enables real-time planning and control, permitting organizations to be flexible and agile in responding to rapidly changing conditions; for example, by faster reacting to changes in demand, supply, and prices, companies can reduce planning cycles and frozen periods [34]. Future events and trends, such as consumer behavior, delivery time, and industrial output, can be predicted using business analytics techniques. Real-time delivery routing and tracking also allow logistics operations to be more flexible, efficient, and agile [44].

Accuracy and Efficiency. Industry 4.0 technologies provide better decision-making by providing real-time, consistent, and accurate data. As a result, next-generation performance management systems will improve end-to-end visibility across the value chain. The data includes everything from key top-level performance metrics like customer service and order fulfillment to detailed process data like a truck position in the logistics network. The automation of physical tasks, planning, control, and information exchange processes improves supply chain (SC) efficiency. Automated technologies are used by a large number of businesses, particularly in their logistics operations [44]. Companies choose cross-company transportation optimization to optimize truck utilization and boost transport flexibility by cooperating and sharing facilities. The entire SC network design is constantly optimized to ensure that it is a perfect fit for business needs [34].

6. Key drivers and obstacles or barriers of industry 4.0

6.1 Key drivers of industry 4.0

Despite the rapid rise of Industry 4.0, research related to the identification of potential drivers and hurdles to its implementation are scarce. To better understand the motivations and challenges to the adoption and use of Industry 4.0 technologies, a literature review was conducted. The following are the primary drivers for Industry 4.0 implementation, as determined by the review:

Agility and Customization. Industry 4.0 implementation enables real-time planning and control, permitting organizations to be flexible and agile in responding to rapidly changing conditions; for example, by faster reacting to changes in demand, supply, and prices, companies can reduce planning cycles and frozen periods [34]. Future events and trends, such as consumer behavior, delivery time, and industrial output, can be predicted using business analytics techniques. Real-time delivery routing and tracking also allow logistics operations to be more flexible, efficient, and agile [44].

Accuracy and Efficiency. Industry 4.0 technologies provide better decision-making by providing real-time, consistent, and accurate data. As a result, next-generation performance management systems will improve end-to-end visibility across the value chain. The data includes everything from key top-level performance metrics like customer service and order fulfillment to detailed process data like a truck position in the logistics network. The automation of physical tasks, planning, control, and information exchange processes improves SC efficiency. Automated technologies are used by a large number of businesses, particularly in their logistics operations [44].

6.2 Applications of fourth industrial revolution

In this section, we introduce an overview of some applications of the Fourth Industrial Revolution. Also, we provide a case study for these applications by *KUKA Group* in many fields. KUKA is an international automation corporation based in Augsburg, Germany. As a world-class provider of intelligent automation solutions. In areas such as automotive, electronics, metal & plastic, consumer products, e-commerce/retail, and healthcare, KUKA provides everything from a single source: from robots and cells to completely automated systems and their networking [45].

The "*Smart Factories*" are automation solutions from KUKA, which is able to transport aircraft components around the production hangar with millimeter precision. The employees at the Airbus production plant move enormous A380 fuselage sections, weighing 90 tons and measuring 15 meters in length around a building the size of a football stadium. This is made possible by the KUKA omniMove mobile transport platform, a transport vehicle for heavy loads that is equipped with omnidirectional Mecanum wheels [46].

Similarly, using techniques such as *Machine-to-Machine* (M-2-M) and *intelligent robots* as applications from the KUKA company. Robot-based KUKA system technology for machine tool automation is used, among other things, for the loading and unloading of machines and supports elements of Industries 4.0 [47]. In the KUKA's site in Augsburg, work 7 robots, which is a typical production environment at an international machine manufacturer [48].

Another application of industry 4.0 in the *medical sector*, automation solutions for greater efficiency in hospitals, in areas of diagnosis and surgery to therapy, KUKA robots meet the stringent requirements of the medical sector and are well-suited to a wide range of medical technology applications. For this, KUKA offers a wide range of medical high-tech products, ranging from robot-based help systems for surgery to assistive components for diagnosis or rehabilitation [45].

There are several applications for industry 4.0, for example, the KUKA corporation which works in the areas, for instance, smart factories, M-2-M, computing cloud, intelligent robots, e-commerce, and so on.

6.3 Key obstacles or barriers of industry 4.0

There are also some intimidating resisting forces, barriers, for implementing Industry 4.0 practices. These obstacles may be classified under the following business dimensions: *Firstly, Financial constraints*. Financial constraints are a fundamental issue in implementing Industry 4.0 in terms of developing sophisticated contemporary infrastructure and sustainable process improvements [28]. *Secondly,* the *technical competency* of the focal organization is the key focus that influences the scale of investment. The economic perspective, on the other hand, is still in its infancy; a lack of clarity about cost–benefit analysis and monetary rewards on digital investments is a critical issue for deploying Industry 4.0 [40].

Thirdly, Organizational nature. Other obstacles that businesses aiming to integrate Industry 4.0 technologies confront include insufficient research and development procedures, a lack of infrastructure, poor data quality, a lack of digital culture, and a lack of trust among partners [17]. Poor infrastructure and internet connectivity are significant impediments to any digital transformation or adoption [22]. As well as *fourthly, Lack of management support and Resistance to change*. Industry 4.0 transformative changes are fast-paced and necessitate proper skill development and training, which is difficult to do without a high degree of management support, which is the most important requirement for launching Industry 4.0. Industries are unsure and unfamiliar with the term Industry 4.0 and are ignorant of the benefits of digital transformation due to which there is reluctance in adopting it [22].

Additionally, *Legal Issues*. The big data transaction brings cybersecurity risk; therefore, privacy and security concerns must be considered when implementing Industry 4.0 [44]. Finally, *Lack of policies and support from the government*. In most nations, governments supply the infrastructure for the digital world (such as the internet and communication networks). However, there is a lack of a roadmap for transforming industrial infrastructure, owing to a lack of clarity (for example, the development of the 5G network and its benefits for Industry 4) about the implications of Industry 4.0 [22].

7. Conclusion

This study contributes to bridging the critical gap, by discussing the key components, characteristics, effects on many dimensions, drivers, barriers, and other implementation challenges of Industry 4.0, the fourth industrial revolution describes a future production system's vision. Industry 4.0 is an inevitable revolution covering a wide range of innovative technologies, such as cyber-physical systems, RFID technologies, IoT, cloud computing, big data analytics, advanced robotics, smart factories, etc. The Industry 4.0 paradigm is transforming business in many industries, e.g., automotive, logistics, aerospace, and energy sectors, etc. Industry 4.0 realizes the development and integration of information and communication technologies into business processes. The capabilities or components of Industry 4.0 bring significant advantages to organizations, including customization of products, real-time data analysis, increased visibility, autonomous monitoring and control, dynamic product design and development, enhanced productivity, and competitiveness.

The key characteristic features of Industry 4.0 are collaboration and integration of schemes, both horizontal and vertical. In vertical integration, Information and Communication Technology (ICT) is integrated into various hierarchical levels of the organization, from floor-level control to production, operations, and management levels. This vertical integration networking empowers the use of components of Industry 4.0 for production to respond to demand disparity or the fluctuations in stock levels. In horizontal integration, ICT is used to exchange information between many players. Integration of these systems for a flawless collaboration, integration, and exchange of data with all the stakeholders is a complicated scenario. Implementation of Industry 4.0 apps support to reduce costs, improves productivity, efficiency, and flexibility, and enhance product customization.

Innovation and technological advancements perform an essential role in organizations, sectors, countries. However, the digital transformation improvements and the rising interconnectivity will bring new challenges to societies, since Industry 4.0 will significantly change the products and manufacturing systems regarding design, processes, operations, and services. Industry 4.0 uses several advanced tools and technologies, thus helping to redefine conventional industrial processes. Industry 4.0 has enormous potential effect in many areas, and its application will have an impact across the entire value chain, improving production and engineering processes, improving product and service quality, optimizing customer-organization relationships, bringing new business opportunities and economic benefits, changing educational requirements, and transforming the current work environment. Digitization and interconnection of industrial processes (Industry 4.0), leading to potentials in all three dimensions of sustainability.

There are several applications for industry 4.0, applied by the KUKA corporation which works in the areas, for instance, smart factories, M-2-M, computing cloud, intelligent robots, e-commerce, etc., these technologies or applications help the industry 4.0 to separate rapidly. On the other hand, there are also some barriers, for implementing Industry 4.0 practices. These obstacles may be classified into many business dimensions: financial constraints, technical competency of the focal, organizational nature, lack of management support and resistance to change, legal issues, lack of policies and support from the government.

Author details

FathyElsayed Youssef Abdelmajied
Faculty of Commerce, Benha University, Cairo, Egypt

*Address all correspondence to: fathy.abdelmagid@fcom.bu.edu.eg

References

[1] Pereira AC, Romero F. A review of the meanings and the implications of the industry 4.0 concept. Procedia Manufacturing. 2017;**13**:1206-1214. DOI: 10.1016/j.promfg.2017.09.032

[2] Mukha D. Impact of industry 4.0 on global value chains, business models and foreign direct investment. Экономическаянаукасегодня. 2021;**13**: 75-84. DOI: 10.21122/2309-6667-2021-13-75-84

[3] Mhlanga D. Artificial intelligence in the industry 4.0, and its impact on poverty, innovation, infrastructure development, and the sustainable development goals: Lessons from emerging economies? Sustainability (Switzerland). 2021;**13**(11):1-16. DOI: 10.3390/su13115788

[4] Oztemel E, Gursev S. Literature review of industry 4.0 and related technologies. Journal of Intelligent Manufacturing. 2020;**31**(1):127-182. DOI: 10.1007/s10845-018-1433-8

[5] Deloitte AG. Industry 4.0. Challenges and solutions for the digital transformation and use of exponential technologies. 2015:1-30

[6] Tay SI, Lee TC, Hamid NZA, Ahmad ANA. An overview of industry 4.0: Definition, components, and government initiatives. Journal of Advanced Research in Dynamical and Control Systems. 2018;**10**(14):1379-1387

[7] Ojra A. Revisiting industry 4.0: A new definition. Advances in Intelligent Systems and Computing. 2019;**858**:1156-1162. DOI: 10.1007/978-3-030-01174-1_88

[8] Beier G, Ullrich A, Niehoff S, Reißig M, Habich M. Industry 4.0: How it is defined from a sociotechnical perspective and how much sustainability it includes – A literature review. Journal of Cleaner Production. 2020;**259**:1-13. DOI: 10.1016/j.jclepro.2020.120856

[9] Culot G, Nassimbeni G, Orzes G, Sartor M. Behind the definition of industry 4.0: Analysis and open questions. International Journal of Production Economics. 2020;**226**:107617. DOI: 10.1016/j.ijpe.2020.107617

[10] Nosalska K, Piątek ZM, Mazurek G, Rządca R. Industry 4.0: Coherent definition framework with technological and organizational interdependencies. Journal of Manufacturing Technology Management. 2020;**31**(5):837-862. DOI: 10.1108/JMTM-08-2018-0238

[11] Pereira AC, Romero F. A review of the meanings and the implications of the industry 4.0 concept. Procedia Manufacturing. 2017;**13**:1206-1214. DOI: 10.1016/j.promfg.2017.09.032

[12] Wahlster H, Helbig J, Hellinger A, Wahlster W. Recommendations for implementing the strategic initiative INDUSTRIE 4.0. Securing the future of German manufacturing industry; final report of the Industrie 4.0" Working Group. Forschungsunion, 2013. München Retrieved from: http://forschungsunion.de/pdf/industrie_4_0_final_report.pdf

[13] Qin J, Liu Y, Grosvenor R. A categorical framework of manufacturing for industry 4.0 and beyond. Procedia CIRP. 2016;**52**:173-178. DOI: 10.1016/j.procir.2016.08.005

[14] Bai C, Dallasega P, Orzes G, Sarkis J. Industry 4.0 technologies assessment: A sustainability perspective.

International Journal of Production Economics. 2020;**229**. DOI: 10.1016/j.ijpe.2020.107776

[15] Schwab K. The Fourth Industrial Revolution: what it means and how to respond| World Economic Forum. World Economic Forum. Vol. 21. 2016. Retrieved from: https://www.weforum.org/agenda/2016/01/thefourth-industrial-revolution-what-it-meansand-how-to-respond [Accessed July 2016]

[16] Philbeck T, Davis N. The fourth industrial revolution: Shaping a new era. Journal of International Affairs. 2019;**72**(1)

[17] Wang S, Wan J, Zhang D, Li D, Zhang C. Towards smart factory for industry 4.0: A self-organized multi-agent system with big data based feedback and coordination. Computer Networks. 2016;**101**. DOI: 10.1016/j.comnet.2015.12.017

[18] Mrugalska B, Wyrwicka MK. Towards lean production in industry 4.0. Procedia Engineering. 2017;**182**. DOI: 10.1016/j.proeng.2017.03.135

[19] Bauernhansl T, Schatz A, Jäger J. Complexity management - industry 4.0 and the consequences: New challenges for sociotechnical production systems [Komplexitätbewirtschaften – Industrie 4.0 und die Folgen: Neue Herausforderungenfürsozio-technische Produktionssysteme]. ZWF ZeitschriftfuerWirtschaftlichen Fabrikbetrieb. 2014;**109**(5)

[20] Santos L, Brittes G, Fabián N, Germán A. International journal of production economics the expected contribution of industry 4.0 technologies for industrial performance. International Journal of Production Economics. 2018;**204**

[21] Berger C, Hees A, Braunreuther S, Reinhart G. Characterization of cyber-physical sensor systems. Procedia CIRP. 2016;**41**. DOI: 10.1016/j.procir.2015.12.019

[22] Ghadge A, Er Kara M, Moradlou H, Goswami M. The impact of industry 4.0 implementation on supply chains. Journal of Manufacturing Technology Management. 2020;**31**(4). DOI: 10.1108/JMTM-10-2019-0368

[23] Chen M. Towards smart city: M2M communications with software agent intelligence. Multimedia Tools and Applications. 2013;**67**(1). DOI: 10.1007/s11042-012-1013-4

[24] Biral A, Centenaro M, Zanella A, Vangelista L, Zorzi M. The challenges of M2M massive access in wireless cellular networks. Digital Communications and Networks. 2015;**1**(1). DOI: 10.1016/j.dcan.2015.02.001

[25] Karnik N, Bora U, Bhadri K, Kadambi P, Dhatrak P. A comprehensive study on current and future trends towards the characteristics and enablers of industry 4.0. Journal of Industrial Information Integration. 2021;**Oct**:100294. DOI: 10.1016/j.jii.2021.100294

[26] Mohammed A, Wang L. Brainwaves driven human-robot collaborative assembly. CIRP Annals. 2018;**67**(1). DOI: 10.1016/j.cirp.2018.04.048

[27] Sunhare P, Chowdhary RR, Chattopadhyay MK. Internet of things and data mining: An application oriented survey. Journal of King Saud University - Computer and Information Sciences. 2020; In press (1), pp. 1-22. DOI: 10.1016/j.jksuci.2020.07.002

[28] Wang L, Liu S, Cooper C, Wang XV, Gao RX. Function block-based

human-robot collaborative assembly driven by brainwaves. CIRP Annals. 2021;**70**(1). DOI: 10.1016/j.cirp.2021.04.091

[29] Lima F et al. Digital manufacturing tools in the simulation of collaborative robots: Towards industry 4.0. Brazilian Journal of Operations & Production Management. 2019;**16**(2). DOI: 10.14488/bjopm.2019.v16.n2.a8

[30] Tay SI, Lee TC, Hamid NZA, Ahmad ANA. An overview of industry 4.0: Definition, components, and government initiatives. Journal of Advanced Research in Dynamical and Control Systems. 2018;**10**(14):1379-1387

[31] Ahmed MB, Sanin C, Szczerbicki E. Smart virtual product development (SVPD) to enhance product manufacturing in industry 4.0. In: Procedia Computer Science. Vol. 159. 2019. DOI: 10.1016/j.procs.2019.09.398

[32] Aoun A, Ilinca A, Ghandour M, Ibrahim H. A review of Industry 4.0 characteristics and challenges, with potential improvements using Blockchain technology. Computers & Industrial Engineering; 2021;**162**:1-11. DOI: 10.1016/j.cie.2021.107746

[33] Karnik N, Bora U, Bhadri K, Kadambi P, Dhatrak P. A comprehensive study on current and future trends towards the characteristics and enablers of industry 4.0. Journal of Industrial Information Integration. 2021;**10**:100294. DOI: 10.1016/j.jii.2021.100294

[34] Barreto L, Amaral A, Pereira T. Industry 4.0 implications in logistics: An overview. Procedia Manufacturing. 2017;**13**. DOI: 10.1016/j.promfg.2017.09.045

[35] Erol S, Jäger A, Hold P, Ott K, Sihn W. Tangible industry 4.0: A scenario-based approach to learning for the future of production. Procedia CIRP. 2016;**54**. DOI: 10.1016/j.procir.2016.03.162

[36] Roblek V, Meško M, Krapež A. A complex view of industry 4.0. SAGE Open. 2016;**6**(2). DOI: 10.1177/2158244016653987

[37] Rojko K, Erman N, Jelovac D. Impacts of the transformation to industry 4.0 in the manufacturing sector: The case of the U.S. The Organ. 2020;**53**(4). DOI: 10.2478/orga-2020-0019

[38] Müller JM, Kiel D, Voigt KI. What drives the implementation of industry 4.0? The role of opportunities and challenges in the context of sustainability. Sustainability (Switzerland). 2018;**10**(1). DOI: 10.3390/su10010247

[39] Mastos TD et al. Industry 4.0 sustainable supply chains: An application of an IoT enabled scrap metal management solution. Journal of Cleaner Production. 2020;**269**. DOI: 10.1016/j.jclepro.2020.122377

[40] Ghobakhloo M. The future of manufacturing industry: A strategic roadmap toward industry 4.0. Journal of Manufacturing Technology Management. 2018;**29**(6):910-936. DOI: 10.1108/JMTM-02-2018-0057

[41] Mastos TD et al. Introducing an application of an industry 4.0 solution for circular supply chain management. Journal of Cleaner Production. 2021;**300**. DOI: 10.1016/j.jclepro.2021.126886

[42] Nagy J, Oláh J, Erdei E, Máté D, Popp J. The role and impact of industry 4.0 and the internet of things on the business strategy of the value chain-the case of Hungary. Sustainability

(Switzerland). 2018;**10**(10). DOI: 10.3390/su10103491

[43] Leonhardt F, Wiedemann A. Realigning risk Management in the Light of industry 4.0. SSRN Electronic Journal. 23 October 2015:1-22. DOI: 10.2139/ssrn.2678947

[44] Ghadge A, Er Kara M, Moradlou H, Goswami M. The impact of industry 4.0 on supply chains. Journal of Manufacturing Technology Management. 2020;**31**(4):669-686. DOI: 10.1108/JMTM-10-2019-0368

[45] Xu T et al. Dynamic identification of the KUKA LBR iiwa robot with retrieval of physical parameters using global optimization. IEEE Access. 2020;**8**. DOI: 10.1109/ACCESS.2020.3000997

[46] Carstensen J et al. Condition monitoring and cloud-based energy analysis for autonomous Mobile manipulation - smart factory concept with LUHbots. Procedia Technology. 2016;**26**. DOI: 10.1016/j.protcy.2016.08.070

[47] Maldonado-Ramirez A, Rios-Cabrera R, Lopez-Juarez I. A visual path-following learning approach for industrial robots using DRL. Robotics and Computer-Integrated Manufacturing. 2021;**71**. DOI: 10.1016/j.rcim.2021.102130

[48] Wuest T, Weimer D, Irgens C, Thoben K-D. Machine learning in manufacturing: advantages, challenges, and applications, Production & Manufacturing Research. 2016;**4**(1:)23-45. Retrieved from: https://www.tandfonline.com/doi/full/10.1080/21693277.2016.1192517

Chapter 2

Enabling Sustainable Supply Chains in the Industrial 4.0 Era

Thuso Mphela, Christopher J. Savage and Alejandro Gutierrez

Abstract

Sustainability has become a global policy agenda following the United Nations adoption of Sustainable Development Goals 2030. Supply chains can contribute to this by adoption of eco-friendly technologies, sustainable materials, reducing waste, among others. Adopting and scaling innovative technologies such as machine learning, blockchain, internet of things (IoT), and 3D printing has potential to improve efficiency through improved visibility, flexibility and decision making across the supply chain. Efficiency and lean operations may induce vulnerability in supply chains, due to disruptions like the Covid-19 pandemic which can compromise business. The concept of sustainability is explored from both the business and customer perspectives, as well as in the broader policy environment that includes politics, the economy and society. Businesses are likely to adopt sustainable practices if there are financial incentives. However, environmental sustainability cannot be pursued at the expense of business survival. Therefore, the adoption of different technologies has potential to bring us closer to solving the sustainability-profitability paradox.

Keywords: sustainability, logistics, supply chains, internet of things, blockchain, machine learning, 3D printing, efficiency, supply chain risk

1. Introduction

Sustainability is not a new phenomenon in business and its associated literature but started receiving greater attention in the supply chain management (SCM) research in the mid-1990s. Unfortunately, a review of literature reveals that most SCM research is slightly detached from the real sustainability problems of the world which include environmental sustainability, reduction in biodiversity, and others [1]. Sustainability is becoming increasingly important not only because of the negative impacts business has had on the environment, but also because customers are starting to use their purchasing power to patronise organisations that are inclined towards sustainability. Although this change in attitude is currently negligible it must have an impact eventually. Recent studies have revealed that despite customers knowing that their choices may contribute to harming the environment, their actions and behaviours seem to not change much [2]. In some instances, customers simply lack understanding on how their choices impact on sustainability. For example, when a customer selects Amazon Prime that promises expedited delivery times, it creates excess packaging, and poor loading, routeing, and scheduling. While the customer may be satisfied, the net effect is an increase in unsustainable outcomes.

Logistics remains a critical component in the delivery of these products and services, and for many companies it is a strategic competitive asset [3]. It is this desire and focus on competitive advantage that may come at the cost of sustainability. The advancement of technology and online instantaneous delivery models have created a customer and society dependent on instant gratification [4]. It is estimated that due to the heightened use of e-commerce the last-mile transportation (B2C) will see delivery vehicles grow by 36% which will result in a 32% increase in emissions in the top 100 cities globally by 2030 [5]. Supply chains have become increasingly more connected, interdependent, and complex, reducing the desired levels of visibility leading to negative ecological and social consequences [6]. Technology may offer solutions to some of these challenges. Current trends of global warming and extreme weather dictate that concerted global effort is vital in adopting sustainable practices. Yet, long payback periods in sustainability initiatives may prove to be a disincentive for businesses [7]. For the latter, financial sustainability, without which they will collapse, remains critical. Therefore, a balance is needed.

The objectives of the chapter are to:

1. Define the concept of sustainability and its application in business operations, with a specific reference to financial sustainability.

2. Discuss components and activities of supply chains and their contributions to environmental sustainability.

3. Demonstrate how technology can be used to integrate sustainability into supply chain decisions in relation to the supply chain components and activities, through the improvement of information and financial flows.

4. Offer a sustainable supply chain governance model that incorporates and balances competing multi-stakeholder interests.

2. Methodology

The Chapter adopts a pragmatist paradigm [8] using a narrative literature review [9], given that the objectives are focused on presenting the current knowledge on sustainable supply chains and showing gaps in their practices, while offering practical tools for improvement. Pragmatism offers flexibility on the choice of methods used in research as guided by the research questions. Therefore, the following approach was taken; (1) Objectives and structure of the chapter (topics to be covered) were discussed and agreed by the authors; (2) Literature was searched from a few databases including Science Direct (predominantly), Ebscohost and Google scholar; (3) Grey literature was added to capture practitioner knowledge and current practices as the subject is constantly evolving; (4) Synthesis of the literature was conducted.

3. Sustainability within the supply chain

As stated in the Introduction, sustainability is not a new concept, and it is a term that is used quite broadly. It therefore tends to take different forms depending on the respective disciplines. For example, a systematic literature review [10] revealed rather divergent areas of sustainability that include Ecological Sustainability, Economic Sustainability and Social Sustainability. Literature commonly presents these as independent concepts. According to the authors, definitions of sustainability in supply chains are disjointed across the literature which makes frameworks for research and practice challenging. In many instances, the concept of sustainability has been narrowed down to very specific areas such as sustainable procurement, production, packaging, and transportation, among others, leading to fragmentation. Generally, sustainability in supply chains has been viewed as attaining a balance between economic, environmental, and social objectives, a concept commonly referred to as the triple bottom line (TBL), and sometimes referred to as Profit, Planet, and People (3Ps). This is reflected and expanded in Searcy's [11] idea of focal firm, supply chain, and sustainability context within which the firm operates. Critically, Searcy emphasises the need for the focal firm and its supply chain partners to consider broader social and environmental boundaries at local, regional, and global levels. This is motivated by the understanding that economic advancement is inherently linked to long-term stability of the environment. To date, the definition of sustainability [12] that posits that sustainability is achieved when current needs are met without compromising the ability of the future generations to meet their needs, remains pivotal both in practice and academia. Incorporating this ideology into SCM to create sustainable supply chain management (SSCM), the authors propose the following definition.

> *Sustainable supply chain management is the attainment of efficiency, visibility, and security of supply chain member interactions for profit by harnessing technological capabilities in a way that the current and future economic, ecological, and societal interests are integrated and not compromised.*

This definition brings two new aspects to the definition of SSCM. First, the belief that technology will be a critical driving force given the desired and realistic SCM future. Second, given the need for urgent action to reverse and slow climate change, the ability to meet the needs of the identified stakeholders is already compromised. To put this into perspective, Brundtland made this assertion more than three decades ago.

4. Role of supply chains and logistics in sustainability

Logistics has become the backbone of business globally. Today, more than ever, the Covid-19 pandemic has demonstrated how the world desperately depends on the movement of goods with container prices growing tenfold from 2019 to 2021. Despite the global disruptions, supply chains have shown resilience in moving what needs to be moved. According to UNCTAD [13], the world ship carrying capacity reached 2.1 billion dead-weight tonnes (dwt) after increasing by 81 million dwt by January 2021. The classical contribution by Converse [14] that recognises logistics as the other half of marketing simply emphasises the position the function occupies in the broader business environment. A supply chain consists of many players (local or international) that work together to create value in an arrangement sometimes referred to as value chains. **Figure 1** below shows a graphical representation of the traditional logistics and value chain activities by Porter [15], made up of primary and

Figure 1.
Logistics and value chain activities. Source: Porter [15].

secondary activities. Primary activities that involve inbound logistics, operations, and outbound logistics among others depend a lot on movement of raw materials, semi-finished, finished goods, services, information, and financial resources between the different players using different modes. Most of the inefficiencies and waste occur when the coordination of these activities fails. For example, wrong forecasts may lead to bullwhip effects creating huge disruptions in supply chains, building up inventory or necessitating expedited shipments. Two cases that are cited [16] of the "Norwegian salmon" and "Rolls Royce wheels" where these high-end products (despite efforts to make their production environmentally friendly), reverse all these gains through increased movement for purposes of "value addition". In the case of the salmon, it goes to China from Europe for processing only to be shipped back to the west for consumption. This increases the carbon footprint of these products, which unfortunately, is not often captured as a cost in supply chains. Equally, there are still controversies around net benefits on the use of electric cars when the industries that produce them and the cars themselves are still powered by fossil fuels generated energy.

In responding to environmental concerns businesses have adopted concepts such as green logistics and circular economy [17]. The green concept forces businesses to infuse sustainability in every decision made—that holistic optimisation in supply chains should go beyond operational and profit efficiencies but also consider environmental and societal impacts with a view to reduce waste at source. On the other hand, the circular economy concept is driven by the idea that waste can be fed back into the system to harness its value as long as it is possible to do so [18]. In other words, business activities can be arranged in a way that one's waste serves as an input for another's production. Materials are re-used until they can no longer be useful, thereby delaying their disposal. To that extent, ecosystem- models like business clustering have made this possible. Some traditional industries have incorporated partial recycling simply as a cost saving measure without being concerned with sustainability - for example, steel production uses scrap iron as a component (often 15–25%) of refined steel finished products. By contrast Just in Time (JIT) has led to clustering of component industries around major manufactures - e.g., in the European automotive industry.

5. Augmenting sustainability efforts through technology

The Fourth Industrial Revolution (4IR) presents great opportunities to revolutionise supply chains, changing how products and services are designed, produced, distributed, and disposed [19]. Broadly, integration of 4IR and sustainability goals has potential to improve chances of attaining positive environmental and ecological outcomes [20]. Despite this, challenges in the adoption and implementation of 4IR initiatives for sustainable supply chains range from organisational, technological, strategic, ethical and legal issues. These are especially true for the developing world. Faced with these challenges, the following technologies are potential gamechangers. By far the greatest benefits are improved visibility, flexibility, security, and integration over a complex web of different supply chains, with sustainability as the likely outcome.

5.1 Machine learning

Inventory and warehousing are some of the main contributors to inefficiencies in the supply chain. Overstocking is a common practice across warehouses around the world. The main reason behind this is the limited information available to decision makers regarding how external factors can impact their operations.

Machine learning provides solutions in the form of inventory control towers that enables recommendations based on data previously gathered. The algorithms created can identify the impact of external and internal factors on inventory cycles upstream and downstream [21]. Also, it allows prediction of potential imbalances in supply chain networks providing reaction time to redistribute goods in a more efficient manner. The result of this is improved energy efficiency and reduced greenhouse gases (GHG) emissions.

5.2 Blockchain and internet of things (IoT)

Supply chain sustainability risk (SCSR) is prevalent because buying firms possess little information about their suppliers and their operations [22]. New technologies like Blockchain and IoT devices are providing a path for companies to solve issues related to visibility (provenance, fraud, and democratisation of data). It is important to mention that lack of visibility can create inefficiencies within supply chains directly impacting on the sustainability of company operations. IoT leads to improved profitability through in-built supply chain flexibility, optimised shipments and reduction of excess production [23].

IoT devices can be defined as the latest generation sensors that have the capabilities to track, collect and transmit multiple parameters like geo-positioning, temperature, pressure, gas concentration among others in real time. Having access to this data in real time allows supply chain practices not only to take better decisions, but also have a better data for future analysis. IoTs have been successfully used to define the provenance of sensitive goods allowing customers to take better decisions on their sustainable journeys.

Blockchain is defined as a "public ledger in which each node in the blockchain network stores the same ledger" [24]. The adoption of Distributed Ledger Technologies (DLT), like Blockchain, in supply chain management is advancing rapidly in top tier companies. Blockchain is providing a foundation to reduce silos across the supply chain flows (physical, financial and informational) as it allows for integration of multiple legacy platforms with new solutions like IoTs. One of the most important characteristics of DLTs, which is also very attractive to the business community, is the immutability of the data recorded [25]. This feature provides companies and customers with a level playing field, resulting from distribution of power [26], where concepts like greenwashing are not relevant anymore due to visibility and the provenance provided. Furthermore, DLTs provide a chance for brands to involve customers in their validation frameworks due to the decentralised nature of these solutions.

5.3 3D printing

Companies are integrating critical parts of their supply chains in order to have better controls and increased suitability efficiencies. 3D printing has become a perfect initiative for companies to regain control of their own supply chains. The Covid-19 pandemic has highlighted how companies have become extremely dependent on outsourced manufacturers located in places far from where their markets are.

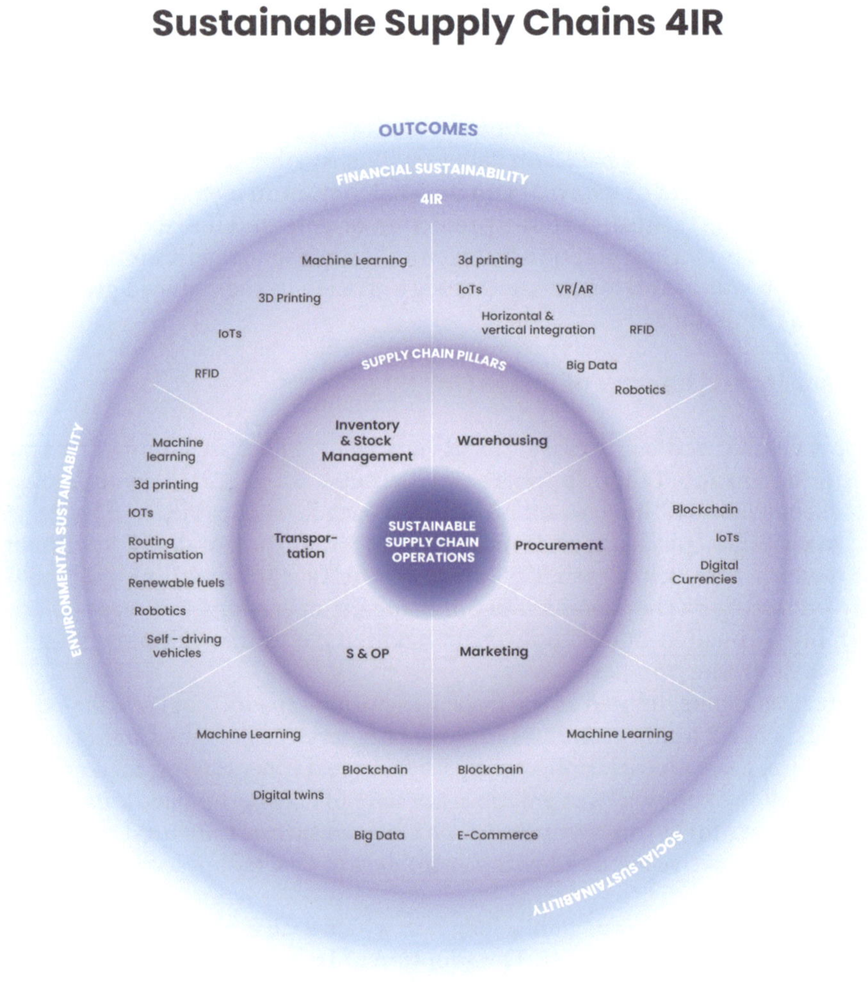

Figure 2.
Sustainable supply chains 4IR. Source: Authors illustration.

3D printing and point of sale production can have a dramatic impact in the sustainable strategies that companies are putting forward. One of the benefits that can be identified from 3D printing is the decrease in long-distance shipping and fossil fuel consumption. The idea is that as long-distance shipping decreases, the last mile will increase due to production sites being closer to final consumers. Also, 3D printing will have a long-term impact in physical warehousing as the need for spare parts and storage will be minimised. Parts will be replaced by blueprints that can be used when required. These actions will save resources currently needed to run facilities and greatly reduce the waste coming from obsolete stock and unused spare parts.

It is worth mentioning that 3D printing can be more energy intensive than traditional methods, but overall, across the whole supply chain there is a greater positive impact when considering not just the manufacturing processes.

Since Porter's value chain framework was introduced in 1985, supply chains have evolved with environmental and societal concerns becoming more significant. Cashflow as opposed to profitability has also become a critical indicator for a healthy business. The advent of 4IR has catalysed this trend, promising accelerated positive outcomes if done right. **Figure 2** above shows a transformed value chain whose players are more integrated in a complex network than before, enhancing visibility and thus offering the potential for flexibility and agility in response to changing circumstances.

6. Why does sustainability matter?

This section discusses the views of the different stakeholders on sustainability. In the beginning, the divergent views are discussed independently and subsequently synthesised to demonstrate their congruence and incongruence at the same time. The bigger question is whether these seemingly competitive views can be reconciled or not.

6.1 Policy view

Governments play a critical role in sustainability through policy, law, and investments. Despite the urgency to cut carbon emissions significantly, the United States of America (which is the second highest emitter after China) withdrew from the Paris Agreement under the Trump administration, only to re-join when President Biden took over. Law on methane taxation and tax credits on electric cars is facing resistance from both the Republican party, petroleum companies and third-party lobbyists. China is still non-committal on its plans to cut emissions. On a positive note, the European continent through its Green Deal has aligned its development agenda to attain 55% emission cuts by 2030. Substantial financial resources have been committed towards the eight actions identified including transportation, energy, industry, research, and innovation [27]. By contrast, the developing world does not have the luxury of resources commanded by their developed counterparts. Inevitably, this will keep sustainability off the developing countries' tables as they have more pressing priorities such as dealing with poverty, hunger and failing healthcare. In 2015, the United Nations COP21 agreed that the developed member countries will jointly raise USD100 billion to fund climate mitigation and adaptation plans for the developing world. Six years later, this is proving to be a challenge. On the other hand, politics, especially in working democracies can bring about change if the electorates are informed and demand sustainable development policy. The decarbonisation of development has catalysed investments in clean energy, sustainable industry, development of electric cars, intensified research, and development in sustainable solutions. In the Netherlands, every new law passed, and policy made has to reflect their effects on sustainable development goals. At global level, the United Nations (UN) sustainable development goals (SDGs) 2030 have set the tone with the desire to achieve a sustainable future for all.

6.2 Business view

The need for businesses to be financially sustainable cannot be over emphasised. Again, businesses remain committed to creating wealth for investors, unless they have very clear social goals. Even then, [28] who claims to have coined the term triple bottom line (TBL), observes that 25 years later business thinking has not changed much. He asserts that business executives would "move heaven and earth" to ensure they reach their profit targets but the same cannot be said about the other two dimensions – people and planet. Part of the reason why businesses were reluctant to fully embrace sustainability was the idea that it only added costs and constrained economic performance [29]. Does sustainability pay? Using game theory, findings [30] demonstrated that businesses would invest in sustainability only if the demand-enhancing effect supersedes the cost-increasing effects especially when managerial incentives are subjected to negative rewards. From a business perspective, they may need government policy incentives to nudge them into sustainable practices [31]. Unless integrated global policies that motivate businesses to adopt sustainable practices are developed, the future looks bleak for both the planet and people.

6.3 Customer view

In the Introduction section of this Chapter, the customer is identified as a critical stakeholder through their choices of products and services. Their purchasing power gives them leverage as agents of change to influence business decisions, especially where sustainability is an important consideration in product choices. Whereas knowledge can be (and remains) critical, in some cases it does not shape action. In the UK, a study by Hornibrook et al. [32] that followed an observation of no discernible effect of carbon labelling on customer product choices, concluded that lack of awareness and understanding of carbon labelling were among the major contributors to low carbon products unfavourable uptake. The evidence points to either an informed customer but little will, or uninformed customers (who are the majority) with no appreciation and requisite tools to make sustainable decisions. Knowledge on sustainable practices is even limited in high institutions of learning in present-day USA [33]. Heeren et al. [34], however, demonstrated that knowledge was insignificant in predicting behaviour when controlling for attitudes, norms, and perceived behavioural control variables of the Theory of Planned Behaviour. Even though this study was also carried out on university students in the USA, the message is that there needs to be more than knowledge to realise the desired change in behaviour towards sustainable practices.

6.4 Societal view

Recent years have seen socio-economic inequalities widen despite the advancement of technology and innovation that promised democratisation of economies.

According to the International Labour Organisation (ILO) [35] it is estimated that modern day slavery reached almost 25 million cases globally as of 2016. On the other hand, poor countries and those with low latitudes are disproportionally affected by climate change [36]. From a societal perspective, despite supply chains offering them choices, if not practised in a responsible manner, they have the potential of impacting lives and the future of the next generations negatively. Families are separated through forced labour while other vulnerable societies are exposed to harsh climate consequences. An existential threat is a reality. In the early 1990s, businesses started the incorporation of more socially responsible practices and the triple bottom line (TBL) reporting was born. According to Slaper and Hall [37], comprehensive investments that considered the people, planet and profit will likely support sustainable goals. The idea is that society through its forms (legal and political) can exert some pressure on business to act both ethically and morally. Society also desires to see governments taking action against polluters and irresponsible supply chains by making them pay for their deeds [11]. Unfortunately, global society hardly has a unified view on a wide variety of issues including sustainability. Societies tend to be heterogenous and have low issue agreement, making them very weak in putting pressure on the market players [38]. It makes sense to argue that societies are part of a political system that continually polarises them. On the world stage we have already seen how polarising politics can be on issues of sustainability in the USA elections. If society is to have any significant influence on sustainability, there is a need to confront an arena where power dominates knowledge [39].

6.5 Conglomerate (or summary) view

Societies, especially those that are vulnerable see sustainability as an urgent matter that should be prioritised by policy. Ironically, when the same society assumes the customer cap, they lose their power of influence driven by either selfish gains (instant gratification) or lack of appropriate tools to exercise this power. The business community is looking for incentives to do what is "right", but in some instances doing the right thing may lead to bankruptcy and collapse. On the other hand, government becomes the hope through policy—this may prove ineffective when political mileage is the ultimate goal of politicians, overpowering scientific evidence. At the end of it all, no matter what the view or interest is, everyone shall pay for the severe consequences of nature when supply chains practices are oblivious of sustainability concerns.

7. Sustainability vs. financial sustainability

Ever since the concept of 'supply chain sustainability' was first mooted, there has been a debate around its possible conflict with profitability. One problem is that, in some cases, there is confusion between environmental (green issues) and commercial sustainability. This phenomenon is particularly noticeable in developing countries' small transport businesses, where a typical reaction from an operator when asked about sustainability could be, 'I don't have time to worry about that green stuff, I have to concentrate on paying my bills and putting food on my family's plates' [40].

There is a genuine fear in many businesses, especially small and medium sized ones, that the short-term costs of operating in a sustainable manner will outweigh any longer-term benefits. This fear can become acute in businesses that operate in a hand to mouth manner, i.e., those that need all their available cash to operate and pay wages and so have insufficient money with which to make provision for the future. In some cases, this fear can be very real, businesses do not fail because of lack of profitability but they will fail, sometimes very quickly, when the cash-flow dries up [41]. In other words, if there is a risk that the immediate investment needed to generate sustainable benefits could lead to business failure and even bankruptcy, there is very little chance that those investments will be made. This is particularly sad because, in many cases, strategies designed to give environmental benefits will also create operational cost reductions. For example; efficient routeing and scheduling will reduce fuel bills and allow more 'drops' to be completed in a given time [42], whilst good warehouse management systems can have a major positive impact on supply chain efficiency and effectiveness [43] and therefore on both sustainability and operating costs.

Seeking long-term benefits can also cause problems. For example, extending one's supply chain with a view to taking advantage of the low prices or variety offered by globalisation, increases the risk of failure as has been unfortunately demonstrated by supply problems encountered during the Covid-19 crisis. This has led to many companies reversing their globalisation efforts (e.g., by re-shoring) to shorten their supply chains and reduce risks, sometimes at a short-term reduction of profit or even financial loss to enhance longer term viability. Some businesses, that were unable to react quickly to the changing circumstances, failed.

Nevertheless, the key would seem to be to take a long-term view, but this can be difficult when one is fighting for survival. One way to reduce the short-term cost of implementing sustainability measures is to co-operate not just with one's own partners and suppliers but across, as well as, up and down supply chains, even with competitors. Such practices, which hitherto would have been an anathema to many businesses, have come to the fore in recent years where sharing data and even transport can be shown to be mutually beneficial to facilitate survival and enhance sustainability [44].

Green supply chain management and other sustainable concepts are slowly gaining popularity in developing countries. If sustainable supply chain management practices are to be fully adopted by all organisations, a demonstrable link between such measures and improving economic performance and competitiveness will be needed [45]. In particular it is essential that any short-term operational costs are not allowed to inhibit potentially beneficial moves towards sustainability. Perhaps the key is to be found in collaboration through technology to minimise both costs and risks, whilst avoiding cyber information risks [46].

8. Governance and sustainability

One of the principles that runs through this Chapter is the need to consider sustainability of the varied stakeholders. Only when economic, environmental, and social sustainability concerns are integrated throughout the decision-making process can you achieve sustainable development [47]. One of the reflections is that despite knowledge of the need to balance these three concerns, in practice, this has been harder to achieve. Even though sustainability in principle is an inclusive concept and possesses broader stakeholder interests, some of the interests have not been sufficiently represented. Consistent with the 'leave no one behind' principle embedded in the SDG 2030, the governance framework on sustainability should be formulated to include even the least of interests. Access to accurate, immutable, and timely data on local, regional, and global supply chain networks and activities promises information symmetry that allows accountability and gives power to policymakers and society in decision making and influences the conduct of the supply chains. The same technological capabilities driving global supply chain excellence can be harnessed to facilitate sustainability in them.

Calls for governance models that decentralise and realign decision-making in a manner that drives inclusion through stakeholder engagement, empowered participation and engaged decision making have been made by researchers [48]. Sustainability governance models have taken different forms including community, state, or private-led initiatives. Debates on which approach(es) is effective ensue. Private governance is normally driven by certification processes based on standard norms that individual companies across the chain commit to adhering to. Companies are incentivised through access to premium markets using certification that is recognised and practised by both producers and buyers. According to Grabs [49], the ability of private governance initiatives to play any meaningful role, depends on whether they can be scaled and institutionalised in a given sector. Grabs' study found that, despite the advancement in the sustainable norms and institutionalisation of standard setting, integration of social and environmental externalities into production and procurement of highly priced certified products remains a challenge. Considering the complexity of global supply chains, sustainability governance presents a huge challenge. Advancement in technological tools affords an opportunity to counter this. Generation of sustainability data that can be visibly and timely circulated among the critical stakeholders can re-shape power balances and accountability in supply chains [26]. Using a sustainability matrix in the US agri-food supply chains private-ordering systems proved that continuous improvement in sustainability, can be achieved.

9. Conclusion

It is axiomatic that supply chains are not only essential to the twenty-first century way of life but that they have a major influence on the environment and therefore on their own sustainability and that of our planet. It is also apparent that most people that have the luxury of being able to think about it, would like to minimise and ideally reverse their impact. Unfortunately, 'thinking' and 'doing' are often worlds apart from each other and reality.

Even if one accepts people's good intentions, it is apparent from this chapter that, confusion reigns. So many things influence sustainability through supply chains, that it is difficult to know where to start, but some things are very clear:

- Technology offers many techniques to tackle the problem or (in the modern idiom) 'provide a -solution'. For example:

- Physical distribution aids such as: Drone technology and its adoption into mainstream parcels delivery can assist addressing the 'last mile problem'.

- Technology such as: 4IR can provide data and visibility of supply chains.

- Such tools are simply enablers. Like every claim made by a software salesman, the savings can only be achieved if people act effectively on the information they provide.

This chapter has shown that 4IR technologies offer an unprecedented, if confusing, wealth of data and visibility with which to manage our supply chains so that, if we desire, they can become sustainable both environmentally and commercially. Importantly, that opportunity is only meaningful if the right policies, as well as leadership, exist and that global supply chains should be made more honest and open to scrutiny. Above all, environmental sustainability can only be achieved if, at all levels, from corporate down to personal, we put the planet before people and people before profit – in other words, we all aspire to use 4IR technology to become 'global citizens'.

Acknowledgements

The authors extend their gratitude to Caroline Savage for her assistance and great professionalism in proofreading and editing the final manuscript. Further appreciation goes to Defactor DAO for the open access publication fee funding.

Author details

Thuso Mphela[1*], Christopher J. Savage[2] and Alejandro Gutierrez[3]

1 Faculty of Business, Department of Management, University of Botswana, Botswana

2 Zorro Logistics Ltd, United Kingdom

3 Defactor, Ireland

*Address all correspondence to: mphelat@ub.ac.bw

References

[1] Quarshie AM, Salmi A, Leuschner R. Sustainability and corporate social responsibility in supply chains: The state of research in supply chain management and business ethics journals. Journal of Purchasing and Supply Management. 2016;**22**(2):82-97. DOI: 10.1016/j.pursup.2015.11.001

[2] Pereira L, Carvalho R, Dias Á, Costa R, António N. How does sustainability affect consumer choices in the fashion industry? Resources. 2021;**10**(4):38. DOI: 10.3390/resources10040038

[3] Sandberg E, Abrahamsson M. Logistics capabilities for sustainable competitive advantage. International Journal of Logistics Research and Applications. 2011;**14**(1):61-75. DOI: 10.1080/13675567.2010.551110

[4] Arbuthnott KD. Taking the long view: Environmental sustainability and delay of gratification. Analyses of Social Issues and Public Policy. 2010;**10**(1):4-22. DOI: 10.1111/j.1530-2415.2009.01196.x

[5] World Economic Forum. The Future of the Last-Mile Ecosystem: Transition Roadmaps for Public - and Private-Sector Players. Cologny, Geneva, Switzerland; 2020. pp. 1-28. Available from: https://www3.weforum.org/docs/WEF_Future_of_the_last_mile_ecosystem.pdf

[6] Erhun F, Kraft T, Wijnsma S. Sustainable triple-A supply chains. Production and Operations Management. 2021;**30**(3):644-655. DOI: 10.1111/poms.13306

[7] Rademaekers K, Williams R, Ellis R, Smith M, Svatikova K, Bilsen V. Study on Incentives Driving Improvement of Environmental Performance of Companies. Rotterdam, The Netherlands: Ecorys; 2012

[8] Goldkuhl G. Pragmatism vs interpretivism in qualitative information systems research. European Journal of Information Systems. 2012;**21**(2):135-146. DOI: 10.1057/ejis.2011.54

[9] Pautasso M. The structure and conduct of a narrative literature review. In: A Guide to the Scientific Career: Virtues, Communication, Research and Academic Writing. John Wiley & Sons, Inc. 2019. pp. 299-310. DOI: 10.1002/9781118907283.ch31

[10] Bhanot N, Rao PV, Deshmukh SG. Sustainable Scenario: A Systematic Review of Definitions of Sustainability and Agenda for Future Research. South Asian Journal of Management. 2019;**26**(4):32-70

[11] Searcy C. Measuring enterprise sustainability. Business Strategy and the Environment. 2016;**25**(2):120-133. DOI: 10.1002/bse.1861

[12] Brundtland GH. Our common future—Call for action. Environmental Conservation. 1987;**14**(4):291-294. DOI: 10.1017/S0376892900016805

[13] UNCTAD. Marine Time: Merchant Fleet. 2020. Available from: https://stats.unctad.org/handbook/MaritimeTransport/MerchantFleet.html.

[14] Converse PD. The other half of marketing. In: Proceedings of the Twenty-Sixth Boston Conference on Distribution. Boston, MA: Boston Trade Board; 1954. pp. 22-25

[15] Porter ME. Competitive Advantage: Creating and Sustaining Superior Performance. New York: Free Press; 1985

[16] Prusa P, Savage CJ. Global supply chains: The cost of sourcing? In:

Proceedings of Aktualni problemy v doprave. Pardubice, Czech Republic: Jan Pernera Institute of Transport; 2007. pp. 103-107

[17] Seroka-Stolka O, Ociepa-Kubicka A. Green logistics and circular economy. Transportation Research Procedia. 2019;**39**:471-479. DOI: 10.1016/j.trpro.2019.06.049

[18] Ying J, Li-jun Z. Study on green supply chain management based on circular economy. Physics Procedia. 2012;**25**:1682-1688. DOI: 10.1016/j.phpro.2012.03.295

[19] Luthra S, Mangla SK. Evaluating challenges to Industry 4.0 initiatives for supply chain sustainability in emerging economies. Process Safety and Environmental Protection. 2018;**117**:168-179. DOI: 10.1016/j.psep.2018.04.018

[20] Oláh J, Aburumman N, Popp J, Khan MA, Haddad H, Kitukutha N. Impact of Industry 4.0 on environmental sustainability. Sustainability. 2020;**12**(11):4674. DOI: 10.3390/su12114674

[21] Bousqaoui H, Achchab S, Tikito K. Machine learning applications in supply chains: An emphasis on neural network applications. In: 2017 3rd International Conference of Cloud Computing Technologies and Applications (CloudTech). Rabat, Morocco: Institute of Electrical and Electronics Engineers (IEEE). 2017. pp. 1-7. DOI: 10.1109/CloudTech.2017.8284722

[22] Busse C, Schleper MC, Weilenmann J, Wagner SM. Extending the supply chain visibility boundary: Utilizing stakeholders for identifying supply chain sustainability risks. International Journal of Physical Distribution & Logistics Management. 2017;**47**(1):18-40. DOI: 10.1108/IJPDLM-02-2015-0043

[23] Haddud A, DeSouza A, Khare A, Lee H. Examining potential benefits and challenges associated with the Internet of Things integration in supply chains. Journal of Manufacturing Technology Management. 2017;**28**(8):1055-1085. DOI: 10.1108/JMTM-05-2017-0094

[24] Tian Z, Li M, Qiu M, Sun Y, Su S. Block-DEF: A secure digital evidence framework using blockchain. Information Sciences. 2019;**491**:151-165. DOI: 10.1016/j.ins.2019.04.011

[25] Gonczol P, Katsikouli P, Herskind L, Dragoni N. Blockchain implementations and use cases for supply chains-a survey. IEEE Access. 2020;**8**:11856-11871. DOI: 10.1109/ACCESS.2020.2964880

[26] Strube J, Glenna L, Hatanaka M, Konefal J, Conner D. How data-driven, privately ordered sustainability governance shapes US food supply chains: The case of field to market. Journal of Rural Studies. 2021;**86**:684-693 https://doi.org/10.1016/j.jrurstud.2021.05.028

[27] European Commission. A European Deal: Striving to be the First Climate-Neutral Continents. Available from: https://ec.europa.eu/info/strategy/priorities-2019-2024/european-green-deal_en. [Accessed 1 November 2021]

[28] Elkington J. 25 years ago I coined the phrase "triple bottom line." Here's why it's time to rethink it. Harvard Business Review. 2018;**25**:2-5

[29] Cerin P, Karlson L. Business incentives for sustainability: A property rights approach. Ecological Economics. 2002;**40**(1):13-22. DOI: 10.1016/S0921-8009(01)00275-0

[30] Veldman J, Gaalman G. On the design of managerial incentives for sustainability investments in the presence of competitors. Journal of

Cleaner Production. 2020;**258**:120925. DOI: 10.1016/j.jclepro.2020.120925

[31] Ding H, Liu Q, Zheng L. Assessing the economic performance of an environmental sustainable supply chain in reducing environmental externalities. European Journal of Operational Research. 2016;**255**(2):463-480. DOI: 10.1016/j.ejor.2016.05.003

[32] Hornibrook S, May C, Fearne A. Sustainable development and the consumer: Exploring the role of carbon labelling in retail supply chains. Business Strategy and the Environment. 2015;**24**(4):266-276. DOI: 10.1002/bse.1823

[33] Msengi I, Doe R, Wilson T, Fowler D, Wigginton C, Olorunyomi S, et al. Assessment of knowledge and awareness of "sustainability" initiatives among college students. Renewable Energy and Environmental Sustainability. 2019;**4**:6. DOI: 10.1051/rees/2019003

[34] Heeren AJ, Singh AS, Zwickle A, Koontz TM, Slagle KM, McCreery AC. Is sustainability knowledge half the battle? An examination of sustainability knowledge, attitudes, norms, and efficacy to understand sustainable behaviours. International Journal of Sustainability in Higher Education. 2016;**17**(5):613-632. DOI: 10.1108/IJSHE-02-2015-0014

[35] International Labour Organisation (ILO). Forced Labour, Modern Slavery and Human Trafficking. 2017. Available from: https://www.ilo.org/global/topics/forced-labour/lang--en/index.htm

[36] Mendelsohn R, Dinar A, Williams L. The distributional impact of climate change on rich and poor countries. Environment and Development Economics. 2006;**11**(2):159-178

[37] Slaper TF, Hall TJ. The triple bottom line: What is it and how does it work. Indiana Business Review. 2011;**86**(1):4-8

[38] Bartley T. Institutional emergence in an era of globalization: The rise of transnational private regulation of labor and environmental conditions. American Journal of Sociology. 2007;**113**(2):297-351. DOI: 10.1086/518871

[39] Wiek A, Farioli F, Fukushi K, Yarime M. Sustainability science: Bridging the gap between science and society. Sustainability Science. 2012;7(1):1-4. DOI: 10.1007/s11625-011-0154-0

[40] Fransman L, Jenkins A, Savage C. Logistics in Namibia: Issues and Challenges – Re-Engineering For Competitiveness. Birmingham, UK: Logistics Research Network Conference; 2013

[41] Uwonda G, Okello N. Cash flow management and sustainability of small medium enterprises (SMEs) in Northern Uganda. International Journal of Social Science and Economics Invention (IJSSEI). 2015;**01**(03). DOI: 10.23958/ijssei/vol01-i03/02

[42] Maden W, Eglese R, Black D. Vehicle routing and scheduling with time-varying data: A case study. Journal of Operational Research Society. 2010;**61**:515-522. DOI: 10.1057/jors.2009.116

[43] Ramaa A, Subramanya K, Rangaswamy T. Impact of warehouse management system in a supply chain. International Journal of Computer Applications. 2012;**54**(1):0975-8887

[44] Andriolo A, Battini D, Persona A, Sgarbossa F. Haulage sharing approach to achieve sustainability in material

purchasing: New method and numerical applications. International Journal of Production Economics. 2016;**164**:308-318. DOI: 10.1016/j.ijpe.2014.12.011

[45] Rao P, Holt D. Do green supply chains lead to competitiveness and economic performance? International Journal of Operations & Production Management. 2005;**25**(9):898-916. DOI: 10.1108/01443570510613956

[46] Colicchia C, Creazza A, Menachof D. Managing cyber and information risks in supply chains: Insights from an exploratory analysis. Supply Chain Management. 2019;**24**(2):215-240. DOI: 10.1108/SCM-09-2017-0289

[47] Emas R. The concept of sustainable development: Definition and defining principles. In: Brief for GSDR. Florida, USA: Florida International University; 2015. pp. 1-3

[48] Denburg AE, Ramirez A, Pavuluri S, McCann E, Shah S, Alcasabas T, et al. Political priority and pathways to scale-up of childhood cancer care in five nations. PLOS One. 2019;**14**(8):e0221292. DOI: 10.1371/journal.pone.0221292

[49] Grabs J. Assessing the institutionalization of private sustainability governance in a changing coffee sector. Regulation & Governance. 2020;**14**(2):362-387. DOI: 10.1111/rego.12212

Chapter 3

Industry 4.0: The Tenets of the Next Generation of Supply Chain Management

Andre T. Mayounga

Abstract

The supply chain industry is at the crossroads of the business revolution through the Fourth Industrial Revolution (4IR), impacting business activities across industries. The transformative elements of 4IR offer individual consumers, corporations, and governments unprecedented opportunities to link, collaborate, process, and manage rising consumer and business data to boost decision-making, efficiency, and productivity. Evidence shows that have applied a mix of collaborative and innovative technologies to internal and external activities to manage supply chain disruptions. The groundbreaking technological advancements paved the way for the supply industry to shift supply business prototypes from traditional supply chain models to supply web models. The shift has helped firms resolve national and global supply chain disruptions. The present chapter introduces the Supply Web (SW) concept and its distinctive tenets by adding to the growing body of the evolving Industry 4.0 field, knowledge to help advance the field. The author calls on governments, the global supply industry, and academia to consider embracing the new SW paradigm evolving under 4IR to help resolve societal and consumer challenges emerging in the 21st Century.

Keywords: Industry 4.0, supply web, supply web management, SWM, fourth industrial revolution, 4IR, supply chain management, supply, SCM, artificial intelligence, big data, IoT, Internet of Things, innovation

1. Introduction

The coronavirus pandemic 2019 (COVID-19) and the 2021 delay of cargo ships along the California coastline illustrated recent challenges facing the supply industry and governments across the globe. Evidence shows that supply and demand challenges in the last years resulted from improper collaboration. The global supply industry saw nearly half a million containers of goods stuck off the coast of Southern California as state seaports operated below optimal capacity due to the coronavirus 2019 (COVID-19). The delay of containers disrupted services and delivery of goods in the United States and globally pre-2021 holiday season. Cargo ships could not return to their ports of origin to drop off or pick up more goods while customers canceled orders impacting business bottom lines. Meanwhile, much of the global supply chain difficulties anticipating to anticipate COVID-19 pandemic-induced lockdowns and closures, which reduced the ability of firms to satisfy global market demands.

At the pick of COVID-19 and the Los Angeles seaport congestion, many firms satisfied consumer demands by utilizing a series of innovative digital technologies which include the Internet of Things, big data to machine learning (ML). COVID-19 pandemic and the California seaport crisis demonstrate the challenges facing firms that applied 20th century supply chain models to 21st-century problems. Today, evidence suggests that companies that employed a blend of new technologies during recent crises registered efficiency and productivity by addressing customer or industry needs in real-time (Imran Ali). The concoction of new technologies gave many firms opportunities to increase productivity and efficiency through big data, intelligent software, Internet of Things (IoT), and hardware. The 4IR is setting to disrupt orthodox supply chain knowledge by offering groundbreaking ways to meet and satisfy customer needs amid crises [1].

Meanwhile, many countries and firms still lack the basic infrastructure desirable to reap the benefits of the 4IR despite the usefulness and potential for the supply industry. The succeeding sections provide a background, methodology, results and discussion introducing the concept of the Supply Web and its tenets.

2. Literature review

2.1 Earlier industrial revolutions and supply chains

History shows technological innovation has always been at the center of business productivity and social emancipation. It brought individuals and firms to mass-produce by moving from manual and small-scale trade activities to mechanization and large-scale engineering productions. Material and services that evolved from the revolutionary innovations impacted every aspect of economic activities [2]. Makers of goods and service providers from agriculture to factories practiced primitive forms of trades to address the challenges and conditions of their respective eras. Previous industrial transformation exacerbated economic activities and created processes and concepts suitable to describe and resolve enduring challenges.

Business concepts relating to earlier supply chain activities, procedures, and actions did not develop until later. The academia, industry, and governments described the activities associated with the phenomenon after they had already happened [3]. However, identifying and describing developing innovative technologies and related processes offered the supply industry concepts and procedures to structure and shape future business activities.

Figure 1 illustrates the typical model of the supply chain showing the association between firms from raw material to end-use. While the linear nature of the supply chain models was suitable to satisfy earlier business practices, it is no longer practical to address problems facing value chains in the 21st Century.

For instance, as figure one illustrates, end-users lack the capability or option to collaborate with material (A), Transformation (B), and so forth if they were a desire to do so. The absence of these options in the linear supply chain model reduces the potential of firms to collaborate within a broader supply chain at the national or global scale.

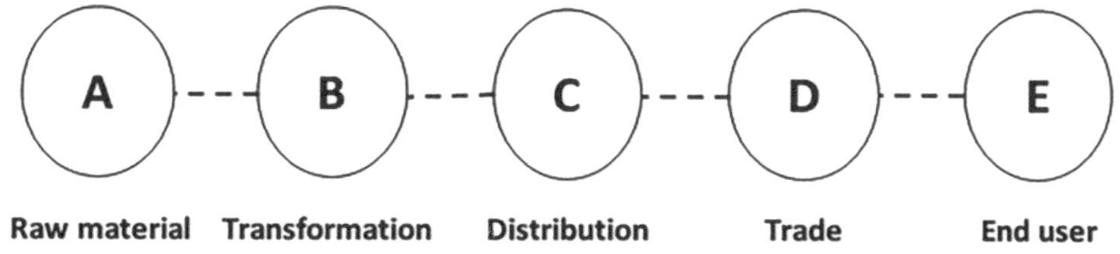

Figure 1.
Supply chain architype.

2.2 Paradigm shift

To understand the urgency to shift supply paradigms, one must grasp the current business environment. The global population doubled since the 1980s when only a handful of companies utilized computers for business. Many companies used computer technologies for small tasks, ranging from storing essential inventory data to chart display. At the time, most firms only performed business activities without computers due to the affordability of the technology. Nevertheless, the business industry and its concepts still evolved along with the adoption of computer technology. For instance, the radio frequency identification (RFID) technology helped the retailer industry and governments describe policies and procedures associated with tracking and tracing consumer products. Hence, though RFID technology did not exist earlier, most producers and retailers could still manage data and track and trace goods through traditional bookkeeping.

Meanwhile, as consumer demand evolved, so did the supply industry by adopting technologies such as RFID in various applications, including product recalls [4]. Referring to the linear supply chain (**Figure 1**), RFID sensors in most retail products often connect trade and distribution, removing end-users from collaboration despite the ability of the technology to do so. However, the linear supply chain paradigm does not envisage a collaborative transaction between the consumer and the manufacturer.

As civilizations progress, the global supply industry and governments must adopt emerging technologies and concepts to address current challenges. Industry 4.0 not only gives governments and the global supply industry the necessary tools and ideas to manage challenges, but it equally provides consumers the prospect to be a part of the solution. The current supply chain models have not successfully predicted and evaded supply chain-related predicaments. The failure is arguably in how the concept of the supply chain itself.

Today, while most supply chain firms employ computer technologies, many still lack the essential technology to collaborate successfully with partners. While many firms remain indifferent in linking their pieces of machinery with others, the speed of technology advancement equally makes it difficult to address security shortfalls as they occur. Nonetheless, a partner's lack of understanding and awareness of existing technological innovation will lead firms not to take advantage of the innovative technologies despite the rationality. In one instance, a farmer revealed during an interview to have never heard of blockchain or cloud computing [5], which many have come to consider as the cornerstone of business security and operations. Since a lack of coordination and collaboration could result in the absence of visibility and synchronized strategy between partners, firms not adopting the industry 4.0 technologies would become the gateways to substandard products and services [6]. The inability of a farmer or supply partner to

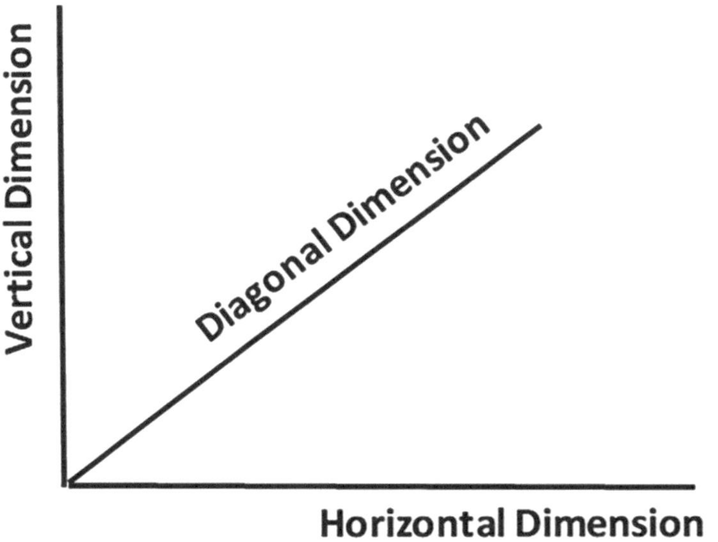

Figure 2.
Three-dimensional collaboration.

successfully and securely collaborate with others at various ends of the supply spectrum could only negatively impact the resiliency of the chain.

Linear supply chain models do not provide the necessary collaboration needed to connect valued chains at various levels of the industry. The current consumer and business data necessitate supply firms connect not only with businesses but also with consumers; hence, the necessity for multidimensional collaboration. As **Figure 2** shows, Industry 4.0 allows firms to exercise cooperation in terms of vertical, diagonal, and horizontal dimensions. When supply firms implement the 4IR technological tools, they enhance their ability to exchange business data internally, externally, and between partners beyond primary products (PBPP).

2.3 Dimensional collaboration

The Horizontal Dimension denotes the breadth of internal transactions within the main production effort. These transactions represent activities that enhance the internal collaboration between firms with direct equities on the primary production effort. Firms could have a mutual horizontal dimension when one adds value directly to the product line. For instance, tire, and windshield manufacturers add value to producing a motor vehicle a car. The three companies from the tire, windshield and carmaker have internal transactions that impact making a motor vehicle. A new motor vehicle would necessitate, among others, tires and a windshield for it to be complete. In this instance, the business transactions from the windshield and tire manufacturers make up the internal transaction of motor vehicles (main production effort).

The Vertical Dimension denotes the scope of transactions external to the main production effort. The transactions represent activities that enhance the external collaboration between firms having indirect equities on the primary production effort. Firms have a mutual vertical when one adds value indirectly to the main production effort. Using the motor vehicle example from the Horizontal Dimension, car dealers and transportation services do not directly add to the main production effort. In this instance, neither transportation services that take the finished car from the plant to the dealership nor the car dealership adds directly to the main production effort. While car dealerships and transportation services could negatively impact production, they do not generate the main production effort. However, they add value to the overall supply web production of the motor vehicle.

The Diagonal Dimension symbolizes the breadth of transactions that could occur internally and externally to the main production effort. These transactions represent activities that enhance both internal and external collaboration between firms having direct and indirect equities on the primary production effort. Firms have a mutual diagonal dimension when they complement value directly and indirectly to the primary production effort. In the above example of a motor vehicle's main production effort case, the tire, windshield, and carmakers would add value to one another when engaged in active (direct) or passive (indirect) joint activities that enhance firms' resiliency and purpose. Meanwhile, the Diagonal Dimension also includes other value partners supporting internal and external business transactions. The value partners range from financial, government, security, and others supporting institutions that directly or indirectly impact the firms' overall business operation value.

The global supply industry no longer relies on the next mile or the input from the value chain to remain resilient and anticipate the next medical shortage or cargo ships bottleneck crisis. As COVID-19 pandemic and the Los Angeles cargo crises proved, the global supply industry needs better tools and concepts to anticipate an evolving global turmoil. As opposed to employing linear supply chain models, supply firms desiring competitive advantage at the international stage should implement supply web models that integrate horizontal, vertical, and diagonal dimensional business models.

3. Methodology

This chapter intends to explain how Industry 4.0 innovative technologies impact the supply industry and introduce the tenets of the next generation of the supply chain. A qualitative exploratory design method helped to gather Industry 4.0 technologies and related concepts with impact on the supply industry to find patterns in data [7]. The mining of associated technologies and ideas was achieved utilizing codes and developing terms, which helped analyze and describe emerging themes [8]. The data used in the analysis originated from government, non-government, business, and peer-review texts.

4. Results and discussion

4.1 Results

The Supply web is the next generation of a supply chain that integrates valued chains horizontal, vertical, and diagonal dimensions through collaboration. Through Industry 4.0, supply web management (SWM) would allow firms to perform a hundred times better at fractions of the price similar firms achieved nearly fifty years ago. For instance, an iPhone device can store terabytes of data and process hundreds of business transactions in fractions of the time it would have taken a hundred 1980-era computers housed in a large building. In so far, not only the device holds a storage capacity of over a hundred earlier computers, but it is also capable of executing thousands of transactions in a record time. Modern technology has enabled businesses, individuals, and governments to conduct virtual meetings miles away, real-time monitoring of product manufacturing and delivery using automation. The current technology innovation has changed societies and demonstrates a 'creative destruction' currently trending to extinguish old industries [9]. Experts believe that Industry 4.0 is comparably helping developing countries as mobile phones did with personal communication. The use of trucks and drones to deliver goods in secluded and urban areas across the globe showed efficiency in developing countries [10]. Industry 4.0 enabled real-time vendor and subcontractors monitoring to manage rapid change and inventory [11] and reduce supply–demand misalignment [5]. Evidence suggests 4IR technologies or Industry 4.0 enhance visibility, interoperability, modularity, decentralization, virtualization, and service orientation [12].

Nonetheless, despite the potential of 4IR in the global supply industry, challenges remain without a deeper understanding of barriers and drivers. While a business' lack of collaboration, awareness, and organizational inertia bare, among others, its ability to execute supply web, a firm likewise needs to master and adopt processes and tools that add value to the supply web. For instance, a firm's plan to adopt strategies that address the reduction of supply–demand misalignment, fast-changing consumer needs, threats of legal penalties, and cost optimization could enhance its Implementation [5].

By addressing the barriers and implementing the drivers to Industry 4.0, the global supply industry would benefit of the 4IR [11]. In the interim, the adoption of Industry 4.0 necessitates investment. In contrast to small firms during the first industrial revolutions, today's small enterprises can reap the benefits of evolving technologies at affordable costs [12]. For instance, a small firm could subcontract its operations or services to large and specialized corporations. Businesses source several activities to lower operating costs, increase market access, enhance scalability, and diminish risks [11, 13].

4.2 Supply web: The next generation of supply chain

The Supply web is the next generation of a supply chain that integrates valued chains horizontal, vertical, and diagonal dimensions through collaboration. Through Industry 4.0, supply web management (SWM).

Which Industry 4.0 strategy supports the tenets of the next generation of the supply chain into a supply web? The answer cannot fundamentally be linear, as the strategy would be dependent on the industry. Nonetheless, firms would want strategies that can integrate basic tenets of the supply web. In so doing, firms would need to employ a blend of technologies into their business operation. While not inclusive, such technology could range from cloud computing, big data, artificial intelligence (AI), machine learning (ML), commodity sensors, robotics to automation. For the clarity and organization of concepts into the figure, the collaborative dimensions are categorized into levels: One, Two, and Three.

Figure 3 illustrates how the supply web incorporates the three-dimensional (vertical, diagonal, and horizontal) collaborations into a framework. The vertical Dimension or Level one (L1) represents internal business activities between firms that impact the main production effort. The level 1 collaborative dimension concerns firms within the same product line as A-A, B-B, and C-C.

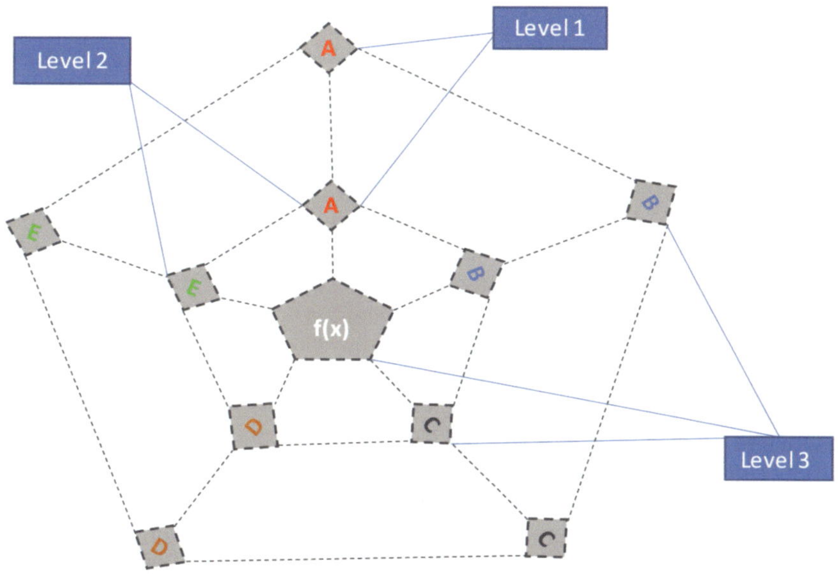

Figure 3.
Unit of supply web.

4.3 Tenets

The main production effort is the final service product can a single, or multiple firms produce conjointly. Meanwhile, a horizontal collaborative dimension or Level Two (L2) outside the primary production when as in A-B, C-D, A-E.... For instance, a transportation firm that delivers parts or final products participates in the collaboration under this category. Finally, firms maintain a diagonal collaborative dimension or Level Three (L3) collaboration when they have business transactions that impact the main production effort's internal and external activities. Level 3: A-A-B-B-C-C... The preponderance of Industry 4.0 elements that enable SW within and outside the main production effort would occur at this level. Firms that provide innovative technologies services from cloud computing, Big Data, ML, AI, RFID, IoT, and others add value to the supply web by enabling collaborative Dimension.

The tenets that enable tenets supply web include among others:

Big Data. Consumer and company data collection and storage paved the way for extensive data trends analysis. Data has become the most valued asset of any organization today, enabling analytics and market intelligence on customers' behavior, business practice, and decision-king [12]. Businesses and governments could use crowdsourcing technology to reinforce manufacturing standards. Many firms also offer to monitor and track production processes to support the supply industry, enhancing the efficacy of production control and decision making [11]. Comparatively, researchers from the Boston University School of Medicine applied big data analytics to realize early exposure to unsafe food products [14]. In so doing, they discovered that hazardous consumer products in the market could have been possible without the current state of technology [15].

Artificial Intelligence (AI). A survey found because of COVID, 55% of companies fast-tracked their way onto AI implementation in 2020, with more companies expected to do the same in 2021 and beyond [16]. With the help of AI, it is possible to depict trends out of large amounts of data. Governments and corporations now employ AI technology in place of human intelligence to enhance decision-making capabilities in machines, which apply scientific models for swift trends analysis. AI technology proved to accurately forecast consumer behavior and business trends crucial to sustaining commodities' management.

Internet of Things (IoT) digitizes business and social activities. Intelligent factories, for instance, enable customers, companies, machines to communicate with workers, other technologies, and resources [12] to facilitate collaborative planning, goal setting, and sharing decision-making with stakeholders. The Just-In-Time or JIT model is an efficient inventory management concept used to lessen the need for warehousing and decrease warehousing-associated costs. Thought JIT model antedates Industry 4.0 when applied within IoT, strengthening collaboration. "Much of what people say about the New Economy is not all that new. A series of discontinuous technological changes before the industrial age sparked technological innovations in the 18th Century. The inventions that the steam engine, railroads, steel, electrification, and telecommunications characterized improved internal and external collaboration with various industries [5]. For instance, a home device equipped with intelligent technology could detect and place an order when certain goods reach a set limit. The sensor submits an order processed through the web and informs what follows. The customer and all other statehooders could monitor the order fulfillment and address any issues accordingly.

Throughout humankind, societies implemented innovative technologies to fix the crisis of their time. The massive backlog of cargo ships in Los Angeles ports and across the globe in October 2021 illustrates some of the issues of the state of the early supply chain models. During an interview on CNN, the Executive Director of Port of Los Angeles noted that the orchestra of players needs to get on the same schedule. COVID-19 pandemic reaffirmed that efficient inventory management continued to be a common business challenge for many firms [12]. COVID-19 induced lockdowns disrupted medical and other supply chains creating impacting commodities supply chain [6]. There is evidence that there is a need for greater collaboration between industries and governments to minimize supply disruption at the national and global scales. Firms that collaborate with multiple stakeholders have better business strategies [6].

5. Discussions

This chapter provides a synopsis of 4IR innovative technologies and related concepts for the next generation of the supply chain. Industry 4.0 is setting the next generation of the supply chain by making it more agile and efficient than the traditional supply chain [17]. The next generation of supply chain management ought to integrate processes that share data among partners through collaborative efforts and automation enabled by the Internet of Things, machine learning to artificial intelligence.

The current global environment enables businesses to expand and connect internal processes with customers and suppliers [18]. The expansion and connections require collaboration, flexibility, redundancy, and integration impact supply chain resilience [19]. The collaboration empowers customized configuration processes and is an essential element in tracking products from suppliers to customers with customized configuration [20] I4.0 offers a set of tools to support decision making through collaboration [21].

DOI: http://dx.doi.org/10.5772/intechopen.102979

The impact of the COVID-19 pandemic and other recent supply chain crises offered the supply industry compelling arguments for implementing4.0 [22]. The adoption of I4.0 has grown in the manufacturing and supply chain sector [23].

Several barriers and drivers exist to Industry 4.0 implementation in the supply chain, including economic, technological, social, organizational, environmental, and inter-relationships [24]. A study found the reduction in supply–demand misalignment, changing consumer needs, legal penalties, and cost optimization as drivers of I4.0. At the same time, a lack of collaboration, organizational inertia, and lack of awareness are designated as barriers [5, 25]. Despite its advantages, firms still face challenges in implementing the I4.0 and in sustaining the security requirements. The cyber community continues to register attacks on secure systems that include attacks in web applications using TLS to secure HTTP communications [17, 26].

Not enough knowledge exists on the implementation strategies of Industry 4.0 concepts for small and medium-sized enterprises [27]. Additionally, no evidence of a conceptual SCM integrates the fundamentals of Industry 4.0, henceforth suggesting the development of business models that tolerate integrative and collaborative connectivity [28].

6. Conclusion

The next generation of supply chain management needs to integrate automation of processes from manufacturing, distribution, retailing to customers through Industry 4.0. The capability gives the supply industry compelling arguments to shift from traditional supply chain models to a supply web for enhanced collaboration and efficiency. The supply web paradigm offers the supply industry to generate and transfer business data internally, externally, and between PBPP. The chapter presented and defined *Supply Web* (SW) and suggested the basic tenets. Firms need to have their business operation participate in the three collaborative levels to integrate SW. Primarily, firms need to maintain an internal Collaborative Dimension with other firms that add value to the primary product or service. Next, a firm must maintain another level with firms external to the main product or service. Lastly, firms will equally require a collaborative dimension that impacts internal and external operations.

Acknowledgements

I wish to thank IntechOpen for considering the chapter.

Conflict of interest

None.

Author details

Andre T. Mayounga
Northcentral University, USA

*Address all correspondence to: a.mayounga3239@email.ncu.edu

References

[1] Schwab K. The fourth industrial revolution: What it means and how to respond. Foreign Affairs. 2015. Retrieved from: https://www.foreignaffairs.com/

[2] Ayres RU. Technological transformations and long waves. Technological Forecasting and Social Change. 1990;**37**:1-37

[3] Cooper MC, Lambert DM, Pagh JD. Supply chain management: More than a new name for logistics. The International Journal of Logistics Management. 1997;**8**:1-14

[4] Mayounga AT. Antecedents of recalls prevention: Analysis and synthesis of research on product recalls. Supply Chain Forum: An International Journal. 2018;**19**:164-177

[5] Ali I, Aboelmaged MGS. Implementation of supply chain 4.0 in the food and beverage industry: Perceived drivers and barriers. International Journal of Productivity and Performance Management. 2021. ISSN: 1741-0401

[6] Okafor GU et al. Global impact of COVID-19 pandemic on public health supply chainl. Rijeka: IntechOpen; 2020

[7] Behrens JT. Principles and procedures of exploratory data analysis. Psychological Methods. 1997;**2**(2):130-161

[8] Sofaer S. Qualitative research methods. International Journal for Quality in Health Care. 2002;**4**:329-336

[9] Senge PM, Carstedt G, Porter PL. Innovating our way to the next industrial revolution. MIT Sloan Management Review. 2001;**42**:24-38

[10] Scott JE, Scott CH. Drone delivery models for healthcare. In: Proceedings of the 50th Hawaii International Conference on System Sciences, Hawaii. 2017

[11] Butdee S. Automotive industrial supply chain performance evaluation under uncertain constraints on cloud computing system. In: Moynihan G, editor. Concepts, Applications, and Emerging Opportunities in Industrial Engineering. London: IntechOpen Limited; 2020

[12] Xue-Ming Y. Impact of Industry 4.0 on Inventory Systems and Optimization. In: Bányai T, De Felice A, editors. Industry 4.0 - Impact on Intelligent Logistics and Manufacturing. IntechOpen; 2020

[13] Mayounga AT. Strategic sourcing in Africa: The case for the labor market. Journal of Global Operations and Strategic Sourcing. 2021;**14**:397-413

[14] Maharana A et al. Detecting reports of unsafe foods in consumer product. JAMIA Open. 2019;**2**(3):330-338

[15] Allianz. Product recall: Managing the impact of the new risk landscape. Allianz. 2017:1-17

[16] McKendrick J. AI adoption skyrocketed over the last 18 months. Harvard Business Review. 2021. Available from: https://hbr.org/

[17] al., A. Esfahani et. An efficient web authentication mechanism preventing man-In-the-middle attacks in industry 4.0 supply chain. IEEE Access. 2019;7: 58981-58989

[18] Raji IO, Rossi T. Exploring industry 4.0 technologies as drivers of lean and agile

supply chain strategies. In: Proceedings of the International Conference on Industrial Engineering and Operations Management, Toronto, Canada. 2019

[19] Gružauskas V, Vilkas M. Managing capabilities for supply chain resilience throiugh IT integration. Economics and Business. 2017;**31**:30-43

[20] Katsaliaki K, Mustafee N. Distributed simulation of supply chains in the industry 4.0 Era: A state of the art field overview. In: Gunal M editor. Simulation for Industry 4.0. Springer Series in Advanced Manufacturing. Cham: Springer; 2019. pp. 55-80

[21] Sonia CC, Grigory P, Pedro S, Nikolay M, Zixu L, Sophia K. An approach and decision support tool for forming Industry 4.0 supply chain collaborations. In: Computers in Industry. 2021;**125**:1-16

[22] Dmitry I, Alexandre D. A digital supply chain twin for managing the disruption risks and resilience in the era of Industry 4.0. Production Planning & Control. 2019;**32**:9

[23] Raut RD et al. Enabling technologies for industry 4.0 manufacturing and supply chain: Concepts, current status, and adoption challenges. IEEE Engineering Management Review. 2020;**48**:83-102

[24] Sharma M et al. Industry 4.0 adoption for sustainability in multi-tier manufacturing supply chain in emerging economies. Journal of Cleaner Production. 2021;**281**:125013

[25] Coping strategy to counter the challenges towards Implementation of industry 4.0 in Thailand: Role of supply chain agility and resilience. International Journal of Supply Chain Management, 2019;**8**:733-744

[26] Mayounga AT. Cyber-supply chain visibility: A grounded theory of cybersecurity with supply chain management. ProQuest. 2017:1-138

[27] Kristina B, Herbert-Hansen ZNL, Khalid W. Considering Industry 4.0 aspects in the supply chain for an SME. Production Management. 2018;**12**

[28] Garay-Rondero CL et al. Digital supply chain model in Industry 4.0. Journal of Manufacturing Technology Management. 2020;**31**:5

Chapter 4

Application of Internet of Things in the Movement of Goods at Customs Level during Covid-19 Pandemic

Erica Varese, Maria Chiara Cesarani and Magdalena Wojnarowska

Abstract

The rapid growth of trade volume makes it necessary on the one hand to increase the safety and security of international trade and, on the other hand, to leave the flow of goods unobstructed. The Covid-19 pandemic severely impacted the world goods and services trade which, after almost 2 years, are still not back to December 2019's volumes. This chapter investigates some of the different suggestions proposed by international organizations to mitigate the pandemic effect on international trade, with a specific focus on trade facilitation measures such as international certifications (i.e., Authorized Economic Operator), risk management strategies and new technologies which are deeply transforming and helping the movement of goods at customs level. After reviewing published reports, this chapter aims to verify which are the most feasible solution to be implemented by the government at the customs level for improving customs operations enhancing their efficiency and effectiveness.

Keywords: Covid-19, trade facilitators, Internet of Things (IoT), authorized economic operator (AEO), customs

1. Introduction

As of March 2020, the Covid-19 pandemic has had an enormous impact on trade volume, disrupting international and sometimes even national trade exchange for several months [1]. As experienced worldwide, the first common reaction to the widespread of the SARS-CoV-2 has been the implementation of travel restrictions and closures of borders, with the obvious consequence of directly affecting goods and services trade. From the first case identified in Wuhan (China) on December, 31st 2019 until March, 11th 2020 when the World Health Organization declared the pandemic, as shown in **Figure 1**, most countries have progressively introduced severe travel restrictions and border closures with the highest expression of this hard situation reached between April and May 2020, leading to a constant increase of shipping costs and transport duration [2].

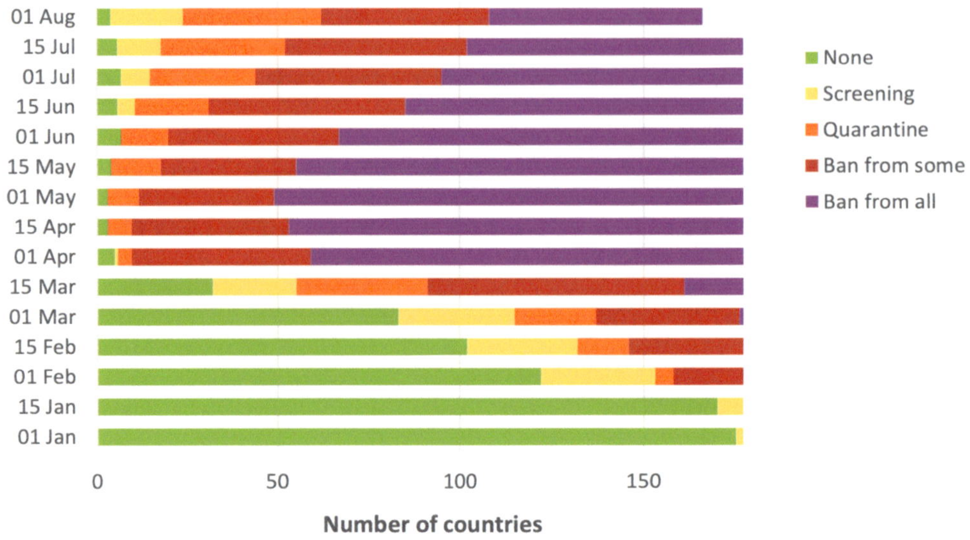

Figure 1.
International travel controls by stringency and date (1st January–1st August 2020). Source: World Trade Organization [2].

Given that, it is estimated that regulatory and legislative differences, as well as trade policy barriers, still count for no less than 10 per cent of trade cost [2] it is of the utmost importance to ensure a safer and faster international trade: this concern is even truer in hard times as the one we are facing. As known, safety is often defined, in international trade, as the condition in which the various risk, which is linked to the exercised activity, has been acknowledged, in which the likelihood of some specific adverse events have been identified and in which all the feasible special measures have been taken to limit, as far as possible, the associated risks [3]. To achieve safety and velocity, several instruments could be taken into consideration, including trade facilitation. In this regard, the World Trade Organization (WTO) specifically highlights that, as done in the current pandemic time on medical products and personal protective equipment, countries should put in place electronic systems and certificates [2] to achieve the above-mentioned goals. Before specifically focusing on this issue, it is useful to recall some of the most efficient tools proposed and adopted by the World Customs Organization (WCO) Council in the last 20 years to reach velocity and safety in international trade: (i) SAFE Framework of Standards to Secure and Facilitate Global Trade (SAFE Framework) in 2005 and (ii) the Authorized Economic Operators (AEO) Program in 2007. The SAFE Framework is a non-binding unique international instrument that ushered in the supply chain which comprised technical security customs standards without obstructing international trade and creating a closer partnership between customs and business operators [4, 5], while the AEO is a voluntary certification that allows traders who meet certain criteria to assure the supply chain security and then to enjoy customs benefits throughout the European Union [6, 7]. Although, the SAFE Framework has proved to work well, in 2021 the WCO undertook a revision of it aiming at "*strengthen[ing] co-operation between Customs and Other Government Agencies; promot[ing] smart security devices to optimize Customs control and effectively monitor the movement of goods in a real-time basis; and, includ[ing] baseline provisions on the development of regional Customs union AEO programmes and the implementation of mutual recognition*" [8].

Similarly, after the period 2016-2020 where the goal was to support European Union's (EU) competitiveness on the world markets, the—at the time—EU Commission's candidate U. Von Der Leyen highlighted those further steps should be taken to lead Customs Union up to the next level, as it is necessary to equip it with new and stronger legislation and framework which would eventually allow the Union to better protect the single market and the citizens [9]. As a result of the Covid-19 pandemic, the 2020–2024 Strategic Plan developed by the European Commission's Directorate-General for Taxation and Customs Union (DG TAXUD) highlights that the European Union needs today more than ever tax and customs policies which can support economic recovery and to guarantee that all the financial resources are correctly and sustainably allocated to create a level playing field capable of higher protection to both the citizens and the Single Market [10]. To achieve this ambitious plan, DG TAXUD started developing trader portals and single EU access points accelerating electronic exchanges between customs authorities and traders enabling 24/7 operativity to Union customs.

As known, to effectively guarantee safety and security in goods and services' trade, it is essential to develop a close partnership between national customs and businesses. To do so, one of the aspects to be taken into consideration consists in ensuring to have implemented an in-depth risk analysis enabling each custom to correctly assess its own procedures. A tool that is commonly accepted and that is gaining more and more importance is the Authorized Economic Operator (AEO) together with the information management and information technology (IT) tools.

As above-mentioned, AEO is recognized as a certification scheme using shared information to assess and lower risks associated with trade. The companies which can gain such certification are allowed to have softer or removed border controls that other companies normally undergo [11].

Given the above, this chapter presents an analysis of some of the Covid response papers issued by international organizations and bodies in the period 2020–2021 with a focus on the new technologies, to understand whether there could be some efficient trade facilitator in this global pandemic era to implement the performance of the whole supply chain.

With the purpose to achieve the aim of this research, the following hypothesis has been developed:

H. In international trade there is an increasing need to monitor the supply chain also about the movement of goods, furthermore, it is necessary to increase and facilitate the safety and velocity of these exchanges particularly in this pandemic period. Since the Internet of Things is considered a strategic tool in many sectors, it would be significant to identify nowadays strategies to help international trade to recover during the Covid-19 pandemic.

To the Author's knowledge, this is the first manuscript that analyses the international bodies' responses to the impact of Covid-19 and the different suggestions issued by the International Organizations.

The study is therefore organized in 3 further sections: Section 2, review on international bodies recommendation; Section 3, discussions and implications and, in Section 4, conclusions are presented.

2. Review on international bodies recommendation

The International Chamber of Commerce (ICC) [12] after reminding that every exceptional time increase the risk for illicit behavior affecting business such as corruption, money-laundering and fraud, called for the drivers that businesses and policy makers should follow not to be overcome by the pandemic: transparency and integrity in all procurement stages which are helped by the digitalization of permits and licensing; keeping the due diligence process ongoing to mitigate supply chain's risks; fighting corruption in the context of borders and customs; and, protecting the rule of law.

In such a contest, where states closed upon themselves and made trade extremely difficult, in the last 2 years several international organizations presented different suggestions to mitigate the Covid-19 trade-related effects.

The United Nations Industrial Development Organization estimated in July 2020 that, among the 49 countries which represent almost 87% of world manufacturing value-added, about 81% of countries faced a decrease of an average of 6% in industrial production comparing the dataset in December 2019 and March 2020, and an average of 20% in 93% of nations comparing December 2019 and April 2020 [13]. The situation has not changed afterward, with several and severe economic consequences hitting countries until June 2020 [14] where the index of industrial production kept on decreasing, although with a small improvement: from −5.6% in March 2020 to −2.5% in June 2020.

The export of goods has had a particular trend which is indicated in **Table 1** from the 4th quarterly 2019 to the 3rd quarterly 2021 (Q4-2019–Q3-2021), the tendency is expressed in billions of US dollars, for each member of the Group 20 (G20). **Figure 2**, furthermore, highlights that the export of goods of these countries has marginally been impacted in 2020 Q1-2020, and then has had a strong downshift in Q2-2020. Starting from Q3-2020, G20 countries have seen a positive trend of it and in Q4-2020 they exported more goods than in Q4-2019, the quarterly previous the start of the pandemic. In the following quarterlies (Q1-2021 and Q2-2021), this trend has continuously increased reaching, in Q3-2021, the amount of 4262.96 billion US dollars.

Given the above, in 2020, the United Nations Conference on Trade and Development (UNCTAD) drafted a report suggesting some measures to efficiently manage the pandemic consequences [16]. While the world would have needed higher agility and efficiency, trade experienced extensive disruptions, with medical devices and personal protective equipment firstly affected by the export restriction. Therefore, four main interventions categories were identified:

i. Process optimization;

ii. Cost reduction;

iii. Transparency and cooperation;

iv. Technology.

With regards to "process optimization", UNCTAD recommended following the criteria specified by art. 7.8 of the WTO Trade Facilitation Agreement introducing, among others, fast tracks lanes, prioritization, implementing the trusted traders such as the AEO and simplifying the declarations. About "cost reduction", the UNCTAD remarked the importance of reducing some tariff, accepting some goods received as gifts by approved organizations free of charges, while on point (iii)—"transparency and cooperation"—it highlighted the necessity of having prompt and transparent information among all countries not only about the pandemic itself but also on the

Time	2019	2020				2021		
	Q4-2019	Q1-2020	Q2-2020	Q3-2020	Q4-2020	Q1-2021	Q2-2021	Q3-2021
Country								
Argentina	15.25	17.41	13.26	13.53	12.85	17.82	18.83	21.37
Australia	64.92	61.21	59.57	60.79	68.06	80.01	88.26	90.79
Brazil	51.98	55.37	51.32	52.19	52.81	60.60	78.44	73.21
Canada	110.75	105.19	76.86	101.81	107.09	118.85	123.53	126.08
China (People's Republic of)	537.83	610.89	627.36	676.10	711.99	844.08	822.95	835.76
France	140.42	131.44	93.17	126.17	137.49	141.89	144.02	145.57
Germany	370.83	358.48	277.83	355.92	383.74	400.96	406.73	399.44
India	72.07	80.05	52.14	75.16	76.20	86.24	97.29	104.10
Indonesia	42.77	42.22	35.23	39.88	45.00	50.59	54.94	58.50
Italy	135.65	128.02	94.04	132.73	143.59	147.67	153.66	151.45
Japan	174.47	167.25	133.35	158.21	180.19	184.39	189.74	190.23
Korea (Republic of)	133.38	135.04	108.97	129.50	138.89	151.79	155.04	163.84
Mexico	112.09	113.74	73.30	110.31	118.38	119.14	122.37	121.98
Russia	90.57	100.85	75.12	81.44	83.77	95.32	124.04	138.14
Saudi Arabia	52.97	61.05	33.81	43.03	43.93	58.54	65.76	73.72
South Africa	22.98	21.97	15.56	21.93	25.01	29.33	35.48	30.03
Turkey	45.53	43.38	32.62	43.63	48.48	51.35	55.39	57.66
United Kingdom	109.09	101.25	76.27	92.92	105.12	98.72	111.23	106.27
United States	407.15	396.38	289.37	356.01	383.17	407.25	434.93	439.34
European Union—27 countries (from February 01, 2020)	1448.62	1406.18	1107.99	1415.85	1525.91	1596.34	1650.68	1646.72
G20	3595.82	3416.03	2862.11	3472.27	3726.85	4050.35	4228.90	4262.96

Source: authors' own elaboration on Organization for Economic Co-Operation and Development [15].

Table 1.
Quarterly (Q4-2019–Q3-2021) of G20 export of goods (value—US dollar, billions).

transported goods. Lastly, about "technology" it remarks that efficient, rapid, and centralized processing should be further implemented.

Linked to this remark, in 2021 WCO together with WTO, drafted a paper [17] whose objective was to provide an evidence-based picture on three different

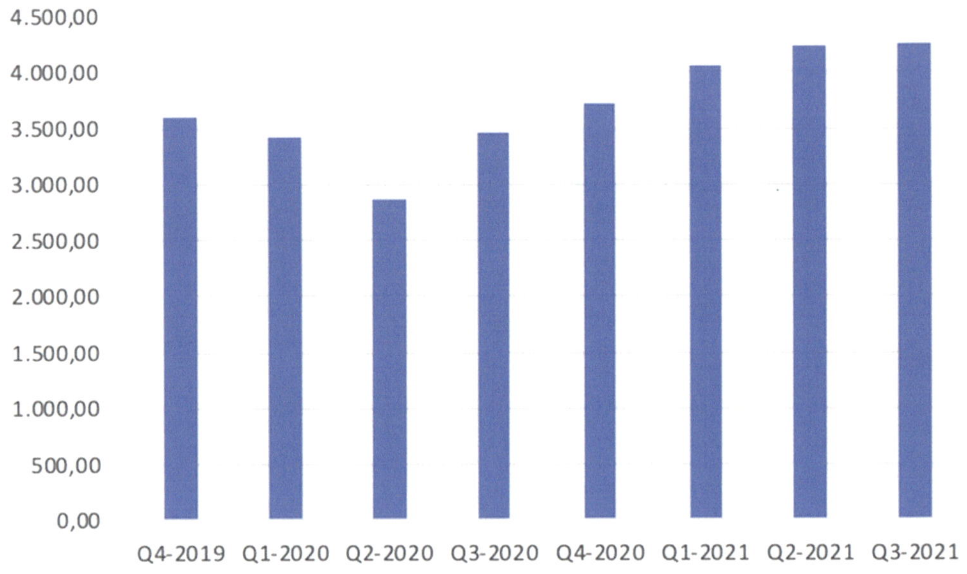

Figure 2.
Export of goods of G20 members (Q4-2019–Q3-2021)—US dollars, billions. Source: authors' own elaboration on Organization for Economic Co-Operation and Development [15].

technologies that Customs could utilize as trade facilitators to achieve safety and velocity, fundamental main stones in this period. The suggested tools are blockchain; IoT and Big Data. Specifically, WCO found that blockchain is still enduring an experimental phase, mainly involving private and permissioned blockchains. Many customs faced a certain hesitancy towards this technology, but the WCO paper highlight that there is a common "*reasonably optimistic concern*" towards blockchain's potential as it could lead to greater efficiency and reliability in risk management, revenue collection, and trade facilitation as well as creating an environment where public authorities can cooperate with private industry from the early stage of production and trade. Further recognized benefits were identified in transparency, immutability and accessibility of information, lower transaction and verifications costs, and increased availability of information and quality data from different sources. About IoT, WCO found that these tools are used by more than 50% of the respondent, mostly in the area of X-ray and computed tomography, QR Code and barcode readers, electronic seals and automated license plate readers, and radio frequency identification (RFID) antennas or e-seals to ensure traceability of mean of transport and goods. It has also been highlighted the importance of implementing IoT solutions, as they enable them to have better risk management, greater customs clearance process efficiency and improved analytics. Regarding Big Data, data analytics, artificial intelligence and machine learning even if it is quite commonly utilized, there still are multiple obstacles in common usage. Particularly, benefits linked to these technologies have been identified in risk management, fraud detection, and audits' facilitations, while the barriers were identified in associated costs, and lack of expertise and good practices.

Again in 2021, the United Nations Economic Commission for Europe (UNECE)—United Nation Center for Trade Facilitation and Electronic Business (UN/CEFACT) published a white paper [18] to provide some best practices ensuring efficient trade control together with facilitation measures to be implemented during the pandemic to avoid a total interruption of commercial trade. The measures to mitigate the impact on trade should involve several stakeholders, including the public sector (i.e., customs, and border authorities), public-private partnership (i.e., National Trade Facilitation Bodies), and private sector stakeholders (i.e., logistic, transport, production, and manufacturing sector) and shall be aimed to cross border cooperation with an increase of trust between partners. This could be achieved with special regimes, special economic zones, expedite pre-arrival clearance procedures, reliable exchange of information, and coordination between integrated risk management and sharing and combination of data into governmental databases accessible by other interested agencies. Similarly, further inputs should be given to National Trade Facilitation Body and external coordination within multilateral, regional and bilateral agreements as well as to trusted trader schemes. The last category includes, as known, the AEO together with the trusted trader. Given the strict requirements provided by the regulations governing the two schemes, governments can trust certified companies which shared with their border authority's information on how they are structured, and on the management procedures and internal structures (i.e., compliance functions, supply chain management, and codes of conduct). Another proposed solution is to efficiently involve private sector actors who mainly run logistical supply chains who can control their workforce and share the records collected with the border authorities or by using packaging materials that are less likely to keep the coronavirus alive for long hours. Finally, a strong recommendation is given on the usage of technologies. The UNECE reminds that to reduce contagions it is important to limit human contact which can be done by introducing system-to-system electronic data interchange (EDI) such as the National Single Window[1], the port community systems and single submission portals. All these automated systems may have several usages in commercial, logistics, and transport exchanges as well as in the regulatory field.

3. Discussions and implications

Covid-19 pandemic has presented a never seen before (at least in the last century) threat to international trade, leading to an important economic downturn. From the 1,179 billion dollars value of word exports of commercial services in 1995 to the 4,872 billion dollars value in 2014 [20] to 5,898 billion dollars in 2019 [21], the trend has almost always been upwards.

In 2020 Q2 [22], commercial services plunged by 30% and merchandise trade volume by 14.3% [23] on a year-on-year review and while they are now rising back up (respectively, +26% and +1.6% on a year-on-year comparison [24, 25] it will take time for them to be back at the pre-crisis level.

To reach a faster recovery, technological tools are definitely something States and governments should invest on.

The first one to invest on is blockchain, which has been recognized as an instrument that facilitates trade by helping risk management [17]. Nevertheless, it has only been fully deployed by 2% of WCO Members, while more than 40% do not even yet start planning its introduction [17].

[1] The National Single Window is defined as "*a facility providing trade facilitation that allows parties involved in trade and transport to lodge standardized information and documents with a single entry point to fulfill all import, export, and transit-related regulatory requirements. Individual data elements should only be submitted once electronically*" [19].

Introducing a standardized dataset between economic operators and government agencies as well as developing common, interconnected, and interoperability blockchain solutions, shared legal requirements and definition of blockchain technology should help a wider usage of this particular tool.

Nevertheless, the actual usage of blockchain covers different areas in the countries where it has been fully or partially used: it may be found in e-commerce environments, in supply chain interconnectivity as well as in electronic certifications and licensing. Particularly, the EU started both a research program to investigate the usage of blockchain in protecting geographical indications, and certification of product origin and in helping VAT collection [17, 26], and the TRICK project in the context of the textile industry funded by Horizon 2020 [17, 27]. Indonesia is currently experimenting with blockchain to automate documentation, simplify the exchange of goods and increase communication and cooperation between counterparts [17].

Other countries are seeking to link it with AEO and container movements: it has been hypothesized that using blockchain in these contexts may faster registration systems and entrust the system and the relationship between counterparts. Among these, it can be named the Malesia experience [17] trying to make the system more competitive and the example of the CADENA project which is a blockchain solution that enables efficient, automated and secure information sharing on AEOs among the Border and Customs authorities of Costa Rica, Peru and Mexico in the context of further implement the mutual recognition agreements [28].

These experiences shall be of guidance and the positive effects that they proved out shall be replicated in other geographical areas.

A second instrument is IoT, which is wildly used to share information with different stakeholders, leading to better risk management, data analysis and efficiency in the Customs clearance process [17]. For example, the usage of QR Codes for transit, the usage of e-lock, GPS tracking, X-ray scanners, and CCTVs cameras interconnected with national or regional Customs are services that help an automatization of border crossing procedures. For example, the Italian Customs and Monopolies Agency is conducting IoT projects based on IoT_ID code to completely digitalize the procedures for goods transported by road and rail transiting in Italian ports [29] while Hong Kong has implemented the GPS technology and e-lock connecting their data with the one of China Mainland [17].

Other instruments that stakeholders can implement are linked to big data, data analytics, artificial intelligence ad machine learning technologies. The more common advantages are seen in data quality, predicting future trends and facilitating customs audits [17]. These have been utilized, among other uses, to ameliorate the efficiency of financial and tax data, to respond to the most common questions through chatbots, to find anomalies in high revenue areas, to find illicit traffic and goods, to enhance Customs clearance efficiency.

Almost half of the WCO members already use them [17] and only less than a quarter have not started planning to introduce them.

To implement such technologies would require States to invest money in new technologies, to overcome the lack of knowledge and expertise, to find a common and shared legal background, and to strengthen trust between counterparts, finally leaving aside cautiousness and lack of trust towards technologies. Nevertheless, governments, as highlighted in the literature [30], face other challenges such as handling the complexity arising from a massive data extraction and converting it into a meaningful model parameter.

4. Conclusion

This chapter has analyzed several strategies related to the movement of goods during the Covid-19 pandemic and expressed by international organizations, including ICC, WTO and WCO. Knowing that the pandemic is not likely to end soon, and that automatization may be the path to be followed to pursue a faster and more secure trade exchange, the common idea is to emphasize the usage of new technologies such as blockchain, IoT, machine learning, data analytics, artificial intelligence, and big data.

Although, most countries have already started implementing some or all of them, getting several advantages by their use such as speed control and tracking—as collected in the WCO annual consolidated survey—, there still are several issues to face to have widespread usage. Costs, lack of knowledge, good practices and/or trust, legislation and privacy issues, and lack of governmental strategy and coordination are the one to be faced shortly to ensure an interconnected international customs system.

This chapter focuses only on strategies proposed by international organizations, without acknowledging national responses to the pandemic, and this may represent a limit in the investigation.

Future research directions may be, on the one hand, understanding whether any country would be able to implement the proposed approaches, investing in new technologies for its borders and Customs, and seeing the actual improvements in the relationship among the international trade stakeholders; on the other hand, selecting a specific geographical scope, examining regional and national response to the downshift of international trade and the proposed solutions at a local level.

Conflict of interest

The authors declare no conflict of interest.

Other declarations

All authors have equally contributed to this chapter.

Author details

Erica Varese[1*], Maria Chiara Cesarani[1] and Magdalena Wojnarowska[2]

1 Department of Management, University of Turin, Turin, Italy

2 College of Management and Quality, University of Economics, Cracow, Poland

*Address all correspondence to: erica.varese@unito.it

References

[1] World Trade Organization. COVID-19 and world trade [Internet]. 2021. Available from: https://www.wto.org/english/tratop_e/covid19_e/covid19_e.htm [Accessed: December 24, 2021]

[2] World Trade Organization. Trade costs in the time of global pandemic [Internet]. 2020. Available from: https://www.wto.org/english/tratop_e/covid19_e/trade_costs_report_e.pdf [Accessed: December 24, 2021]

[3] Grottelli M. The safety and security of international trade as a determinant of the business strategy off the Polish Customs Service. European Integration Studies. 2015;**9**(1):139-154

[4] Ireland R. The WCO SAFE framework of standards: Avoiding excess in global supply chain security policy. Global Trade and Customs Journal. 2009;**4**(11/12):341-352

[5] United Nations. WCO Framework of Standards to Secure and Facilitate Trade (SAFE) [Internet]. Available from: https://tfig.unece.org/contents/wco-safe.htm [Accessed: December 24, 2021]

[6] European Commission, Taxation and Custom Union. Authorised Economic Operator (AEO) [Internet]. Available from: https://ec.europa.eu/taxation_customs/authorised-economic-operator-aeo_en [Accessed: December 24, 2021]

[7] Jażdżewska-Gutta M, Grottel M, Wach D. AEO certification–necessity or privilege for supply chain participants. Supply Chain Management. 2020;**25**(6):679-691. DOI: 10.1108/SCM-07-2019-0253

[8] World Customs Organization. WCO SAFE Package—WCO tools to secure and facilitate global trade [Internet]. 2021. Available from: http://www.wcoomd.org/en/topics/facilitation/instrument-and-tools/frameworks-of-standards/safe_package.aspx [Accessed: December 24, 2021]

[9] Von Der Leyen U. A Union that Strives for More. My Agenda for Europe. Luxembourg: Publications Office of the European Union; 2019. DOI: 10.2775/018127

[10] European Commission. Strategic Plan 2020-2024. DG Taxation and Customs Union [Internet]. 2020. Available from: https://ec.europa.eu/info/publications/strategic-plan-2020-2024-taxation-and-customs-union_en [Accessed: December 24, 2021]

[11] Ugaz P, Sun S. How countries can leverage trade facilitation to defeat the Covid-19 pandemic [Internet]. 2021. Available from: https://unctad.org/system/files/official-document/dtlinf2020d2_en.pdf [Accessed: December 24, 2021]

[12] International Chamber of Commerce. ICC Guidance—Integrity for a resilient response and rebuild after Covid-19 [Internet]. 2020. Available from: https://iccwbo.org/content/uploads/sites/3/2020/07/icc-guidance-integrity-for-a-resilient-response-and-rebuild-after-covid-19.pdf [Accessed: December 24, 2021]

[13] United Nations Industrial Development Organization. Coronavirus: The economic impact—10 July 2020—a health pandemic or a pandemic for the economy? [Internet]. 2020. Available from: https://www.unido.org/stories/coronavirus-economic-impact-10-july-2020 [Accessed: December 24, 2021]

[14] United Nations Industrial Development Organization. Coronavirus: The economic impact—21 October 2020—Recovery or protracted economic downturn? The role of policies based on evidence [Internet]. 2020. Available from: https://www.unido.org/stories/coronavirus-economic-impact-21-october-2020 [Accessed: December 24, 2021]

[15] Organisation for Economic Co-Operation and Development. Monthly International Merchandise Trade (IMTS). Headline Series: G20 International Trade [Internet]. Available from: https://stats.oecd.org/Index.aspx?DataSetCode=MEI_TRD# [Accessed: December 24, 2021]

[16] United Nations Conference on Trade and Development. How countries can leverage trade facilitation to defeat the Covid-19 pandemic [Internet]. 2020. Available from: https://unctad.org/system/files/official-document/dtlinf2020d2_en.pdf [Accessed: December 24, 2021]

[17] World Customs Organization—World Trade Organization. Customs use of advanced technologies to facilitate and secure cross border trade [Internet]. 2021. Available from: http://www.wcoomd.org/-/media/wco/public/global/pdf/topics/facilitation/instruments-and-tools/tools/wco-wto-paper/wco_wto-paper-on-disruptive-technologies-en.pdf [Accessed: December 24, 2021]

[18] United Nations Economic Commission for Europe—United Nation Center for Trade Facilitation and Electronic Business. White paper pandemic crisis trade-related response [Internet]. 2021. Available from: https://unece.org/sites/default/files/2021-01/ECE-TRADE-456E_WhitePaperPandemicCrisis_0.pdf [Accessed: December 24, 2021]

[19] United Nation Center for Trade Facilitation and Electronic Business. Recommendation and guidelines on establishing a Single Window—To enhance the efficient exchange of international trade information between trade and government—Recommendation no. 33 [Internet]. 2020. Available form: https://unece.org/fileadmin/DAM/cefact/recommendations/rec33/ECE-TRADE-352_Rev.1E_Rec33_2020Edition.pdf [Accessed: December 24, 2021]

[20] World Trade Organization. International trade statistics 2015 [Internet]. 2015. Available from: https://www.wto.org/english/res_e/statis_e/its2015_e/its15_highlights_e.pdf [Accessed: December 24, 2021]

[21] World Trade Organization. World trade statistical review 2020 [Internet]. 2020. Available from: https://www.wto.org/english/res_e/statis_e/wts2020_e/wts2020_e.pdf [Accessed: December 24, 2021]

[22] World Trade Organization. Latest trade trends [Internet]. 2021. Available from: https://www.wto.org/english/res_e/statis_e/daily_update_e/serv_2020q2.pdf [Accessed: December 24, 2021]

[23] World Trade Organization. Latest trade trends [Internet]. 2021. Available from: https://www.wto.org/english/res_e/statis_e/daily_update_e/merch_2020q2.pdf [Accessed: December 24, 2021]

[24] World Trade Organization. Latest trade trends [Internet]. 2021. Available from: https://www.wto.org/english/res_e/statis_e/latest_trends_e.htm [Accessed: December 24, 2021]

[25] World Trade Organization. Latest trade trends [Internet]. 2021. Available from: https://www.wto.org/english/res_e/statis_e/daily_update_e/

merchvol_2021q2.pdf [Accessed: December 24, 2021]

[26] Intrasoft International S.A. European Commission DG TAXUD. SEED-on-Blockchain [Internet]. 2021. Available from: https://www.intrasoft-intl.com/case-studies/seed-blockchain [Accessed: December 24, 2021]

[27] Community Research and Development Information Service. Product data traceability from cradle to cradle by blockchains interoperability and sustainability service marketplace [Internet]. 2021. Available from: https://cordis.europa.eu/project/id/958352 [Accessed: December 24, 2021]

[28] World Customs Organization. CADENA, a blockchain enabled solution for the implementation of Mutual Recognition Arrangements/Agreements [Internet]. 2018. Available from: https://mag.wcoomd.org/magazine/wco-news-87/cadena-a-blockchain-enabled-solution-for-the-implementation-of-mutual-recognition-arrangements-agreements/ [Accessed: December 24, 2021]

[29] Agenzia delle Dogane e Monopoli. Modello di interoperabilità per la digitalizzazione delle procedure doganali nei porti [Internet]. 2019. In Italian. Available from: https://www.adm.gov.it/portale/documents/20182/5008381/Modello+di+interoperabilit%C3%A0_+porti.pdf/4d189440-bd74-4fb1-8307-aaff364d42f4 [Accessed: December 24, 2021]

[30] Chung S-H. Applications of smart technologies in logistics and transport: A review. Transportation Research Part E. 2021;**153**:102455. DOI: 10.1016/j.tre.2021.102455

Chapter 5

Industry 4.0 Technologies Impact on Supply Chain Sustainability

Mohammad Akhtar

Abstract

A supply chain is a network that links technology, activities, resources and organisations involved in the manufacturing and distribution of product and services. Supply Chain Operations Reference model (SCOR) defines basic processes of the supply chain (SC) into five categories as Plan, Source, Make, Delivery and Return. The search for a more sustainable production and consumption system is so relevant today that the United Nations (UN) have selected it as one of their paramount societal objectives for sustainable development. The implementation of sustainability in production and consumption processes aims to mitigate negative pressures on the ecosystem generated by products, services, and transportation. Industry 4.0 (I40) technologies have sparked interest in recent years. The advanced digital technologies of I40 such as big data analytics (BDA), artificial intelligence (AI), machine learning (ML), internet of things (IoT) and sensors, block chain technology (BCT), robotic systems (RS), cloud computing (CC), cyber-physical system (CPS), additive manufacturing (AM) /3D printing (3D), virtual reality (VR), augmented reality (AR), autonomous vehicles (AV), and drones have found applications in many processes of manufacturing, logistics and SC. The benefits are sustainability, efficiency, cost reduction, transparency, traceability, and collaboration. In addition to benefits, I40 implementation is not free from challenges.

Keywords: Industry 4.0, sustainable supply chain, triple bottom line, industrial internet of things

1. Introduction of industry 4.0 technologies

Industry 4.0, often known as smart manufacturing, is built on information technology (IT)-driven industrial processes [1]. It combines smart factories and products with the Internet of Things [2, 3], with the goal of providing real-time information on production, machines, and component flow, and integrating this data to assist managers in making decisions, monitoring performance, and tracking parts and products.

1.1 Industry 4.0 technologies

1.1.1 Big data analytics

Big data analytics (BDA) is the collecting of real-time data, the use of analytical tools, and the use of computer algorithms to derive relevant insights and patterns for better decision-making using data, text, audio, video [4]. Big Data 6Vs framework describe Volume, a very large amount of data; Velocity, the data are generated very quickly and must be processed in a very short time; Variety, a large number of structured and unstructured data types are processed; Value, the goal is to generate significant value for the organisation; Veracity, reliability of the processed data; and Variability, flexibility to adapt to new data formats by collecting, storing, and processing them. BDA aids in the achievement of long-term corporate success and competitive advantage [5].

1.1.2 Internet of things

Internet of Things (IoT) allows devices to communicate with one another without the need for human involvement [6]. The Internet of Things is based on a network of devices, each of which has its own unique identity to the computer system to which it is attached. IoT-controlled industrial systems are intelligent because they can accurately and efficiently operate all linked equipment from afar [7]. For example, big data has been utilised to enhance product development [8], SC demand forecasts [9], and green production strategies [8, 10].

1.1.3 Block chain technology

Blockchain is a distributed data structure—a distributed ledger—in which the data is shared on a peer-to-peer network. The network members and nodes communicate and validate the data following a predefined protocol without a central authority. Distributed ledgers can be either decentralised, giving equal rights to all users or centralised, providing specific users with special rights.

1.1.4 Artificial intelligence

Artificial intelligence (AI) is a field in computer science encompassing the development of systems capable of performing tasks that normally necessitate human intelligence. The science of making machines do things that would require intelligence if done by men. Three main functions are sensing and interacting, learning from the data and decision making.

1.1.5 Autonomous robotic vehicle

Autonomous vehicles as more environmentally friendly automobiles are capable of sensing its navigation without human input, thus the costs, emission level and working time can be reduced dramatically. They can be used not only for long distances, but also for operational level of the supply chain.

1.1.6 Additive manufacturing (3D printing)

Additive manufacturing (AM) begins with the creation of a three-dimensional digital model using computer-aided design software, followed by the formation of the finished object using a 3D printer [11]. AM helps to Industry 4.0 goals by generating personalised items in small batches and producing complex and lightweight designs with great precision [3].

1.1.7 Cloud manufacturing

Cloud manufacturing is a method of providing a shared network of manufacturing resources and capabilities through the internet by establishing a virtual and global environment. The logic of cloud manufacturing is service-based, which means providers and consumers interact to sell and acquire services such as product design, simulation, production, and assembly [12].

1.1.8 Cloud computing

The Cloud computing (CC) is an Internet-based third-party service provider for data or database storage. The cloud is housed at a faraway location, not at the area where production takes place [12]. The CC has the advantages of lower operating costs, faster service, and simple accessibility [13].

1.2 Sustainability

Sustainability is a multi-dimensional concept incorporating economic, environmental, and social dimensions of business. Primary goal of any commercial enterprise is to make profit for long tern economic sustainability by balancing costs and revenues in sourcing, production and distribution of goods and services. Due to global pressure, climate change and pollution, environmental sustainability has taken centre stage in today's business [14]. The focus is to minimise natural resources use, waste and pollution (air, water, land), and increased renewable energy use in production and distribution. Social sustainability includes working environment, employee morale and satisfaction, equity and social integration of communities. Industry 4.0 technologies (I4T) help manufacturing companies achieve long-term goals by reducing lead times, providing customised goods, improving product quality, improving the working environment, and employee morale [15]. Organisations have been compelled to adapt smart production systems which are more adaptable, intelligent, and agile, and allows to address the demands of a dynamic and global market [16].

2. Literature review

Sustainable development is crucial necessity for the survival of humankind, which should integrate sustainable production and consumption [17]. Sustainability is three-dimensional concept encompassing economic, environmental and social (triple bottom line). Sustainable supply chain enables the management of material, information and capital flows as well as the cooperation among companies along the supply chain while taking goals from all three dimensions of sustainable development (economic, environmental and social) into account which are derived from customer and stakeholder requirements [18]. One of the key features of Industry 4.0 enabled by CPS, IoT, and big data analytics, is data accessibility and real-time information, which may help companies achieve low cost, high quality, low risk sharing, more flexible SC planning and effective decision making. Industry 4.0 allows for long-term purchase of more personalised items [19]. I40 opens up new and long-term commercial prospects by maximising resource efficiency, enhancing manufacturing flexibility, and reducing time to market [20]. IoT controlled industrial systems are clever as they can accurately and efficiently operate all linked equipment from afar [7]. Various I4T is shown to have a good influence on the organisations' long-term success. However, there is a dearth of empirical evidence in the literature to substantiate the influence of I4T on sustainable operating practices in various industries [15]. I4T contribute to long-term operations management choices and new business models by connecting value chains through data collection and exchange [3, 21]. As a result, long-term operations management decisions help to establish a link between circular economy (CE) principles and Industry 4.0 concepts.

The search for a more sustainable production and consumption system is so important now that the United Nations Organisation (UNO) has made it one of their most important social goals for long-term development [22]. The ultimate goal of implementing sustainability into production is to take the industry to a world-class level of sustainable manufacturing [23]. Moghaddam et al. [24] developed several reference designs for sustainable smart I40 factories to dealt with the production of environmentally friendly products. Nascimento et al. [25] proposed a circular economy (CE) business model using I4T for recycling garbage. Kiel et al. [26] classified Internet of Things (IoT) issues and benefits that centred on the long-term value creation. Waibel et al. [20] investigated the effects of smart production systems in terms of resource efficiency and sustainability. Zambon et al. [27] proposed an Agriculture 4.0 through the virtualization of the Agro-food chain. Ding [28] conducted a literature review to identify the barriers of incorporating sustainability into the pharmaceutical SC and proposed I40 application in SC known as Pharma 4.0. Bag et al. [29] developed a framework incorporating thirteen enablers I40 affecting SC sustainability. Tsai and Lu [30] developed a I40 based production planning and control framework using a carbon price. Ghadimi et al. [31] suggested a multiagent system to automatically analyse and choose suppliers that contribute to sustainable SC. Belaud et al. [32] developed agriculture 4.0 by integrating I40 into a SC and waste valorization using big data to improve sustainability management. Sensing, smart, and sustainable technologies were identified as crucial aspects of future sustainable goods [33]. Bibaud-Alves et al. [34] used I4T to establish a relationship between the development process of new goods, digital transformation, and sustainable development. Paravizo et al. [35] offered a conceptual framework using I40 for developing gamified apps that focus on sustainable manufacturing. Kamble et al. [15] reviewed 85 articles on I40 and established a sustainable industry 4.0 framework. Stock et al. [36] carried out qualitative assessment of I40 that enables ecological and social sustainable development. Hidayatno et al. [37] proposed a conceptual model to assess the effect I40 technology on sustainable energy in Indonesian industries. Bonilla et al. [38] used multiple development scenarios to assess the impact and challenges of I40 implementation on long-term sustainable development. Man and Strandhagen [21] presented I40 and sustainability adoption into various business operations. Luthra and Mangla [39] conducted a literature analysis and categorised eighteen I40 implementation challenges of sustainable SC into four categories: organisational, strategical, legal, and ethical. Ardanza et al. [40] demonstrated a human–machine interface using I40 that enable operators to be more productive and safer. Meng et al. [41] carried out literature review on sustainability and energy efficiency in smart factories, their interaction, benefits and issues. Chaim et al. [42] examined the feasibility of using key performance indicators (KPIs) to assess sustainability in I40 virtual learning environment. Kamble et al. [43] analysed the barriers of I40 adoption in manufacturing industry.

Manavalan and Jayakrishna [44] examined the IoT application for a sustainable SC and suggested software to organise material resources in businesses. Birkel et al. [45] proposed a risk framework using I40 for sustainable manufacturing in SMEs using a long-term strategy. Jabbour et al. [46] identified eleven critical success factors for implementing I40 and environmentally sustainable manufacturing and proposed an integrated framework for future research. Kamble et al. [15] investigated the barriers to I40 adoption in Indian manufacturing and analysed their driving and dependence relationship. Monteleone et al. [47] suggested a water management conceptual model in agricultural 4.0. [48, 49] carried out empirical study of 234 manufacturing firms in Pakistan to investigate the effect of I40 on green practices in manufacturing and logistics, which have substantial effect on sustainability of the firms.

Chalmeta and Santos-deLeón [50] carried out literature review on I40, big data and sustainable SC. Mastos et al. [51] provided IoT application for scrap metal waste management. Strandhagen et al. [52] proposed I40 solutions to shipbuilding supply chains sustainability challenges in a case company. Yadav et al. [53] identified 22 I40 and CE based solutions measures to overcome 28 sustainable SC challenges in an automotive industry using BWM-ELECTRE.

Belhadi et al. [54] carried out empirical study by collecting data from 306 organisations in Europe, Asia and Africa to explore the role of digital business transformation, organisational ambidexterity and circular business models on the relationship between I40 capabilities and sustainable performance. Fatorachian and Kazemi [55] conducted exploratory research based on inductive reasoning and systems theory to explore the impact of I4T on SC performance in terms of integration, information sharing and transparency, processes improvement in procurement, production, inventory management and retailing through digitisation, automation, and analytical capabilities. Kumar et al. [56] analysed critical success factors for I40 implementation in circular SC. Kumar et al. [57] studied the barriers of integrating I40 and CE in the agriculture SC using ISM-ANP and concluded that government policies, support and incentives is major barrier. Kusi-Sarpong et al. [58] adopted I40 initiatives for sustainable supplier selection in circular SC. Mastos et al. [59] used I40 technologies to redesign SC for circular economy with key identified benefits of improved availability of personnel and fleet resources, and SC traceability through the full visibility and automation. Mubarik et al. [60] collected data from 154 electrical and electronics Malaysian firms and found that I40 application impact SC mapping and visibility. Sharma et al. [61] found in the study that the environmental and social factors were the highest-ranked drivers while organisational and environmental dimensions as the highly ranked barriers of I40 adoption with the sustainability context in multi-tier manufacturing SC. Umar et al. [48, 49] studied the effect of I40 on sustainable operations and green SC practices.

3. Industry 4.0 technologies enabling supply chain sustainability

Industry 4.0 technologies are intended to play a key role in guiding industrial and social organisations toward long-term sustainability [46]. I4T makes it easier to achieve a high level of process integration, which improves organisational performance across three aspects of sustainability [15]. Braccini and Margherita [62] explored the impact of I40 adoption in a case study of a ceramics manufacturing firm and found that product quality and productivity improvement, energy monitoring and consumption reduction, safe work environment and job satisfaction for workers. Birkel and Muller [63] provided a literature review on potential of I40 on SC triple bottom line of sustainability in planning, sourcing, logistics and recycling logistics. Digital and smart manufacturing processes, machines and devices are likely to offer advantages of manufacturing productivity, resource efficiency, and waste reduction [64].

3.1 Economic sustainability

On the economic front, I4T makes a significant contribution to value creation, production flexibility, and product customization, which lead to higher consumer satisfaction [3]. Automation and digitisation capabilities of I40 help manufacturers achieve shorter lead times, cheaper manufacturing costs, and higher quality [11, 65]. I4T helps in raw material inventory reduction and efficient capacity utilisation [66]. The data offered by cloud manufacturing and IoT may be used to alter the design, production, and logistics choices of sustainable operations management [46]. IoT applications enable the reuse of resources in a remanufacturing process. The data generated by IoT sensors is evaluated using a mathematical model in order to lower expenses and dynamically manage limited resources [67]. Blockchain capabilities can support sustainable supply chains, which can help reduce the product recall and rework, and trace actual footprint of products; and reduce fraud [68]. Dev et al. [69] adopted agent-based modelling and decision trees to facilitate inventory and supply chain reconfiguration issues of a mobile phone supply chain. The information gathered by I40 may be used to improve product life cycle and industry's economic performance. Using Additive manufacturing (AM) and IoT together can help create a more sustainable manufacturing process by increasing resource efficiency and reducing recovery procedures [70]. Big data technology can influence the SC methods in terms of eco-efficiency and long-term performance. Esmaeilian et al. [71] reviewed capabilities of Blockchain as enabler for the successful implementation of sustainability and circular economy concepts under four main categories of (i) promoting green behaviour through designing specialised tokens, (ii) enhancing the visibility of product lifecycle, (iii) increasing systems efficiency and decreasing development and operational costs, and (iv) enhancing corporate performance reporting and sustainability monitoring capabilities. Digital supply chain may offer benefits of higher operational efficiency, ad-hoc dynamic planning, collaborative planning, collaborative product design, marketing effectiveness, financial flow, and deeper customer integration [72]. CPS, IoT, and big data analytics, enable a flexible supply chain planning and effective decision making, which may help to achieve high quality with low cost and risk in sustainable purchasing [19].

3.2 Environmental sustainability

In terms of the environment, real-time data acquired from various value chain partners assists organisations in effectively allocating industrial resources such as materials, energy, water, and products [3, 46]. I4T also support reduced greenhouse gas emissions [73], energy consumption [74], reduced fuel consumption as a result of improved transportation and logistics planning; and the use of advanced tracking and monitoring systems [75]. The Big data offers predictive analytics that improve environmental and social sustainability [76, 77]. The inclusion of sensors in goods enables performance monitoring such as tracking maintenance requirements-allowing businesses to deliver high-quality service to clients on a proactive basis. Further, organisations may invest in extending product life spans by using the 3Rs (reduce, re-use, and recycle) and monitoring items throughout customer usage. Cloud manufacturing and IoT can gather data from processes and things, such as machinery, allowing for the faults detection that might result in waste. Managers may also monitor and regulate the performance of operations based on production and resource consumption criteria, such as energy usage; the use of sensors would allow them to intervene in processes, even during component/product manufacturing. Machine efficiency might also be monitored in real time in order to schedule maintenance and avoid wasting resources [46]. Blockchain offers visibility, transparency, relationship management, and smart contracting which in turn offers environmental as well as economic benefits and plays a positive role in circular economy [78]. Abdella et al. [79] proposed machine learning using a set of environmental, social and governance criteria to predict sustainability performance across the supply chain. The revolution of autonomous vehicles can provide several benefits particularly in transportation part of the supply chain to reduce the damaged products. Automated guided vehicles (AGV) help in efficient materials handling operations improving the environmental and social sustainability. Krueger et al., [80] analysed possibilities of shared autonomous vehicles implementation implemented in a logistic cluster in public transport industry to improve utilisation of assets and reduce environment effect. Additive manufacturing result in less material being used and requires recycling of tiny amounts of trash due to mobility of 3D printers [70]. The usage of AM also helps to improve the sustainability of a manufacturing process by lowering the materials use and energy consumption. I40 help in energy monitoring that will result into increased energy efficiency and lower CO_2 emissions [81]. AM and IoT can aid in improving reverse logistics operations, such as tracking and tracing end of use and end of life items and monitoring recycling activities to pave the way for a long-term route toward circular manufacturing [82]. Cloud technology allows for the capture, exchange, and sharing of dynamic life-cycle data, as well as SC partnerships for environmental footprint assessment [83]. Cloud-based service platform can help in improved decision-making and thereby minimise greenhouse gas emissions in the transportation and logistics industries [84]. Big data analytics in process control, for example, might help in pollution control and natural resource management [85]. Cyber-physical systems aid in production without generating waste or consuming unnecessary resources; the IoT enables mass customization and production that meets demand without producing excess inventory; cloud manufacturing enables controlled resource consumption (e.g., raw materials, energy, water); and additive manufacturing proactively maintains products, saves energy, and reduces waste from defective products [2, 20, 86]. By designing goods based on precise consumption data, cyber-physical systems improve customer satisfaction. As a result, using the 5Rs technique (reduce, repair, re-use, recycle, and remanufacture) [86, 87], it is feasible to develop goods with longer life spans. CPS and IoT aid in the planning of energy and carbon-efficient logistics routes, as well as assisting suppliers in managing their own performance in terms of production planning, delivery quality and reliability, and environmental compliance via remote monitoring [88]. In smart factory, communication efficiency, transparency, surveillance, and control will minimise downtime, waste, defect, and risk across production processes [89].

3.3 Social sustainability

On the social front, I4T provides a plethora of options for employees to learn new technology, boosting morale and motivation [73, 74]. I4T provides employees with a better and safe working environment [15]. AI and data analytics can help in personalised career development programs based on the behaviour, experience, skills, personality, and learning patterns of each employee [90]. I4T will create new jobs in area of informatics, mechatronics, process engineering, and system integration [91]. Industry 4.0 technologies impact on supply chain sustainability is summarised in **Table 1**. Industry 4.0 sustainability benefits are shown in **Table 2**.

Industry 4.0 Technology Features		
Automation	Integration	Modularity
Real-time capability	Flexibility	Interoperability
Virtualisation	Decentralisation	Data quality and availability
Servitisation	Product and service customisation	Transparency

⬇

Supply Chain Sustainability		
Economical	**Environmental**	**Social**
Process and Production efficiency	Material and Resource use reduction	Worker's productivity improvement
Cost effectiveness	Energy Consumption reduction	Working condition improvement
Quality improvement	Water Consumption reduction	Worker's Health and safety improvement
Scalability	Waste reduction	Equity
Profit Margin improvement	Air pollution and GHG emission reduction	
	Reverse logistics reduction	

Table 1.
Industry 4.0 technologies impact on supply chain sustainability.

4. Discussion on Industry 4.0 sustainability

Industry 4.0 technologies such as AI, ML, IoT, Big data, Block chain technology, VR, AR, CPS, Industrial Autonomous Robotics, Cloud computing etc. are being adopted in manufacturing and supply chain throughout the world but slowly. Researchers and professional managers believe that I40 offers integration, interoperability, real-time capability, quality data, modularity, decentralisation, product customisation, servitisation, collaboration, transparency and virtualisation, which may positively impact sustainability. On economic dimension, I4T adoption in supply chain will improve supply chain efficiency, quality, resilience, customer specific planning, production and logistics alignment, on-time delivery, order accuracy, downtime prediction, and repair and maintenance, supplier selection and procurement, and reduce lead time. Economic sustainability will reduce cost and improve profitability. I40 acts environment friendly as its adoption will lead to reduction of raw materials and resources, energy consumption, GHG emission, scrap and waste, physical prototyping, transparency, tracking and traceability. It will enhance sustainability processes and transportation and environmental monitoring. Regarding social sustainability dimension, I4T can offer safe working environment and flexibility, reduce stress and hazardous tasks, and improve learning and development. It is not free from challenges. Human activities such as inventory tracking, quality control, and even product distribution may be performed by Industrial robots, automated vehicles, and intelligent machines and there would be loss of jobs [96]. At the same time, it will provide opportunity for new jobs in I4T. Most of the studies are theoretical. Hence, it needs to be supported by qualitative and case studies.

	Sustainability Benefits	Herrmann et al. [74]	Peng et al. [84]	Despeisse et al. [70]	Hofmann and Rüsch [88]	Waibel et al. [20]	Zhao et al. [85]	Keil et al. [26]	Fatorachian and Kazemi [92]	Ghobakhloo [93]	Jabbour et al. [46]	Kamble et al. [15]	Luthra & Mangla [39]	Muller et al. [94]	Stock et al. [36]	Stone et al. [90]	Tortorella and Fettermann [64]	Ghobakhloo & Fathi [91]	Braccini & Margherita [62]	Saberi et al. [68]	Dev et al. [82]	Garcia-Muina et al. [95]	Khan et al. [78]
Economic	Lead time reduction				x																		
	Customer specific planning				x														x				
	Autonomous supplier selection and procurement				x	x																	
	Improved supply chain resilience				x																		
	Downtime prediction							x						x									
	Aligned production and logistics	c				x								x	x								
	Logistics process efficiency				x									x	x								
	Faster delivery					x					x	x											
	Order accuracy				x																		
	Recycling cost reduction										x	x											
	Repair and maintenance efficiency							x														x	
Environmental	Resource consumption reduction						x				x						x						
	Energy consumption reduction	x									x								x				
	Sustainable Process optimisation																		x				
	Environmental monitoring easier				x																		
	Physical prototyping reduction			x																			
	Scrap reduction																x		x				

	Sustainability Benefits	**Herrmann et al. [74]**	**Peng et al. [84]**	**Despeisse et al. [70]**	**Hofmann and Rüsch [88]**	**Waibel et al. [20]**	**Zhao et al. [85]**	**Keil et al. [26]**	**Fatorachian and Kazemi [92]**	**Ghobakhloo [93]**	**Jabbour et al. [46]**	**Kamble et al. [15]**	**Luthra & Mangla [39]**	**Muller et al. [94]**	**Stock et al. [36]**	**Stone et al. [90]**	**Tortorella and Fettermann [64]**	**Ghobakhloo & Fathi [91]**	**Braccini & Margherita [62]**	**Saberi et al. [68]**	**Dev et al. [82]**	**Garcia-Muina et al. [95]**	**Khan et al. [78]**
	Transport optimisation				x																		
	Transparency																						x
	Tracking and tracing of recycling										x	x		x	x					x	x		
	GHG emission reduction		x				x																
Social	Safe working environment											x	x						x				
	Reduction of hazardous tasks and stress	x						x											x				
	Learning and training improved	x														x							
	Hazardous recycling process reduction										x	x											

Table 2.
Industry 4.0 sustainability benefits.

5. Conclusion

Data collection and monitoring, information sharing, tracking, decision-making, and coordination between organisational areas and SC partners are technical and organisational factors that could influence the integration of Industry 4.0 and environmentally sustainable SC decision-making. This paper argues for an integrated approach to the issues that Industry 4.0 technologies may unleash the full potential of ecologically sustainable SC. The impact of Industry 4.0 technologies in economic dimension of triple bottom line is efficiency, flexibility, productivity and quality, which will enhance economic performance. On the environmental dimension, better resources utilisation, more quantity production, reduction of waste and energy will result into environmental performance. Finally on societal dimension, better labour utilisation and safe working conditions due to digitalisation and automation. The goal of this paper is to highlight the convergence of two important subjects; Industry 4.0 and sustainable SC with triple bottom line considerations. These two aspects have mostly been investigated separately. Industry 4.0 has the potential to increase ecologically sustainable production, distribution and consumption by allowing for the creation of green products, green manufacturing processes, and green SCM in ways that have never been possible before. On the other hand, the synergy between Industry 4.0 and ecologically sustainable production and distribution is contingent on a number of important success factors. Industry 4.0 adoption is faces few challenges. I4T need to be connected continuously and massive data centres will increase energy consumption. Therefore, it is necessary to balance energy savings and additional energy requirement in I40 adoption. I40 device replacement may also create additional waste. In recycling, sharing information about product by manufacturer, product use and transparency is also a matter of concern that needs to be addressed. Initial high investment and return also need to be studied. Major limitation of the study is the theoretical aspect. It is suggested that these theoretical research propositions be further explored, either through qualitative research or further investigated using quantitative methodology.

Author details

Mohammad Akhtar
School of Business, Galgotias University, Greater Noida, UP, India

*Address all correspondence to: mk71b@yahoo.com;
mohammad.akhtar@galgotiasuniversity.edu.in

References

[1] Esmaeilian B, Behdad S, Wang B. The evolution and future of manufacturing: A review. Journal of Manufacturing Systems. 2016;**39**:79-100

[2] Shrouf F, Ordieres J, Miragliotta G. Smart factories in Industry 4.0: A review of the concept and of energy management approached in production based on the internet of things paradigm. Industrial Engineering and Engineering Management (IEEM), IEEE International Conference paper, Selangor, Malaysia. IEEE Xplore; 2014. pp. 697–701. DOI: 10.1109/IEEM.2014.7058728

[3] Stock T, Seliger G. Opportunities of sustainable manufacturing in Industry 4.0. Procedia CIRP. 2016;**40**:536-541

[4] Jeble S, Dubey R, Childe SJ, Papadopoulos T, Roubaud D, Prakash A. Impact of big data and predictive analytics capability on supply chain sustainability. The International Journal of Logistics Management. 2018;**29**(2): 513-538

[5] Wamba SF, Gunasekaran A, Akter S, Ren SJF, Dubey R, Childe SJ. Big data analytics and firm performance: Effects of dynamic capabilities. Journal of Business Research. 2017;**70**: 356-365

[6] Da Xu L, He W, Li S. Internet of Things in industries: A survey. IEEE Transactions on Industrial Informatics. 2014;**10**(4):2233-2243

[7] Lee JY, Yoon JS, Kim BH. A big data analytics platform for smart factories in small and medium-sized manufacturing enterprises: An empirical case study of a die casting factory. International Journal of Precision Engineering and Manufacturing. 2017;**18**(10):1353-1361

[8] Zhan Y, Tan KH, Li Y, Tse YK. Unlocking the power of big data in new product development. Annals of Operations Research. 2018;**270**: 577-595

[9] Li L, Chi T, Hao T, Yu T. Customer demand analysis of the electronic commerce supply chain using Big Data. Annals of Operations Research. 2016; **268**(1):1-16

[10] Du S, Tang W, Zhao J, Nie T. Sell to whom? Firm's green production in competition facing market segmentation. Annals of Operations Research. 2016;**270**(1):1-30

[11] Oesterreich TD, Teuteberg F. Understanding the implications of digitisation and automation in the context of Industry 4.0: A triangulation approach and elements of a research agenda for the construction industry. Computers in Industry. 2016;**83**:121-139

[12] Liu Y, Xu X. Industry 4.0 and cloud manufacturing: A comparative analysis. Journal of Manufacturing Science and Engineering. 2017;**139**(3):34701-34708

[13] Yu Z, Ouyang J, Li S, Peng X. Formal modelling and control of cyber-physical manufacturing systems. Advances in Mechanical Engineering. 2017;**9**(10):1-12. DOI: 10.1177/1687814017725472

[14] Boons F, Montalvo C, Quist J, Wagner M. Sustainable innovation, business models and economic performance: An overview. Journal of Cleaner Production. 2013;**45**:1-8

[15] Kamble SS, Gunasekaran A, Gawankar SA. Sustainable Industry 4.0 framework: A systematic literature

review identifying the current trends and future perspectives. Process Safety and Environmental Protection. 2018a; **117**:408-425

[16] Zhong RY, Xu X, Klotz E, Newman ST. Intelligent manufacturing in the context of industry 4.0: A review. Engineering. 2017;**3**(5):616-630

[17] Akenji L, Bengtsson M. Making sustainable consumption and production the core of sustainable development goals. Sustainability. 2014; **6**(2):513-529

[18] Mardani A, Kannan D, Hooker RE, Ozkul S, Alrasheedi M, Tirkolaee EB. Evaluation of green and sustainable supply chain management using structural equation modelling: A systematic review of the state of the art literature and recommendations for future research. Journal of Cleaner Production. 2020;**249** 119383

[19] Gottge S, Menzel T, Forslund H. Industry 4.0 technologies in the purchasing process. Industrial Management & Data Systems. 2020; **120**(4):730-748

[20] Waibel MW, Steenkamp LP, Moloko N, Oosthuizen GA. Investigating the effects of smart production systems on sustainability elements. Procedia Manufacturing. 2017;**8**:731-737

[21] Man JCD, Strandhagen JO. An Industry 4.0 research agenda for sustainable business models. Procedia CIRP. 2017;**63**:721-726

[22] UN – United Nations, 2015. Sustainable Development Goals—United Nations. https://sdgs.un.org/goals

[23] Dubey R, Gunasekaran A, Childe SJ, Wamba SF, Papadopoulos T. The impact of big data on world-class sustainable manufacturing. The International Journal of Advanced Manufacturing Technology. 2016;**84**(1–4):631-645

[24] Moghaddam M, Cadavid MN, Kenley B, Deshmukh AV. Reference architectures for smart manufacturing: A critical review. Journal of Manufacturing Systems. 2018;**49**:215-225

[25] Nascimento DLM, Alencastro V, Quelhas OLG, Caiado RGG, Garza-Reyes JA, Rocha-Lona L, et al. Exploring Industry 4.0 technologies to enable circular economy practices in a manufacturing context: A business model proposal. Journal of Manufacturing Technology. 2019;**30**(3): 607-627

[26] Kiel D, Müller JM, Arnold C, Voigt K-I. Sustainable industrial value creation: Benefits and challenges of industry 4.0. International Journal of Innovation Management. 2017;**21**(8):1-34

[27] Zambon I, Cecchini M, Egidi G, Saporito MG, Colantoni A. Revolution 4.0: Industry vs. agriculture in a future development for SMEs. Processes. 2019; **7**(1):36

[28] Ding B. Pharma Industry 4.0: Literature review and research opportunities in sustainable pharmaceutical supply chains. Process Safety and Environmental Protection. 2018;**119**:115-130

[29] Bag S, Telukdarie A, Pretorius J, Gupta S. Industry 4.0 and supply chain sustainability: Framework and future research directions. Benchmarking International Journal. 2018;**28**(5): 1410-1450

[30] Tsai W-H, Lu Y-H. A framework of production planning and control with carbon tax under Industry 4.0. Sustainability. 2018;**10**:3221

[31] Ghadimi P, Wang C, Lim MK, Heavey C. Intelligent sustainable supplier selection using multi-agent technology: Theory and application for Industry 4.0 supply chains. Computers & Industrial Engineering. 2019;**127**: 588-600

[32] Belaud J-P, Prioux N, Vialle C, Sablayrolles C. Big data for agri-food 4.0: Application to sustainability management for by-products supply chain. Computers in Industry. 2019;**111**: 41-50

[33] Miranda J, Ponce P, Molina A, Wright P. Sensing, smart and sustainable technologies for Agri-Food 4.0. Computers in Industry. 2019;**108**:21-36

[34] Bibaud-Alves J, El-Haouzi HB, Thomas P, Boucinha V. Toward a sustainable new product development approach based on Industry 4.0 assets. In: International Workshop on Service Orientation in Holonic and Multi-Agent Manufacturing. Cham: Springer; 2018. pp. 156-167

[35] Paravizo E, Chaim OC, Braatz D, Muschard B, Rozenfeld H. Exploring gamification to support manufacturing education on industry 4.0 as an enabler for innovation and sustainability. Procedia Manufacturing. 2018;**21**: 438-445

[36] Stock T, Obenaus M, Kunz S, Kohl H. Industry 4.0 as enabler for a sustainable development: A qualitative assessment of its ecological and social potential. Process Safety and Environmental Protection. 2018;**118**: 254-267

[37] Hidayatno A, Destyanto AR, Hulu CA. Industry 4.0 Technology Implementation Impact to Industrial Sustainable Energy in Indonesia: A Model Conceptualization. Energy Procedia. 2019;**156**:227-233

[38] Bonilla SH, Silva HRO, Da Silva MT, Gonçalves RF, Sacomano JB. Industry 4.0 and sustainability implications: A scenario-based analysis of the impacts and challenges. Sustainability. 2018;**10**: 3740

[39] Luthra S, Mangla SK. Evaluating challenges to Industry 4.0 initiatives for supply chain sustainability in emerging economies. Process Safety and Environmental Protection. 2018;**117**: 168-179

[40] Ardanza A, Moreno A, Segura Á, De La Cruz M, Aguinaga D. Sustainable and flexible industrial human machine interfaces to support adaptable applications in the Industry 4.0 paradigm. International Journal of Production Research. 2019;**57**:4045-4059

[41] Meng Y, Yang Y, Chung H, Lee P-H, Shao C. Enhancing sustainability and energy efficiency in smart factories: A review. Sustainability. 2018;**10**:4779

[42] Chaim O, Muschard B, Cazarini E, Rozenfeld H. Insertion of sustainability performance indicators in an industry 4.0 virtual learning environment. Procedia Manufacturing. 2018;**21**: 446-453

[43] Kamble SS, Gunasekaran A, Sharma R. Analysis of the driving and dependence power of barriers to adopt industry 4.0 in Indian manufacturing industry. Computers in Industry. 2018b; **101**:107-119

[44] Manavalan E, Jayakrishna K. A review of Internet of Things (IoT) embedded sustainable supply chain for industry 4.0 requirements. Computers

& Industrial Engineering. 2019;**127**: 925-953

[45] Birkel H, Veile JW, Müller JM, Hartmann E, Voigt K-I. Development of a risk framework for Industry 4.0 in the context of sustainability for established manufacturers. Sustainability. 2019;**11**: 384

[46] Jabbour ABLDS, Jabboura CJC, Foropona C, Filho MG. When titans meet–Can industry 4.0 revolutionise the environmentally-sustainable manufacturing wave? The role of critical success factors. Technological Forecasting and Social Change. 2018; **132**(1):18-25

[47] Monteleone S, de Moraes EA, Maia RF. Analysis of the variables that affect the intention to adopt precision agriculture for smart water management in Agriculture 4.0 context. In 2019 Global IoT Summit (GIoTS) IEEE. 2019. pp. 1–6.

[48] Umar M, Khan SAR, Zia-ul-haq HM, Yusliza MY, Farooq K. The role of emerging technologies in implementing green practices to achieve sustainable operations. The TQM Journal. 2022a; **34**(2):232-249

[49] Umar M, Khan SAR, Yusoff Yusliza M, Ali S, Yu Z. Industry 4.0 and green supply chain practices: An empirical study. International Journal of Productivity and Performance Management. 2022b;**71**(3):814-832

[50] Chalmeta R, Santos-deLeón NJ. Sustainable supply chain in the era of industry 4.0 and big data: A systematic analysis of literature and research. Sustainability. 2020;**12**(10):4108

[51] Mastos TD, Nizamis A, Vafeiadis T, Alexopoulos N, Ntinas C, Gkortzis D, et al. Industry 4.0 sustainable supply chains: An application of an IoT enabled scrap metal management solution. Journal of Cleaner Production. 2020;**269** 122377

[52] Strandhagen JW, Buer SV, Semini M, Alfnes E, Strandhagen JO. Sustainability challenges and how Industry 4.0 technologies can address them: A case study of a shipbuilding supply chain. Production Planning & Control. 2020: 1-16. DOI: 10.1080/09537287.2020. 1837940 [online. Ahead of print]

[53] Yadav G, Luthra S, Jakhar SK, Mangla SK, Rai DP. A framework to overcome sustainable supply chain challenges through solution measures of industry 4.0 and circular economy: An automotive case. Journal of Cleaner Production. 2020;**254** 120112 [ahead-of-print]

[54] Belhadi A, Kamble S, Gunasekaran A, Mani V. Analyzing the mediating role of organizational ambidexterity and digital business transformation on industry 4.0 capabilities and sustainable supply chain performance. Supply Chain Management. 2021. DOI: 10.1108/SCM-04-2021-0152 [ahead-of-print]

[55] Fatorachian H, Kazemi H. Impact of Industry 4.0 on supply chain performance. Production Planning and Control. 2021;**32**(1):63-81

[56] Kumar A, Choudhary S, Garza-Reyes JA, Kumar V, Rehman Khan SA, Mishra N. Analysis of critical success factors for implementing industry 4.0 integrated circular supply chain–Moving toward sustainable operations. Production Planning & Control. 2021a:1–15. DOI: 10.1080/09537287.2021.1980905 [online. Ahead of print]

[57] Kumar S, Raut RD, Nayal K, Kraus S, Yadav VS, Narkhede BE. To identify industry 4.0 and circular economy

adoption barriers in the agriculture supply chain by using ISM-ANP. Journal of Cleaner Production. 2021b;**293** 126023

[58] Kusi-Sarpong S, Gupta H, Khan SA, Chiappetta Jabbour CJ, Rehman ST, Kusi-Sarpong H. Sustainable supplier selection based on industry 4.0 initiatives within the context of circular economy implementation in supply chain operations. Production Planning & Control. 2021:1-21. DOI: 10.1080/09537287.2021.1980906 [online. Ahead of print]

[59] Mastos TD, Nizamis A, Terzi S, Gkortzis D, Papadopoulos A, Tsagkalidis N, et al. Introducing an application of an industry 4.0 solution for circular supply chain management. Journal of Cleaner Production. 2021;**300** 126886

[60] Mubarik MS, Naghavi N, Mubarik M, Kusi-Sarpong S, Khan SA, Zaman SI, et al. Resilience and cleaner production in industry 4.0: Role of supply chain mapping and visibility. Journal of Cleaner Production. 2021;**292** 126058

[61] Sharma M, Kamble S, Mani V, Sehrawat R, Belhadi A, Sharma V. Industry 4.0 adoption for sustainability in multi-tier manufacturing supply chain in emerging economies. Journal of Cleaner Production. 2021;**281** 125013

[62] Braccini AM, Margherita EG. Exploring organizational sustainability of Industry 4.0 under the triple bottom line: The case of a manufacturing company. Sustainability. 2019;**11**:36

[63] Birkel H, Müller JM. Potentials of industry 4.0 for supply chain management within the triple bottom line of sustainability-A systematic literature review. Journal of Cleaner Production. 2021;**289**:125612

[64] Tortorella GL, Fettermann D. Implementation of Industry 4.0 and lean production in Brazilian manufacturing companies. International Journal of Production Research. 2018;**56**(8): 2975-2987

[65] Ramadan M, Al-Maimani H, Noche B. RFID-enabled smart real-time manufacturing cost tracking system. The International Journal of Advanced Manufacturing Technology. 2017;**89** (1–4):969-985

[66] Wang S, Wan J, Zhang D, Li D, Zhang C. Toward smart factory for Industry 4.0: A Self-organised multi-agent system with big data based feedback and coordination. Computer Networks. 2016;**101**:158-168

[67] Zhang Y, Liu S, Liu Y, Yang H, Li M, Huisingh D, et al. The 'Internet of Things' enabled real-time scheduling for remanufacturing of automobile engines. Journal of Cleaner Production. 2018;**185**: 562-575

[68] Saberi S, Kouhizadeh M, Sarkis J, Shen L. Blockchain technology and its relationships to sustainable supply chain management. International Journal of Production Research. 2019;**57**(7): 2117-2135

[69] Dev NK, Shankar R, Gunasekaran A, Thakur LS. A hybrid adaptive decision system for supply chain reconfiguration. International Journal of Production Research. 2016;**54**(23): 7100-7114

[70] Despeisse M, Baumers M, Brown P, Charnley F, Ford SJ, Garmulewicz A, et al. Unlocking value for a circular economy through 3D printing: A research agenda. Technological Forecasting and Social Change. 2017;**115**: 75-84

[71] Esmaeilian B, Sarkis J, Lewis K, Behdad S. Blockchain for the future of sustainable supply chain management in Industry 4.0. Resources, Conservation and Recycling. 2020;**163**:105064

[72] Dolgui A, Ivanov D, Sethi SP, Sokolov B. Scheduling in production, supply chain and Industry 4.0 systems by optimal control: Fundamentals, state-of-the-art and applications. International Journal of Production Research. 2019; **57**(2):411-432

[73] Peukert B, Benecke S, Clavell J, Neugebauer S, Nissen NF, Uhlmann E, et al. Addressing sustainability and flexibility in manufacturing via smart modular machine tool frames to support sustainable value creation. Procedia CIRP. 2015;**29**:514-519

[74] Herrmann C, Schmidt C, Kurle D, Blume S, Thiede S. Sustainability in Manufacturing and Factories of the Future. International Journal of Precision Engineering and Manufacturing Green Technology. 2014;**1**(4):283-292

[75] Müller J, Dotzauer V, Voigt K-I. Industry 4.0 and its impact on reshoring decisions of german manufacturing enterprises. In: Bode C, Bogaschewsky R, Eßig M, Lasch R, Stölzle W, editors. Supply Management Research — Advanced Studies in Supply Management. Wiesbaden: Springer Gabler; 2017. pp. 165-179

[76] Dubey R, Gunasekaran A, Childe SJ, Papadopoulos T, Luo Z, Wamba SF, et al. Can big data and predictive analytics improve social and environmental sustainability? Technological Forecasting and Social Change. 2019;**144**:534-545

[77] Song M, Cen L, Zheng Z, Fisher R, Liang X, Wang Y, et al. How would big data support societal development and environmental sustainability? Insights and practices. Journal of Cleaner Production. 2017;**142**:489-500

[78] Khan SAR, Yu Z, Sarwat S, Godil DI, Amin S, Shujaat S. The role of block chain technology in circular economy practices to improve organisational performance. International Journal of Logistics Research and Applications. 2021;**1–18**. DOI: 10.1080/13675567.2021.1872512 [online. Ahead of print]

[79] Abdella GM, Kucukvar M, Onat NC, Al-Yafay HM, Bulak ME. Sustainability assessment and modeling based on supervised machine learning techniques: The case for food consumption. Journal of Cleaner Production. 2020;**251**:119661

[80] Krueger R, Rashidi TH, Rose JM. Preferences for shared autonomous vehicles. Transportation Research Part C: Emerging Technologies. 2016;**69**: 343-355

[81] Thiede S. Environmental sustainability of cyber physical production systems. Procedia CIRP. 2018;**69**:644-649

[82] Dev NK, Shankar R, Qaiser FH. Industry 4.0 and circular economy: Operational excellence for sustainable reverse supply chain performance. Resources, Conservation and Recycling. 2020;**153**:104583

[83] Xing K, Qian W, Zaman AU. Development of a cloud-based platform for footprint assessment in green supply chain management. Journal of Cleaner Production. 2016;**139**:191-203

[84] Peng T-K, Shiang W-J. Developing a cloud carbon footprint decision support system for supply chain. International Journal of Electronic Business Management. 2014;**12**(3):200-213

[85] Zhao R, Liu Y, Zhang N, Huang T. An optimization model for green supply chain management by using a big data analytic approach. Journal of Cleaner Production. 2017;**142**: 1085-1097

[86] Tao F, Wang Y, Zuo Y, Yang H, Zhang M. Internet of things in product life cycle energy management. Journal of Industrial Information Integration. 2016; **1**:26-39

[87] Zawadzki P, Żywicki K. Smart product design and production control for effective mass customization in the Industry 4.0 concept. Management and Production Engineering Review. 2016; 7(3):105-112

[88] Hofmann E, Rüsch M. Industry 4.0 and the current status as well as future prospects on logistics. Computers in Industry. 2017;**89**:23-34

[89] Ghobakhloo M, Ng TC. Adoption of digital technologies of smart manufacturing in SMEs. Journal of Industrial Information Integration. 2019; **16**:100107

[90] Stone CB, Neely AR, Lengnick-Hall ML. Human resource management in the digital age: Big data, HR analytics and artificial intelligence. In: Melo PN, Machado C, editors. Management and Technological Challenges in the Digital Age. Boca Raton, Florida, USA: CRC Press; 2018. pp. 13-42

[91] Ghobakhloo M, Fathi M. Corporate survival in Industry 4.0 era: The enabling role of lean-digitised manufacturing. Journal of Manufacturing Technology Management. 2019;**31**(1):1-30

[92] Fatorachian H, Kazemi H. A critical investigation of Industry 4.0 in manufacturing: Theoretical operationalisation framework. Production Planning & Control. 2018; **29**(8):633-644

[93] Ghobakhloo M. The future of manufacturing industry: A strategic roadmap toward Industry 4.0. Journal of Manufacturing Technology Management. 2018;**29**(6):910-936

[94] Müller JM, Kiel D, Voigt KI. What drives the implementation of Industry 4.0? The role of opportunities and challenges in the context of sustainability. Sustainability. 2018;**10**(1): 247-271

[95] García-Muina FE, Medina-Salgado MS, Ferrari AM, Cucchi M. Sustainability transition in industry 4.0 and smart manufacturing with the triple layered business model canvas. Sustainability. 2020;**12**(6):2364

[96] Zheng P, Sang Z, Zhong RY, Liu Y, Liu C, Mubarok K, Xu X. Smart manufacturing systems for Industry 4.0: Conceptual framework, scenarios, and future perspectives. Frontiers of Mechanical Engineering. 2018;**13**(2): 137-150

Chapter 6

Open Innovation Strategies on New Product and Process Development Prospects: A Case of the Automotive Component Manufacturers in South Africa

Arthur Mzwandile Gonyora and Pfano Mashau

Abstract

Competition between South African Automotive Component Manufacturers ACMs has focused on activities associated with supply chain management such as transporting raw materials and finished products. However, these activities are non-value, adding, so they are an area of relative opportunities for cost reduction; hence new product development presents a significant boost to competitiveness. This chapter's primary goal is to determine which open innovation practices can benefit ACMs in developing new products and processes by using a sample survey of 10 ACMs in the automotive manufacturing industry in South Africa. The study adopted a quantitative methodology approach using a 5 Likert structured questionnaire. Data were collected from 33 respondents, including owners, senior and junior managers of ACMs. The results identified that idea generation positively influences the Open Innovation activity of seeking new outside applications for internally developed innovations, knowledge, tools and ideas on new product development. The significant implications are that ACMs should improve their dynamic capabilities to turn ideas generated into new innovative products to remain competitive. This chapter contributes to the existing knowledge by suggesting a contextualised impact of open innovation strategy on sustainable new product development of ACMs in South Africa.

Keywords: automotive component manufacturers, open innovation, new product development, fourth industrial revolution

1. Introduction

The disruptive changes of the 4th Industrial Revolution (4th IR) era have resulted in fierce competition between companies, big or small, focused on supply chain management activities, such as transporting primary and secondary products. However, these activities are non-valve adding to products; instead, there are significant opportunities for cost reduction. On the other hand, Global Original Equipment

Manufacturers (OEMs) seek advanced operational strategies that capacitate the approach towards their target markets while reducing distances, decreasing production costs, on-time delivery, reducing cycle times, and thus improving the overall process and product quality [1]. To respond to the disruptive changes caused by the 4th IR, these big international players have established local subsidiaries to support them in producing automobiles in other countries and position themselves better to access their markets. The benefits derived include government subsidies from the host country, local skilled labour, appropriate infrastructure, and low production costs [2].

Since ACMs are pivotal in the manufacturing supply chain, they face unique challenges of lack of resources, dynamic capabilities, and vulnerabilities in the industry. These challenges result in technical stoppages or unplanned shutdowns, leading to loss of working time, hindering workers from keeping their jobs and companies from retaining skilled human resources. Thus, besides ACMs maintaining their employees, their revenue is significantly compromised and negatively impacts competitiveness. This problem has necessitated management to develop alternatives such as new products and services. This new product development process enables companies to increase their income, become more competitive, and avoid the frequent loss of highly skilled workers, curtailing unintended knowledge transfer.

2. Problem statement

The main markets for ACMs have diminished due to financial crises and the numerous operational challenges they have to overcome. These firms face impermanent shutdowns or technical stoppages in avoiding job losses and retaining valued skilled human resources, notwithstanding the challenges of the 4th IR, which emanate from adopting a big-picture perspective of business and processes to integrate different needs across departments and workers into one common goal. Industry 4.0 brings entirely new capabilities to operations managers, allowing them to respond faster to critical situations and improve on multiple KPIs. The price of holding on to their human resources reduces financial income or risks total work stoppage. This problem has resulted in top managers adopting innovation and developing new products manufactured with the existing infrastructure, robust organisational structure, advanced production systems and competent workforce. Inevitably, the benefits of new product development are an increase in income, competitiveness and retention of highly skilled workers, and managing knowledge transfer. As such, this study sought to compile and categorise the application of OI in the context of the new product development in the 4 IR era by answering the following Research Questions RQs:

RO1: What impact of open innovation strategies on new product development prospects in the 4 IR era?

RO2: What proposed contextual open innovation strategies model will apply to automotive component manufacturers?

The study contributes to the current body of knowledge by addressing the gap that exists in the literature on open innovation strategies by exploring how ACMs in a developing country such as South Africa approach new product development initiatives to escape the intense competition of today's global economy when responding to the competitiveness issues. Open innovation strategies identified in the study impact the competitiveness of the ACMs industry, which plays a vital role in the overall South African economy. The study also identifies how South African ACMs adopt open innovation strategies and the benefits. The field of competitive strategies is dynamic;

thus, the study provides new insights into new product development and the concept of open innovation strategies, which can assist practitioners in developing appropriate open innovation strategies to mitigate new product development challenges and boost competitiveness.

The chapter first reviews available literature on ACMs, open innovation strategies and the benefits to new product development, followed by a description of the research design and methodology, a report of the findings, recommendations and subsequent conclusions.

3. Literature review

ACMs have to develop innovations and new products compared to the traditional innovation process to be competitive. They must identify customers' needs and requirements achievable from their production process capacity and the organisational structure. Their inability to implement drastic changes to their production processes and only be ready and attentive to the requirements of their parent companies makes them vulnerable to competitiveness and innovation [3].

4. Fourth industrial revolution (I4.0)

While the first, second and third industrial revolutions (IRs) changed the industries' shop floors through the use of steam power, electrical power and automation, respectively, the I4.0 is about the communication among cyber-physical systems (CPSs) [4]. The advances in computing power, intelligent control, and connectivity lead to the development of intelligent products and allow for radical changes in several other areas. As in the previous IRs, sweeping changes in the shop floor are causing a cascading effect of changes through all the processes in the value chains, thus supporting the creation of new business models and allowing for the production of improved products, which are impacting customers' uses and behaviours in new ways.

5. ACM open innovation model

The ACM Open Innovation Strategies archetypal represents the various approaches that diverse ACMs are likely to apply to strengthen their organisation's performance by increasing innovation activities, including New Product Development NPD and economic performance. The strategies are responsible for the successful overwhelming core challenges component manufacturers face about their size, otherwise coined (size-related challenges). Referred to in this archetype as 'resource scarcity, inadequate dynamic capabilities, and extreme exposure to risk', This archetypal assumes that ACM's 'knowledge exploration', referred to as 'creation of value', and 'knowledge exploitation', referred to as 'value capture', help to select the appropriate strategic options to follow. It assumes that ACM's leverage changes over time and can hypothetically accept other alternatives in the future.

The open innovation strategies model (**Figure 1**) represents an assumption that ACMs must concentrate on essential elements in the management process, which encompass guidance, reinforcement of absorptive and adsorptive capacities, cultivation

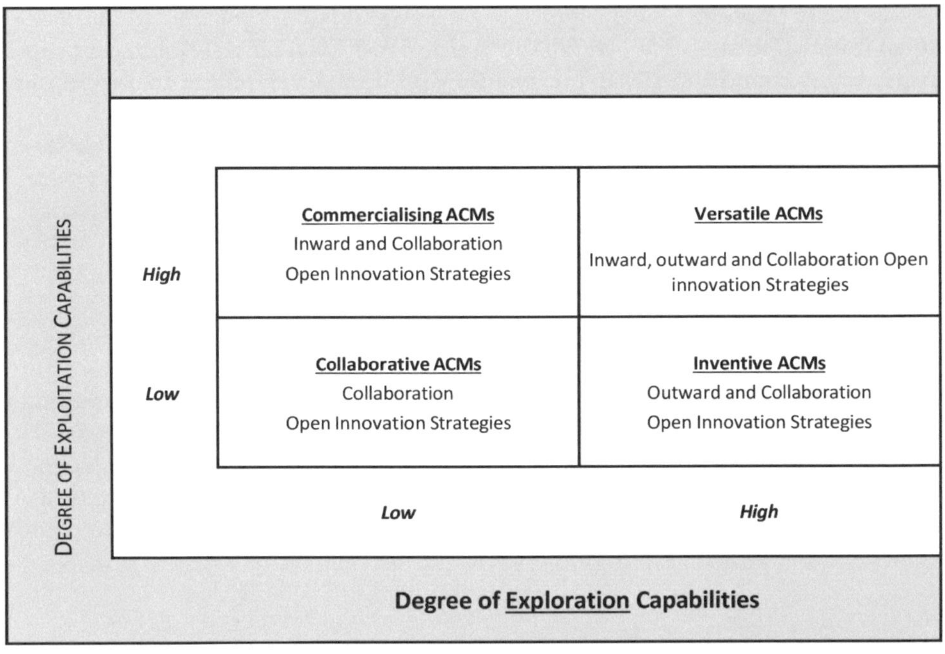

Figure 1.
ACM open innovation strategies. Source: [5].

of risk-taking culture, employee motivation, exploiting functional business systems, effective decision-making and employee assurance and other numerous factors.

The proposed archetype highlights those facets since they are vital in determining which strategy an ACM should pursue. This model incorporates management considerations to focus on lower forms of innovation strategies that can be followed by ACMs who possess unique strengths in competition depending on whether they are "exploration and exploitation capabilities" [5].

With the automotive industry being the focal point, the study authors adopted this archetype to assess a variety of ACM approaches for contending with others in this environment, given ACM's relative innovation exploration and exploitation strengths. There are many combinations of strategies and sub-strategies. For example, inward open innovation is viewed in numerous ways, including procurement or hiring a patent, exchanging stock for a patent, acquiring mutually joint patents, acquisitions, or subcontracting R and D projects. Inward and outward innovation can coincide by combining other unique strategies such as cross-licencing. This model focuses on open innovation's three main groupings (inward, outward, and collaboration strategies). The model pairs them to the categories of ACMs that will use and benefit from them. Each strategy was assessed theoretically about:

- Its ability to increase ACM innovation outputs and financial performance.

- Its strategic mitigation or aggravation of the mentioned challenges are resource scarcity, limited dynamic capabilities and disproportionate risk exposure.

The study intends to establish the link between open innovation strategies in reducing NPD challenges affecting these ACMs to the actual performance outcomes. The study also allows us to evaluate the impact of the strategies in executing NPD activities.

The model indicates that each quadrant is identified by a name that describes the archetypal strategic positioning in that quadrant. As an illustration, ACMs in the lower right quadrant focus on investing in the production of new knowledge, whereas ACMs in the upper left quadrant will focus on commercialisation initiatives. Each quadrant describes all ACMs, and the classification is designed to give an easy reference. All ACMs could follow the collaborative route, but the ACMs in the lower left quadrant could employ only collaborative strategies. This choice is a result of the lack of proficiency in the creation of value, hence classified as "inventive," and the capturing of value capabilities classified as "Commercialising" and combined capabilities classified as "versatile. ACMs in the other quadrants are classified as "collaborative." The collaborative approach is available as a strategic option in every quadrant.

6. Collaborative automotive component manufactures quadrant

The lower left quadrant in the model represents ACMs that collaborate and lack innovative exploration and exploitation capabilities. Besides the lack of explorative or exploitative capabilities, they possess the option to implement various collaboration approaches that permit control of the exploration and exploitation strengths over other organisations. Besides, there are three core classifications of collaborations with employees termed "closed innovation approach." These collaborations are [6]. While collaboration is the primary open innovation strategy available, it is not exceptional for collaborative organisations only since ACMs in supplementary quadrants could, by choice, implement collaboration-interrelated strategies. These subsequent suggestions are about ACMs universally, notwithstanding the quadrant they occupy.

7. Inventive automotive component manufacturers quadrant

The inventive quadrant is at the lower right side of the model. Since the ACMs in this quadrant have strong knowledge creation (exploration) abilities, referred to as "inventive," they are likely to depend on their unique resources and capabilities. Many ACMs belong to this group because they experience challenges with value capture. Additionally, [7] noted that ACMs who possess fewer capabilities to commercialise resort to the option of licencing out their innovations to willing partners.

8. Commercialising automotive component manufactures quadrant

The upper left quadrant of the model is the "Commercialising" ACMs quadrant. These organisations are characterised by intense commercialisation, "exploitation capabilities" matched with not as robust knowledge creation, "exploration capabilities." The conversion of external ideas into new products achieved through Commercialisation and ACMs in this quadrant focus on this activity. There are fewer ACMs in this grouping than in Inventive or Collaborative quadrants because many organisations lack commercialisation capabilities [8]. This grouping includes manufacturers and niche organisations with specialised distribution channels. Other organisations are bound to gain an advantage by obtaining IP since their positioning makes them better positioned to consider IP as a feasible option. "Inward open innovation" gives ACMs a competitive advantage when bringing products to the market.

9. Versatile automotive component manufactures quadrant

The Versatile ACMs quadrant is on the upper right side of the model and depicts the most robust organisations. More established mid-sized and small organisations in this cluster have reached maturity and are deeply rooted in niche markets. They possess robust knowledge creation and exploitation capabilities. They are self-reliant in exploration or exploitation assistance and can opt for a more closed innovation approach. They can benefit by implementing more than one innovation strategy: inward, outward, or collaboration. These ACMs can use different strategies, sub, or coupled strategies to enhance their organisational performance and competitive standing. When negligible benefits derived from the formation of these actions are equal to the marginal costs, these organisations start seeking an approach to change the excellent symmetry of depth (intensity) and breadth (scope) of these activities; hence we reach the final proposition.

10. Innovation and new product development in the automotive industry

Frequently innovation definition is about the adoption of an idea or behaviour [9], the development of new products [10] and the initiation of changes to an established phenomenon [11] utilising the right technology [12]. Innovation is critical to different companies and countries, and Schumpeter was the first economist to pronounce the importance of innovation and development for any entity. Additionally, a recent overview of the economic importance of innovation has found an adjacent relationship between these two variables for any country [13]. Innovation is a strategy used by automotive component manufacturers that adhere to long-term plans based on OEM operational strategy [14], especially in a capitalist environment, where production and consumerism are vibrant [15].

Innovative practices assist automotive component manufacturers and the supply chain that have saturated traditional markets with outdated products. Automotive component manufacturers usually understand their customer requirements and lead times based on long-term forecasting. Minor product modifications can be implemented using the available organisational structures and production processes. Despite this, automotive component manufacturers can expedite proposed products with suitable characteristics thanks to their technical capabilities, which is a great advantage since the time required for the new product development (NPD) process is lengthy in a small company. However, currently, these ACMs have much expertise in product changes and production processes they can swiftly respond to their parent companies' production requirements.

Fortunately, some South African automotive component manufacturers improve product characteristics through innovative practices designed by their product department or a product development department. In contrast, some OEMs have introduced technical development centres that provide technical support to other departments in NPD and component suppliers in their value chains. These companies possess a competitive advantage based on their geographical location, which is strategically a critical success factor in competing with other global players in the automotive industry. Nevertheless, one of the most critical issues concerning innovation in these automotive component manufacturers is the relationship between the different critical factors associated with the success of NPD and competitive advantage [16]. Therefore, this relationship makes it an area of exceptional and consistent attention if competitiveness is achieved.

11. Critical success factors in NPD and innovation

Innovation and NPD present an opportunity for strategic advantage in the automotive and other industries as related processes necessary to identify a firm's activities or critical success factors (CSFs) [17]. Numerous authors have intensified efforts on the role of CSFs; the literature review indicates management commitment as crucial for NPD [18], survival and success. Team development skills are other extensively studied CSFs [18] and the internal processes companies use to retain a trained workforce. Similarly, authors have highlighted the processes for the identification of the following: market needs [19, 20], the translation of those needs into a workable design to be manufactured [21, 22] and the cultural adaptations made as companies introduce the structural changes required to keep people continuously informed in an even developmental process [13, 22].

The present study [15] recently authenticated three dimensions addressed in [21] as CSFs. These dimensions are product, market and process characteristics. Furthermore, [15] confirmed organisational and marketing characteristics, suggesting that these CSFs are relevant in NPD.

Several authors have presented their evidence and finally identified benefits gained from NPD for both customers and companies worldwide. **Table 1** presents the most important benefits. However, the question is, "Are these findings applicable to South African automotive component manufacturers as processes and innovation

Benefits for Companies	**References**
Competitive edge	[16, 19]
Financial performance	[16, 19, 22]
Innovation speed	[16, 22, 23]
Financial profit	[24]
Market share	[25]
Product adaptation to the environment	[22, 23, 25]
Adaptation to customer demands	[19, 25]
Technological upper hand over competitors	[25]
Long-term view	[26]
Reduced product lifecycle	[24]
Market growth	[24]
Product acceptance in the market	[27]
Benefits for Customers	
Customer satisfaction	[16, 22]
Innovation of a new product	[16, 22]
Product quality	[16, 19]
Technological innovations	[16, 25]
Product functionality	[24]
Reliability of the new product	[24]
Technical support and performance	[24]

Table 1.
Benefits of open innovation in ACMs. Source: Own.

practices? The answer is based on the relationship between innovation and NPD and the benefits derived from open innovation explored in the next section.

Open innovation is not a walk in the park [7], especially for start-up ventures which lack adequate capabilities regarding capital investments and research and development activities. Hence, open innovation presents an excellent opportunity for ACMs to venture into new product development [28]. Nevertheless, [29] criticises [30], the founder of open innovation, for exaggerating its applicability to research and development by claiming that it is often long-term, expensive and always risky and requires the protection of consequences. He argues that closed innovation remains an effective way for research and development investment. Internet-based tools such as Web 2.0 are increasingly gaining leverage in the internal and external capabilities of ACMs [31]. Some scholars argue that ACMs are more effective than OEMs in parallel using various open innovation practices because of their unwavering support and dedication to parent companies' requirements [32]. However, [33] found that most ACMs still pursue closed over open innovation. [34] argue that firms that provide their ideas to external parties are more product innovative orientated than non-providers. They found that mutual rather than one-way exchanges are relationships that significantly raise the probability for automotive component manufacturers to experience a substantial benefit from contributing to other firms' new product development projects. [35] explored Danish small and medium enterprises and identified the costs linked to numerous sources of innovation. However, the automotive manufacturers found that market and science sources are related to decreased costs and collaboration, so suppliers of a similar knowledge base are related to the performance of the market and collaboration with customers in lesser project fees.

Nevertheless, they found that novelty in new products is lower than in those embedded with suppliers. Technology scouting is a low cost but valuable alternative for SMEs involved in high-tech activities [36]. Overall, SMEs are increasingly adopting open innovation as a part of operational strategies [37, 38].

A critical study by [38] found that ACMs adopt open innovation primarily for commercial interests such as meeting customer demand and keeping up with competitors. [39] demonstrated that ACMs' interaction with sources of innovation is not essential during the phase of recognising the innovation process but also at the end-stage to facilitate the successful commercialisation of a product or service. Kang et al. [40] asserted that the firm size and government support significantly impact the commercialisation of automotive component manufacturers. They established that appropriability, innovative capabilities and investment in external research and development have profoundly positive impacts on ACMs' commercialisation initiatives. [28] further, argue that ACMs are good at inventions but lack essential commercialisation resources. Hence, ACMs suggest that collaboration with other partners, including intermediaries at the commercial stage, may help overcome their limitations for commercialisation. Collaboration for ACMs is more critical in the commercialisation stage than in other stages such as ideation, research, and development [38–41]. For ACMs, open innovation is less practical than revenue generation [32, 42]. Nevertheless, cooperation with industry incumbents helps to overcome challenges ACMs encounter [38].

12. The theory underpinning the study

Based on the literature review, the study identifies four ACMs' open innovation strategies: commercialisation, collaboration, invention, and versatility. In support of [5], they illustrate the relationship between these four main categories of open innovation

DOI: http://dx.doi.org/10.5772/intechopen.105035

strategies and the theoretical underpinnings to evaluate how they impact competitiveness. This study focuses on how these strategies impact NPD. The resource-related challenges (inputs) are expressed in terms of the resource-based view theory. The firm capability-related challenges (transforming these inputs into outputs) are conceptualised by examining the dynamic capabilities theory. The risk-related challenges (related to the uncertainty of innovation project outcomes) are more effectively comprehended by assessing the portfolio theory. Regardless of the nature of the performance benchmark (financial and philanthropic), these three types of challenges faced by ACMs directly impact competitiveness, which the study proposes to be achieved through new product development.

13. Research design

An exploratory and descriptive method technique was adopted. The empirical research aimed to determine:

1. the impact of open innovation strategies on new product development prospects in the I4.0 era.

2. to propose a contextual open innovation strategies model that will apply to the automotive component manufacturers in the industry.

The chapter's objectives were achieved; by designing a structured questionnaire that consisted of two sections. Section 1 included the profile of the company concerning positions and qualifications. Section 2 required the respondents to indicate to what extent they collaborated with external partners in adopting open innovation strategies during NPD, identified using a five-point Likert scale for each of these constructs. The constructs measured organisational support for innovation projects, collaboration with external partners and the use of external knowledge. The impact of the strategies was measured using a five-point Likert scale varying from 1 (impact to a lesser extent) to 5 (impact to a greater extent). Section 2 of the questionnaire required respondents to rate their agreement, from 1 = strongly disagree to 5 = strongly agree, that there were benefits from each of the four strategies, namely versatility, inventiveness, commercialisation and collaboration under study. A statistician checked the questionnaire prior to conducting the empirical research to ensure that the formulation of the questions was clear and understandable to the respondents.

14. Sampling

The unit of analysis for the study was senior R and D practitioners within the South African automotive component manufacturers who are member companies of the AIDC, an association that represents the South African automotive industry. As the association represents the entire automotive industry in South Africa, it was decided to incorporate members of this association. Four ACMs from the three central automotive manufacturing provinces were included giving a fair geographical spread a total of 33 questionnaires were sent out to the research and development managers representing the ACMs—a census sample.

15. Data collection

By using a survey questionnaire, quantitative data was collected from a sample of 33 managers with research and development responsibilities. Four major automotive component manufacturers participated in the research and provided all 33 respondents. These firms were distributed as Kwazulu natal (2), Gauteng (6) and Eastern cape (2). Some automotive component manufacturers refused to participate in the research, citing confidentiality issues with their clients, Original Equipment Manufacturers with head offices based globally. A total of 33 (75.3%) responses were received.

16. Data analysis

The completed questionnaires were coded, following which the responses were captured in Excel and analysed employing SPSS25, using descriptive statistics and binomial tests.

17. Ethical considerations

The UKZN research office granted the ethical clearance to enable the execution of the study. The researchers ensured that participants signed the consent forms, indicating that they were participating in the research voluntarily. The researchers assured participants of the confidential handling of information divulged in the questionnaires. The researchers were mindful of the effects of leaking business secrets to rival firms and kept all records about the research under lock and key.

18. Reliability analysis of the questionnaire

Reliability is an evaluating measure that tests a measuring instrument's accuracy and consistency. It is how techniques, approaches and methodologies for collecting data provide reliable findings [43]. A reliability test was conducted on each of the four strategies, using Cronbach's coefficient alpha, as illustrated in **Table 2**.

The analysis indicated a high level of reliability with a Cronbach's Alpha of .899, items scoring 89.9%. **Table 2** above reflects the resultant Cronbach's Alpha for the questionnaire used in this study. Bryman and Bell [44] stated that it is essential to appreciate the basic features of what a reliability test means. Whereas Cronbach's alpha determines internal reliability, it essentially calculates the average of all possible split-half reliability coefficients. A computed alpha coefficient will vary between 1 and 0 (denoting perfect internal reliability). As a rule of thumb, Figure 0.80 is typically employed in denoting an acceptable level of internal reliability, though many writers accept a slightly lower figure. For example, in the case of the "Burnout Scale" replicated by several researchers, alpha was 0.7, which they suggested was efficient.

Cronbach's Alpha	No of Items
0.899	54

Table 2.
Cronbach's coefficient alpha.

19. Presentation of quantitative results

The focus of the chapter was on determining the relationship between innovation challenges and the competitiveness of automotive component manufacturers' operations. The competitiveness was achieved by identifying the industry's open innovation challenges and their impact on its competitiveness.

20. Position

Table 3 below indicates that most respondents occupied positions other than top managerial such as Artisans. Artisans provide technical advice to the management, which is a strategic role and function, and above all, they are the implementers of the organisation's open, innovative strategies. However, strategic planning is primarily the responsibility of top management. Cumulatively management constituted 54.5% of the total respondents, with 15.2% being Chief Executive Officers, 27.3% senior managers, and 12.1% research and Development Managers. The researchers believe the respondents were strategically configured and positioned to competently answer the questionnaire and help the researchers gather relevant information and data to solve the research problem.

Position	Frequency	Per cent	Valid Percent	Cumulative Percent
CEO	5	15.2	15.2	15.2
Senior Manager	9	27.3	27.3	42.4
R&D Manager	4	12.1	12.1	54.5
Others	15	45.5	45.5	100.0
Total	33	100.0	100.0	

Table 3.
Respondents' position.

21. Qualification

Table 4 below shows that out of 33 respondents, the majority constituting 30.3% had a master's degree, 27.3% with a Diploma, 8% with first degrees, 12.1% with other qualifications such as relevant Certificates and 6.1% had PhDs. A Master's degree

Qualification	Frequency	Per cent	Valid Percent	Cumulative Percent
Diploma	9	27.3	27.3	27.3
Degree	8	24.2	24.2	51.5
Masters	10	30.3	30.3	81.8
PhD	2	6.1	6.1	87.9
Others	4	12.1	12.1	100.0
Total	33	100.0	100.0	

Table 4.
Respondents qualifications.

Correlation									
		Driven by University and research centers	**From idea generation**	**Seeking new outside applications for internally developed innovations, knowledge, tools, and ideas**	**Synergy created from combining knowledge among participating firms**	**Process of new product/ processes development**	**Introduction of new products/ processes development**	**Introduction of new processes/ services**	**Opening of new markets**
Driven by University and research centres	Pearson Correlation	1	−0.060	−0.183	0.090	−0.014	0.073	0.126	0.081
	Sig. (2-tailed)		0.740	0.309	0.620	0.938	0.685	0.485	0.660
	N	33	33	33	33	33	33	33	32
From idea generation	Pearson Correlation	−0.060	1	0.539**	0.108	0.556**	0.497**	0.324	0.183
	Sig. (2-tailed)	0.740		0.001	0.549	0.001	0.003	0.066	0.317
	N	33	33	33	33	33	33	33	32
Seeking new outside applications for internally developed innovations, knowledge, tools, and ideas	Pearson Correlation	−0.183	0.539**	1	0.115	0.518**	0.222	0.254	0.345
	Sig. (2-tailed)	0.309	0.001		0.523	0.002	0.215	0.154	0.053
	N	33	33	33	33	33	33	33	32
Synergy created from combining knowledge among participating firms	Pearson Correlation	0.090	0.108	0.115	1	0.203	0.110	0.304	0.631**
	Sig. (2-tailed)	0.620	0.549	0.523		0.256	0.541	0.086	0.000

DOI: http://dx.doi.org/10.5772/intechopen.105035

Correlation		Driven by University and research centers	From idea generation	Seeking new outside applications for internally developed innovations, knowledge, tools, and ideas	Synergy created from combining knowledge among participating firms	Process of new product/ processes development	Introduction of new products/ processes development	Introduction of new processes/ services	Opening of new markets
	N	33	33	33	33	33	33	33	32
Process of new product/processes development	Pearson Correlation	−0.014	0.556**	0.518**	0.203	1	0.697**	0.455**	0.269
	Sig. (2-tailed)	0.938	0.001	0.002	0.256		0.000	0.008	0.136
	N	33	33	33	33	33	33	33	32
Introduction of new products/ processes development	Pearson Correlation	0.073	0.497**	0.222	0.110	0.697**	1	0.455**	0.210
	Sig. (2-tailed)	0.685	0.003	0.215	0.541	0.000		0.008	0.248
	N	33	33	33	33	33	33	33	32
Introduction of new processes/ services	Pearson Correlation	0.126	0.324	0.254	0.304	0.455**	0.455**	1	0.459**
	Sig. (2-tailed)	0.485	0.066	0.154	0.086	0.008	0.008		0.008
	N	33	33	33	33	33	33	33	32
Opening of new markets	Pearson Correlation	0.081	0.183	0.345	0.631**	0.269	0.210	0.459**	1
	Sig. (2-tailed)	0.660	0.317	0.053	0.000	0.136	0.248	0.008	
	N	32	32	32	32	32	32	32	32

Table 5.
Impact of open innovation on new product development.

is an international standard managerial qualification. Managers that possess such a high level of qualifications are highly competent in their managerial duties. 81.8% of the respondents fell in suitably and relevantly qualified respondents. As a result, the researcher had no reason to doubt the managerial capabilities of the respondents and their competence to handle the questionnaire.

Table 5 below shows the inferential correlation statistics measuring the impact of open innovation strategies on new product development prospects.

The results in **Table 5** above show that idea generation was found to have a strong positive impact on seeking new outside applications for internally developed innovations, knowledge, tools and ideas, r (0.539**) = 0.539, p = 0.001. From idea generation was also found to be having a strong positive impact on process of new product/ processes development, r (0.556**) = 0.556, p = 0.001, strong positive impact on introduction of new products /processes development r (0.497**) = 0.497, p = 0.003. "Seeking new outside applications for internally developed innovations, knowledge, tools, and ideas" were found to have a strong positive impact on the new product/ processes development process, r (0.518**) = 0.518, p = 0.002.

The results also show that synergy created from combining knowledge among participating firms is having a strong positive impact on the opening of new markets, r (0.631**) = 0.631, p = 0.000. Process of new product/ processes development was found to be having a strong positive impact on introduction of new products/processes development, r (0.697**) = 0.697, p = 0.000 and a strong positive impact on introduction of new processes/ services, r (0.455**) = 0.455, p = 0.008. On the other hand, the introduction of new products/processes development had a strong positive impact on the introduction of new processes/services, r (0.455**) = 0.455, p = 0.008, while the introduction of new processes/services has a strong positive impact on the opening of new markets, r (0.459**) = 0.459, p = 0.008.

22. Discussion of results

This study indicates that idea generation positively influences the open innovation activity of seeking new outside applications for internally developed innovations, knowledge, tools, and ideas for new product development. Idea generation also positively impacts new process development and the introduction of new product development. The results also indicate that the synergies created from combining knowledge among participating firms have a positive, substantial impact on opening new markets for new products. The introduction of new processes or services has a strong positive impact on opening new markets for new products. New processes and services such as distribution channels and value chains are essential and critical for new product development.

Literature suggests that several attempts have proffered open innovation strategies at the centre of openness and its ability to stimulate innovation within firms. This stimulation is achieved by combining large and different pools of external sources resulting in increased diversified products and better processes of matching products to consumer preferences [45–47]. Open innovation management creates and brings monetary values to innovative technological knowledge and individual creativity. Literature has, in recent years, popularised this model of bringing monetary value to innovation as open innovation [3]. However, open innovation is not a one-dimensional concept; it culminates in many tastes and forms, and although it adds to the richness of the open innovation concept, it hinders theory development [45]. Above all, open innovation enables the identification of new product development performances, even in situations where internal R and D activities provide new product development needs solely and goes beyond by engaging external sources such as the knowledge of individuals as well as ideas from customers and technology [46, 48].

The automotive components manufacturers need innovators who create products, develop discovery skills, and believe that they can change the world [49] as they lead these innovative organisations. Organisational leadership and management play an essential role in staffing all organisational departments with innovative individuals [49] and encouraging employee creativity as the basis for innovation [50].

In summary, new product development encompasses physical product development, processes development and services development, of which innovation plays a vital role in their achievement. New product development requires innovative employees, leaders and creative managers who believe in themselves and are driven by the quest for knowledge acquisition.

23. Recommendations

The nature of the automotive components manufacturers demands that their performance be measured in terms of product development productivity. The demand for components parts is exceptionally high and ever-increasing in the automotive industry. Quality determines the life span of the component products; as a result, the need for continuous innovation in new product development overwhelms the automotive components manufacturers. Dynamic capabilities lie at the centre of achieving all these. Therefore, the chapter recommends that the automotive components manufacturers invest in improving their dynamic capabilities to turn ideas generated into new innovative products to remain competitive in the country's automotive industry and globally competitive.

24. Limitations

A study of a strategic nature such as this would naturally face limitations in terms of the target population of corporate executives that might not be willing to divulge information. Predominantly the local or domestic automotive component manufacturers are more reluctant to share information as they perceive threats to their production capabilities and processes, especially regarding the use of external knowledge and contents of materials and local suppliers in fear of the likelihood of being sidelined by the multinational corporations who are dominating the market share of the South African automotive industry.

The study was quantitative, and bulk data were collected using a structured questionnaire. A structured questionnaire limited the respondents. They could not express their personal views and opinions beyond the structured constructs in the questionnaire, unlike the interview protocol would allow.

The study was limited to a small sample drawn from KwaZulu-Natal, Gauteng and the Eastern Cape with the diversity of the automotive component manufacturers compared to the limited number of companies covered externally in this research; this limitation is essential for future research. Not all subsectors of the automotive industry have been covered in the research due to the technical nature of the study, where research and development are not prerequisites among small and micro firms. A more comprehensive sample would have enhanced the potential for the generalisability of the results.

Acknowledgements

The authors would like to express their gratitude to The Graduate School of Business Leadership at the University of KwaZulu Natal for issuing an ethical clearance certificate making it possible to conduct the study.

Authors' contributions

AMG conception and design of the research. AMG collected, analysed and interpreted the data and drafted the manuscript. P.M critically revised the manuscript and approved the final version to be published.

Funding

This research received no specific grant from any funding agency in public, commercial or not-for-profit sectors.

Competing interests

The authors declare that they have no financial or personal relationships that may have inappropriately influenced them in writing this article.

Data availability statement

Data sharing applies to this article as new data were created and analysed. Data can be obtained from the authors upon request.

Disclaimer

The views and opinions expressed in this article are those of the authors and do not necessarily reflect the official policy or position of any affiliated agency of the authors.

DOI: http://dx.doi.org/10.5772/intechopen.105035

Author details

Arthur Mzwandile Gonyora* and Pfano Mashau
Graduate School of Business and Leadership, University of KwaZulu-Natal, Durban, South Africa

*Address all correspondence to: agonyora@icloud.com

References

[1] Feng Y. System dynamics modeling for supply chain information sharing. Physics Procedia. 2012;**25**:1463-1469

[2] Grosse R, Mudd S, Cerchiari CG. Exporting to the far and near abroad. Journal of Business Research. 2013;**66**(3):409-416

[3] Van der Meer H. Open innovation–the Dutch treat: Challenges in thinking in business models. Creativity and Innovation Management. 2007;**16**(2):192-202

[4] Schwab K. The Fourth Industrial Revolution Currency. Cologny, Switzerland: World Economic Forum; 2017

[5] Cornell BT. Open Innovation Strategies for Overcoming Competitive Challenges Facing Small and Mid-sized Enterprises. Maryland: University of Maryland University College; 2012 Dahlander L, Gann DM. How open is innovation? Research Policy. 2010;39(6):699-709

[6] Poot T, Faems D, Vanhaverbeke W. Toward a dynamic perspective on open innovation: A longitudinal assessment of the adoption of internal and external innovation strategies in the Netherlands. International Journal of Innovation Management. 2009;**13**(02):177-200

[7] Lee S, Heo CY. Corporate social responsibility and customer satisfaction among US publicly traded hotels and restaurants. International Journal of Hospitality Management. 2009;**28**(4):635-637

[8] Keupp MM, Gassmann O. The past and the future of international entrepreneurship: a review and suggestions for developing the field. Journal of Management. 2009;**35**(3):600-633

[9] Jiménez-Jiménez D, Sanz-Valle R. Innovation, organizational learning, and performance. Journal of Business Research. 2011;**64**(4):408-417

[10] Gündoğdu MÇ. Re-thinking entrepreneurship, intrapreneurship, and innovation: A multi-concept perspective. Procedia-Social and Behavioral Sciences. 2012;**41**:296-303

[11] Turker H, Bacha S, Chatroux D, Hably A. Low-voltage transformer loss-of-life assessments for a high penetration of plug-in hybrid electric vehicles (PHEVs). IEEE Transactions on Power Delivery. 2012;**27**(3):1323-1331

[12] Creus GL, Gestión operativa de la innovación, Tohidi H, Jabbari MM. The importance of innovation and its crucial role in growth, survival and success of organisations. Procedia Technology. 2012;**1**:535-538

[13] Barnett WA, Diewert WE, Maasoumi E. Innovations in measurement in economics and econometrics: An overview. Journal of Econometrics. 2016;**2**(191):273-275

[14] Wonglimpiyarat J. New economics of innovation: Strategies to support high-tech SMEs. The Journal of High Technology Management Research. 2015;**26**(2):186-195

[15] Murphy P. Design capitalism: Design, economics and innovation in the auto-industrial age. She Ji: The Journal of Design, Economics, and Innovation. 2015;**1**(2):140-149

[16] Molina-Castillo FJ, Jimenez-Jimenez D, Munuera-Aleman JL. Product competence exploitation and exploration strategies: The

impact on new product performance through quality and innovativeness. Industrial Marketing Management. 2011;**40**(7):1172-1182

[17] Huang LS, Lai CP. An investigation on critical success factors for knowledge management using structural equation modeling. Procedia-Social and Behavioral Sciences. 2012;**40**:24-30

[18] Lynn GS, Abel KD, Valentine WS, Wright RC. Key factors in increasing speed to market and improving new product success rates. Industrial Marketing Management. 1999;**28**(4):319-326

[19] Cheng CF, Chang ML, Li CS. Configural paths to successful product innovation. Journal of Business Research. 2013;**66**(12):2561-2573

[20] Henard DH, Szymanski DM. Why some new products are more successful than others. Journal of Marketing Research. 2001;**38**(3):362-375

[21] Evanschitzky H, Eisend M, Calantone RJ, Jiang Y. Success factors of product innovation: An updated meta-analysis. Journal of Product Innovation Management. 2012;**29**:21-37

[22] Chen J, Damanpour F, Reilly RR. Understanding antecedents of new product development speed: A meta-analysis. Journal of Operations Management. 2010;**28**(1):17-33

[23] Carbonell P, Rodriguez AI. The impact of market characteristics and innovation speed on perceptions of positional advantage and new product performance. International Journal of Research in Marketing. 2006;**23**(1):1-2

[24] Chen CJ, Huang JW, Hsiao YC. Knowledge management and innovativeness: The role of organizational climate and structure. International Journal of Manpower. 2010

[25] Huang X, Soutar GN, Brown A. Measuring new product success: An empirical investigation of Australian SMEs. Industrial Marketing Management. 2004;**33**(2):117-123

[26] Tsai KH, Yang SY. Firm innovativeness and business performance: The joint moderating effects of market turbulence and competition. Industrial Marketing Management. 2013;**42**(8):1279-1294

[27] Cankurtaran P, Langerak F, Griffin A. Consequences of new product development speed: A meta-analysis. Journal of Product Innovation Management. 2013;**30**(3):465-486

[28] Lee S, Park G, Yoon B, Park J. Open innovation in SMEs—An intermediated network model. Research Policy. 2010;**39**(2):290-300

[29] Oakey RP. Open innovation and its relevance to industrial research and development: The case of high-technology small firms. International Small Business Journal. 2013;**31**(3):319-336

[30] Chesbrough H. Open Business Models: How to Thrive in the New Innovation Landscape. Boston, Massachusetts, United States: Harvard Business Press; 2006

[31] Bell J, Loane S, McNaughton RB, Servais P. 11 toward a typology of rapidly Internationalising SMEs. International Growth of Small and Medium Enterprises. 2010;**177**:14

[32] Spithoven A, Vanhaverbeke W, Roijakkers N. Open innovation practices in SMEs and large enterprises. Small Business Economics. 2013;**41**(3):537-562

[33] Lichtenthaler U. Integrated roadmaps for open innovation. Research-Technology Management. 2008;**51**(3):45-49

[34] Dries L, Pascucci S, Török Á, Tóth J. Open innovation: A case-study of the Hungarian wine sector. EuroChoices. 2013;**12**(1):53-59

[35] Tranekjer TL, Søndergaard HA. Sources of innovation, their combinations and strengths–benefits at the NPD project level. International Journal of Technology Management. 2013;**61**(3/4):205-236

[36] Parida V, Westerberg M, Frishammar J. Inbound open innovation activities in high-tech SMEs: The impact on innovation performance. Journal of Small Business Management. 2012;**50**(2):283-309

[37] Xiaobao P, Wei S, Yuzhen D. Framework of open innovation in SMEs in an emerging economy: firm characteristics, network openness, and network information. International Journal of Technology Management. 2013;**62**(2/3/4):223-250

[38] Van de Vrande V, De Jong JP, Vanhaverbeke W, De Rochemont M. Open innovation in SMEs: Trends, motives and management challenges. Technovation. 2009;**29**(6-7):423-437

[39] Van Hemert P, Nijkamp P, Masurel E. From innovation to commercialisation through networks and agglomerations: Analysis of sources of innovation, innovation capabilities and performance of Dutch SMEs. The Annals of Regional Science. 2013;**50**(2):425-452

[40] Kang W, Montoya M. The impact of product portfolio strategy on financial performance: The roles of product development and market entry decisions. Journal of Product Innovation Management. 2014;**31**(3):516-534

[41] Theyel N. Extending open innovation throughout the value chain by small and medium-sized manufacturers. International Small Business Journal. 2013;**31**(3):256-274

[42] Chaston I, Scott GJ. Entrepreneurship and Open Innovation in an Emerging Economy. Management Decision. Bingley, United Kingdom: Emerald Publishing; 2012

[43] Sekaran U, Bougie R. Research Methods for Business: A Skill Building Approach. Hoboken, New Jersey, United States: John Wiley & Sons; 2016

[44] Bell E, Harley B, Bryman A. Business Research Methods. Oxford, United Kingdom: Oxford University Press; 2022

[45] Huizingh EK. Open innovation: State of the art and future perspectives. Technovation. 2011;**31**(1):2-9

[46] Chiaroni D, Chiesa V, Frattini F. The open innovation journey: How firms dynamically implement the emerging innovation management paradigm. Technovation. 2011;**31**(1):34-43

[47] Boyer K, Verma R. Operations and Supply Chain Management for the 21st Century (Book Only). Boston, Massachusetts, United States: Cengage Learning; 2009

[48] Trott P. Innovation Management and New Product Development. London, United Kingdom: Pearson Education; 2008

[49] Christensen C, Dyer J, Gregersen H. Le gène de l'innovateur: Cinq compétences qui font la différence. London, United Kingdom: Pearson Education; 2013

[50] Amabile TM, Conti R, Coon H, Lazenby J, Herron M. Assessing the work environment for creativity. Academy of Management Journal. 1996;**39**(5):1154-1184

Chapter 7

Shipping Digitalization and Automation for the Smart Port

Enna Hirata, Daisuke Watanabe and Maria Lambrou

Abstract

Shipping, like most industries, is undergoing a digital transformation process which influences existing business models and operational practices, in a multifaceted way. Today, the shipping business context has been changing to incorporate further social demands, environmental, innovation and sustainability priorities, into fundamental shipping strategies, while taking advantage of technological advancements. In the era of Industry 4.0, which constitutes a recent evolution of advanced communications and information technologies and further promotes sustainable, human-centric, and resilient business development strategies, shipping and port entities need to embrace a broader perspective and a deeper understanding of various elemental technologies, namely: Artificial Intelligence, Blockchain, Cloud Computing, Big Data, and Physical Internet, in addition to core maritime logistics matters. This chapter proposes a descriptive framework of shipping digitalization and port automation, while providing a review of related technologies and business approaches, also international initiatives, for automation in global ports. Hence the chapter offers insights for business practitioners to steer through the current challenging global environment, also for policy makers to gain a more informed understanding of maritime logistics developments, towards necessary coordination and oversight mechanisms implementation.

Keywords: shipping, digitalization, automation, smart port, artificial intelligence, blockchain, physical internet

1. Introduction

In recent years, major ports around the world have been implementing new technologies to realize "Smart Ports," in order to enhance international competitiveness, reduce environmental impact, and improve the workplace environment. In addition to the automation and labor-saving measures that have been actively pursued so far, smart ports are nowadays expected to benefit from the Internet of Things (IoT), Artificial Intelligence (AI), and Big Data[1], as well as more focused initiatives, in specific the Physical Internet (PI), based on the development of

[1] Big data refer to various types of data in various forms and with various characteristics. Big data consist of three V's: Volume (amount of data), Variety (types of data), and Velocity (frequency of data generation and update).

high-speed communication infrastructures, such as the fifth generation mobile communication system (5G). The robust use of the numerous digital technologies, such as the ones above-mentioned, offers substantial business innovation opportunities and requires numerous organizational adjustments [1].

In specific, the digitalization of ports is enabled by 5G networks that provide low latency, high capacity, and increased bandwidth, hence allowing the collection and intelligent processing of vast amounts of data shared over an IoT information network infrastructure. 5G is foremost supporting the PI objectives, namely the widespread adoption of interconnected, sustainable logistics systems and applications.

A smart port is realized by means of wireless devices, smart sensors, actuators, data centers, and other IoT-based systems being connected and exchanging information. The seamless communication of ships, cargoes, and waterway and shore-based facilities, based on 5G and IoT technologies, constitutes the infrastructure of the smart port and shapes the innovation potential of the emergent maritime logistics services and applications. The efficiency, security, and safety of port operations and the achievement of the highly prioritized sustainable development goals are substantially improved by automating port operations, such as vessel management, container terminal operations, and yard automation.

Competitiveness and henceforth the competitive positioning of ports being nodes of multiple, global supply chain networks are of paramount importance and are directly determined by the adopted digital strategy and infrastructures implemented in each port.

This chapter outlines the main technologies' capabilities, as well as the current status of policies and initiatives for the development and deployment of various technologies, primarily for automated terminals and automated ships in ports, as innovations for ships and various automated machinery, mainly for cargo handling, toward the realization of smart ports. Moreover, the chapter introduces a particular technological framework for creating a sustainable next-generation maritime logistics system, by applying PI to digitize maritime logistics networks and BC technology for secure information exchange to improve the overall efficiency of maritime logistics, at ports.

2. Industry 4.0: technologies for next-generation maritime logistics and shipping digitalization

How does modern maritime logistics look like in the era of Industry 4.0? The concept of Industry 4.0, first formulated by the German government, mainly refers to the automation and digitization of manufacturing processes. Industry 4.0 encompasses cyber-physical systems[2], AI[3], IoT[4], cloud computing[5], cognitive computing[6], smart

[2] A Cyber Physical System is a system in which cyber space and physical space are more closely linked, in which information from reality (physical) is taken into a virtual space (cyber) by a computer, and the analysis results of the computer's computational power are fed back to derive optimal results in the real world. It is a system in which cyber space and physical space are more closely linked.

[3] AI, short name of Artificial Intelligence, is a branch of computer science that studies "intelligence" using the concept of "computation" and the tool of "computers."

[4] IoT, or Internet of Things, is a system in which various things (devices) are connected to the Internet to fully utilize the information those devices carried.

[5] Cloud computing is a form of usage in which computer resources are provided in the form of services via a computer network such as the Internet. It is sometimes referred to as cloud for short.

[6] Cognitive computing is a system in which computers not only process instructions given by humans, but also think and learn on their own like humans, and support decision-making.

factories[7], and digital twin[8]. Industry 4.0 has been implemented in many countries besides Germany, including the US, France, the UK, China, Japan, Korea, and Thailand. Particularly in the supply chain area, digitalization, integration of AI and IoT, sharing economy[9], and BC are playing an important role in addition to these core technologies. Logistics has not been associated with high technology for a long time since it was recognized as an industry in the mid of nineteenth century. The situation is changing with the increase of Logistics 4.0 efforts, where innovative technologies such as AI, IoT, and BC are increasingly being implemented in the logistics industry, in parallel with similar efforts to many other industries, presenting even more efficient sustainability and human-centric approaches. However, despite the numerous regional initiatives, there are no adequate frameworks existing for companies in the logistics industry to embrace those technologies to the largest extent. There is a need for guidelines to implement new technologies in the logistics industry for the common good of the entire industry and eventually society as a whole.

Against this background, a closely related development, namely the Physical Internet (PI), has drawn attention from various parties as one of the most effective measures to improve logistics efficiency and reduce greenhouse gas emissions. The features of PI include interoperability, modularity, and standard interfaces and protocols. In order to take advantage of these features, technology to share data while maintaining confidentiality, such as Blockchain (BC) technology, is essential. This technology, also known as a distributed ledger, is difficult to tamper with, requires no administrator, and allows execution of smart contracts. The use of BC technology in PI is expected to dramatically accelerate the construction of a sustainable logistics network. In the following sections, we will present, in more detail, the potential of applying BC technology in the PI network context.

2.1 AI

Artificial Intelligence (AI) is a field of computer science that uses the concept of "computation" and the tool of "computers" to study and implement "intelligence."

AI can be classified into general-purpose AI and specialized AI. General-purpose AI is also referred to as strong AI. It is an AI that is not limited to a specific task but is capable of general-purpose processing; that is, it has the same intelligence as humans. Some examples of general-purpose AI are Doraemon and Astro Boy. None of them exist in the real world yet. Specialized AI is also called weak AI. It is an AI that specializes in performing a specific task. Image recognition, chess, Go, automated driving, human conversation, etc., are all examples of specialized AI.

In a broader sense, AI includes rule-based AI and machine-learning AI. Rule-based AI refers to making decisions according to rules described by humans. It also automates tasks that require hardware and human judgment. It can be described

---

[7] A smart factory is a highly productive and efficient factory that utilizes digital technologies such as AI and IoT.

[8] Digital twin is a technology that reproduces various data collected from the real world on a computer, as if they were twins. Based on the huge amount of data collected, the computer can perform physical simulations that are as close to reality as possible, which is an effective way to improve the manufacturing process of your products and services. Digital twin ship is a recognized prospect in shipping sector that helps optimize fleet management and enhance port and terminal operations.

[9] The sharing economy is a new economic movement in the form of renting, buying, selling, and offering among individuals via an Internet platform.

as an office robot. In contrast, machine-learning AI generally does not require a human to write the rules. It has algorithms for self-learning in machine-learning models, and it behaves intelligently based on those algorithms, building the models automatically. Compared with machine-learning AI, rule-based AI has advantages such as faster to automate tasks, a human can train AI, and lower cost. On the other hand, it also has disadvantages such as unable to learn independently, unable to train AI unless it is explicit knowledge, and unable to make decisions on matters it has not been trained on.

Machine learning can be divided into supervised learning, unsupervised learning, and reinforcement learning in general (**Figure 1**).

2.1.1 Supervised learning

Supervised learning is the process of preparing training data with a set of inputs and correct outputs in advance, and having the computer learn to produce correct outputs when given a certain input. Supervised learning methods are mainly used for prediction and classification (labeling). Examples include image classification. Supervised learning can be applied to forecasting sales and predicting the tendency of customers' churns, etc.

2.1.2 Unsupervised learning

Unsupervised learning is often referred to as self-supervised learning these days. It is used to grasp the inherent structure of data from the input data supplied Unsupervised learning mainly uses clustering techniques to classify data. Examples of applications include product recommendation, customer segmentation, target marketing, etc., based on customer purchase history.

2.1.3 Reinforcement learning

Reinforcement learning is a model that learns to maximize future value instead of giving the correct answer. In other words, it learns to act in a way that maximizes value through trial and error. The problem setting is similar to that of

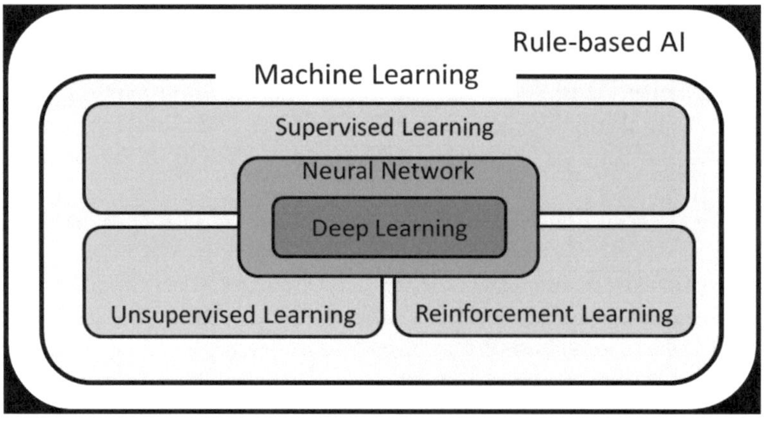

Figure 1.
AI and machine learning relationship diagram.

supervised learning, but it is not enough to learn the output of the given correct answer as it is, but it is necessary to learn the behavior that maximizes value in a broader sense.

Tetris game is a good example to understand the scheme of reinforcement learning. When playing a game of Tetris, the problem of getting the highest possible score can be considered in the framework of reinforcement learning. The best way to score at that point is to play in such a way that even a single row can be eliminated immediately, but in the longer term, the score will be higher if you accumulate as much as possible and then eliminate many rows at once.

AlphaGo, which defeated a human player, also incorporates reinforcement learning in some parts of its games. As in the case of Go, it can learn even when humans do not necessarily know the correct answer, so it is expected to acquire the ability to surpass humans.

2.1.4 Artificial neural network

A neural network is a mathematical model inspired by the function of nerve cells (neurons) and their connections, or neural networks in the human brain, called artificial neurons. When the neural network model is properly constructed according to the problem to be solved, it can make a variety of decisions (i.e., outputs), such as the following:

First, image recognition and binary classification. For example, it answers questions such as: Is the object in front of me a ship or a train?

Second, natural language processing, multi-level classification. For example: which is "Emma Maersk" among various images of vessels online?

2.1.5 Deep learning

Deep Learning is a method of machine learning in which neural networks are combined in multiple layers to enhance their representation and learning capabilities. Currently, it is the most commonly used algorithm for AI.

Deep learning, on the other hand, is often used when complex unstructured data is available and is applied in fields such as speech recognition, image recognition, and natural language processing.

There are many cases where conventional machine-learning methods do not work well for classification and regression without complex function approximation, and deep-learning methods are increasingly being used for such problems. In some cases, deep-learning methods have dramatically improved recognition accuracy compared with conventional methods, and deep learning is currently attracting a great deal of attention in the world. Recently, it has been used in a wide range of fields such as recommendation and automated driving.

2.2 Blockchain

BC is an open distributed ledger technology (DLT) based on a peer-to-peer (P2P) approach that allows transactions to be recorded on thousands of servers simultaneously. On the efficient, verifiable, and immutable BC platform, anyone can see the transactions of others in near real time, making it difficult for one user to manipulate the records and control the network [2]. Applying these features, BC facilitates the digitization of traditional economic, legal, and political systems.

Consensus	PoW (Proof of Work)	PoS (Proof of Stake)	PoI (Proof of Importance)	PoC (Proof of Consensus)	PBFT (Practical Byzantine Fault Tolerance)
Evaluation method	(one's) workload	Workload and coin holdings	Overall evaluation of coin holdings, transaction volume, transaction frequency, etc.	Designated agency	Consensus of two-thirds or more
Benefits	Resistant to transaction tampering	No wasted power consumption	Low power consumption	Fast remittance speed	High speed compared to other methods
Weakness	High-power consumption	How the rich get richer.	Participation is impossible without a certain amount of coins.	centralized	A block will not be created unless a two-thirds majority is agreed.
Representative example	Bitcoin (BTC)	Ethereum (ETH)	Nem (NEM)	Ripple (XRP)	Permitted type consortium type

Table 1.
Typical consensus algorithms.

In BC, cryptography is used to store records (hash values[10]) of transactions that occur in the network in blocks of records called blocks. In each block, it contains three values, the first is the hash value of the previously generated block, the second is the record of the transaction in the current block, and the third is a new hash value generated by a disposable random value called a nonce. The three values are passed to the next block and the accumulated blocks form a chain of blocks in time series. The name BC comes from this data structure.

BC can be divided into public BC, which allows anonymous participation, and permitted BC, which requires permission to participate. Public BC is mainly applied to cryptocurrencies. Since the permitted type of BC is faster than the public type in handling transactions, it has been applied to various business fields such as supply chain and intellectual property management [3].

There have been five main types of algorithms for consensus building in BC (**Table 1**). In public BC, PoW and PoS are mainstream; in the PoW consensus, rewards are evaluated by the amount of work done. In PoW consensus, the reward is evaluated by the amount of work done; in other words, the network participant who performs the appropriate computation the fastest receives the reward. In the PoS consensus, rewards are based on both the amount of work and the amount of cryptocurrencies held. In PoS consensus, rewards are based on both the amount of work done and the amount of cryptocurrencies held, easing the fierce competition in PoWs and saving electricity consumption, it suffers the problem that the rich get richer. On the other hand, in permitted BC, PBFT is the mainstream method. PBFT is faster than other consensus methods but has the disadvantage that blocks will not be created if two-thirds or more of the consensus is not obtained.

[10] A hash value is a fixed length of data created using a hash function. It is unidirectional and is difficult if not impossible to restore the original data from a hash value.

In the maritime industry, many players from different industries, usually in several countries, are involved in currently operating blockchain platforms. This complexity leads to a lack of transparency in the entire supply chain. In addition, the industry has the disadvantage of high transaction costs for information exchange, the possibility of fraud and theft, and vulnerability to the risk of cyber-attacks. BC offers the possibility to solve these problems [3]. To maximize the capacity and productivity of the digital information space, traditional authentication methods and data structures need to be reformed and modern technologies such as BC need to be actively applied.

2.3 Physical internet (PI)

PI was initially proposed by Montreuil in 2010 [4]. He defined PI as an open, global logistics network that efficiently and sustainably interconnects all elements of the logistics process. The PI includes the complete supply chain including storage, movement, supply, and delivery of goods, and the PI network is composed of various logistic providers. The goal of PI is to create a global logistics system based on the interconnection of existing logistic networks. To achieve this, a standardized set of protocols, modular containers, and smart interfaces are combined modular containers, called PI containers (**Figure 2**), which come in various sizes and can be combined and loaded to reduce waste. In addition to modular containers, PI-stores, PI-movers, PI-conveyors, and PI-gateways have also been proposed.

The characteristics of PI include interoperability, modularity, and standard interfaces and protocols. In order to take advantage of these features, technologies to share data while protecting confidentiality, such as BC technology, are essential.

Although it is not difficult to understand the usefulness of PI and BC, specific application measures have not been fully studied. In this chapter, we make a proposal for planning measures to build a BC network in PI, and discuss issues and measures for practical application. Specifically, the next sections also aim to clarify the following two points. First, to clarify the scope of application of BC in PI. Second, we propose a framework for implementing PI and BC technologies.

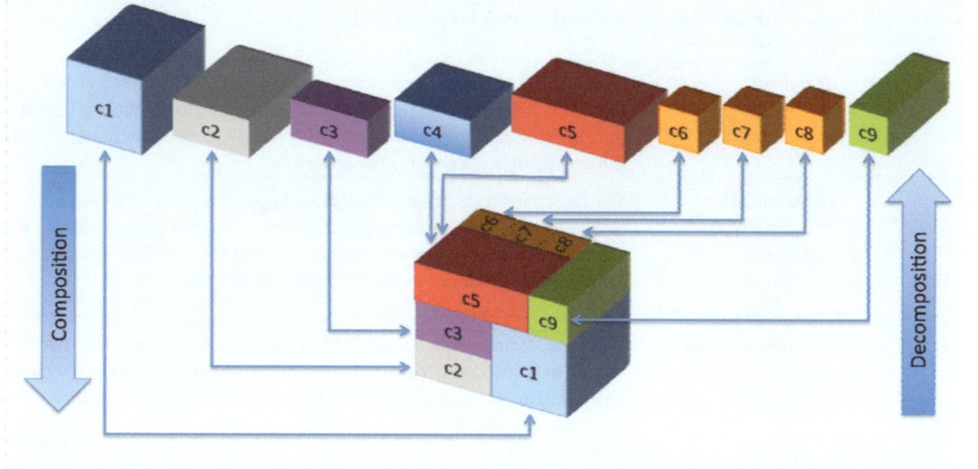

Figure 2.
An example of PI container combination. Source: Montreuil et al., 2010 [4].

3. Digitalization and automation for smart ports

3.1 Smart port initiatives in major countries

Various information systems have been introduced in maritime and port-related operations, such as Terminal Operating System (TOS) for internal terminal operations, Port Community System (PCS) for port logistics, Automatic Identification System (AIS), and the Transport Management System (TMS) for land-side operations such as trucking [5]. A smart port is an initiative that aims to improve the efficiency and safety of the port as a whole and to reduce the environmental impact of the port by integrating these systems through innovations in automation and new digital technologies such as IoT, AI, and 5G. Currently, the Port of Rotterdam (Smart Port Initiative) and the Port of Hamburg (smart port) in Europe, Japan (PORT2030), Korea (Smart Maritime Logistics) and Singapore (Sense-making Analytics For maritime Event Recognition: SAFER) and other major ports around the world are working on various initiatives.

The Port of Rotterdam in the Netherlands has a vision of being the "smartest port in the world" and is working on digitalization, energy transformation, and innovation to become carbon neutral. They have identified four levels of "digital maturity" for a port cargo community as shown in **Table 2** [8]. The Smart Port Initiative is a roadmap that includes projects in energy and industry like recycling, electrification, renewable energy, logistics like BD, automated driving and BC, port infrastructure like quays, dredging, maritime traffic management, and innovation. The Port Call Optimization (PMO) project is underway as part of Port Collaborative Decision Making (PortCDM), an initiative aimed at optimizing the timing of vessel arrival and departure [9]. PortXChange (formerly Pronto), a real-time information sharing platform for PMO between shipping companies, shipping agents, terminals, and other stakeholders, has been in operation since 2018. In the past, about 75% of shipping companies, including major operators such as Maersk and ONE, have participated in

Level	Name	Overview
1	Digitization of individual activities in the port	The individual organizations operating in the port digitize their processes so that they work more efficiently.
2	Integrated systems in a port community	The digital exchange of information within the port community leads to reliable, efficient, and paperless dataflows, resulting in more efficient port operations. The focus at this level is related to securely sharing data. Cybersecurity and cyber resilience are key.
3	Logistics chain integrated with hinterland	The hinterland four players (importers, exporters, logistics hubs, and domestic transporters) are involved in digital communication with the port community. This integration promotes sharing of real-time information on freight and vessel movements, facilitating better planning.
4	Connected ports in the global logistics chain	The port and its hinterland connections are extended to other ports around the world, forming a global network of interconnected ports. This network will allow further reductions of inefficiencies in the global logistics chains by optimizing the use of port capacities and achieving shorter, more reliable transit times.

Source: Buck et al. 2019 [6] and ADB2020 [7].

Table 2.
Definition of maturity levels of smart ports.

the experiment, and the results have shown that PortXChange is effective in reducing the waiting time of ships, especially for departures.

In Japan, one of the main measures in the mid-to long-term port policy "PORT2030" announced in July 2018 is to make ports smarter and more resilient by using information and communication technologies. In addition to the complete computerization of ports, which will be called "Cyber Port" through the construction of a port-related data linkage infrastructure, the policy aims to create container terminals with the world's highest level of productivity and a good working environment (AI terminals) by combining AI, IoT, and automation technologies. In the container terminal field, the introduction of remote-controlled cargo handling machinery and automated gate handling is being promoted, terminal operations are being streamlined and optimized using AI and other technologies, automated vessels, and remote-controlled tugboats are being operated, automated guided vehicles are being introduced, and automated trucks are being driven in convoys. In addition, the next generation high standard unit load terminal will be developed. Furthermore, in the next generation of high standard unit load terminals, the use of automatic driving technology for cross-carriage transport and the linkage with automatic navigation and navigation support technology for ships are mentioned.

3.2 Research and development for the realization of the automated ship

Various efforts have been made by shipping companies to develop navigation support technologies to improve the safety and efficiency of ship operations using IoT and big data. In this context, Maritime Autonomous Surface Ships (MASS) have been attracting attention rapidly in recent years. The term MASS generally describes a ship that is highly automated or remotely controlled to perform some or all of the following shipboard tasks: external situational awareness (watchkeeping), monitoring of equipment status, ship operation, engine control, cargo management, and loading/unloading, take-off and landing, and other shipboard tasks by using the latest technologies such as IoT, ICT, and data analysis technologies, various sensors, and land-based monitoring and control centers connected by broadband communications.

A number of projects are underway, mainly in Europe, with the aim of realizing MASS. In December 2018, Rolls-Royce and FinnFerry successfully demonstrated the world's first fully automated ferry. As an example of an international project, One Sea, a consortium launched in Finland in 2016, is developing a roadmap for practical application and discussing the necessary safety standards and international standardization in order to create an environment for MASS operation by 2025.

There is an ongoing international discussion on the legislative framework for safety standards for MASS. With regard to classification societies' certification systems, in February 2017, the British classification society Lloyd's Register published the LR Unmanned Marine Systems Code, which sets out the performance requirements for automated ships. The International Maritime Organization (IMO) has been considering the regulatory aspects of automated ships since May 2018 and has presented a provisional proposal, as shown in **Table 3**, and is discussing the necessary amendments to IMO rules and new developments. For demonstration tests, the provisional guidelines for safe and efficient demonstration tests of automated ships, jointly proposed by Japan and Norway, have been approved in June 2019. In May 2021, IMO has completed a regulatory scoping exercise on MASS that was designed to assess existing IMO instruments to see how they might apply to ships with varying degrees of automation.

Level	Name	Overview
1	Ship with automated processes and decision support	Seafarers are on board to operate and control shipboard systems and functions. Some operations may be automated and at times be unsupervised but with seafarers on board ready to take control.
2	Remotely controlled ship with seafarers on board	The ship is controlled and operated from another location. Seafarers are available onboard to take control and to operate the shipboard systems and functions.
3	Remotely controlled ship without seafarers on board	The ship is controlled and operated from another location. There are no seafarers on board.
4	Fully autonomous ship	The operating system of the ship is able to make decisions and determine actions by itself.

Source: IMO [10].

Table 3.
Definition of automation levels for MASS.

In Japan, industry, government, and academia have been collaborating since FY2017 to develop technologies, develop infrastructure and systems, and study business models for the realization of MASS through demonstration projects of automatic ship operation, remote ship operation, and automatic docking and unloading functions in order to improve the environment, including the formulation of safety requirements. The ClassNK has been working on the development of the technology through demonstration projects. In January 2020, the ClassNK established requirements and procedures for the functional verification of automation and remote-control systems used on ships and remote-control facilities, from the perspective of ensuring safety at each stage of development and design, ship installation, and operation [11]. The Ship Data Centre was established in December 2015 as a platform for the use of ship big data, with the participation of shipping companies, shipbuilders, marine industry operators, and meteorological information companies. The Ship Data Center was established in December 2015 as a foundation for the use of ship big data, with the participation of shipping companies, shipbuilders, marine industry companies, meteorological information companies, etc. Rules for fair and equitable data use have been established to promote the distribution and use of ship big data, and the effective use of accumulated big data is being promoted.

Based on the results of the economic evaluation of the MASS operation system, efforts are being made to commercialize a manned automated ship operation system (corresponding to automation level 1 in **Table 3**), which is more feasible in the short term. In NYK line, research has been conducted on an action planning system for the decision-making required to execute ship operations, and the world's first demonstration of a manned automated ship based on the provisional guidelines set by the IMO was conducted in September 2019 [12]. Future projections for unmanned automated ships (corresponding to automation level 3 or higher in **Table 3**) for domestic ships suggest that if 50% of ships are replaced by unmanned automated ships in 2040, the annual economic impact will be approximately 1 trillion yen [13]. In June 2020, the Foundation selected five projects for MEGURI 2040, which aims to realize unmanned automated ships by 2025, by conducting the world's first demonstrations in waters with high vessel traffic, long-distance navigation, and using large vessels.

3.3 Deployment of automated terminals at ports

The unmanned and automated handling of cargo at container terminals is expected to increase productivity per worker, improve the working environment and safety, and reduce the effects of weather conditions such as fog and wind. On the other hand, the introduction of the system is not without its challenges, such as high initial investment costs, maintenance costs (e.g., power consumption), and coordination with trade unions. At the ECT Delta Terminal in the Port of Rotterdam, the world's first automated terminal, an Automated Guided Vehicle (AGV) and an Automated Stacking Crane (ASC) were introduced in 1993. However, the introduction of these systems did not proceed due to technical and economic problems and difficulties in coordinating with labor unions, and there were only a few cases until the mid-2000s. However, since the mid-2000s, and especially since the 2010s, the number of automated terminals has been increasing rapidly, with nearly 60 terminals worldwide having installed the system so far. The number of automated terminals has increased rapidly since the mid-2000s, especially in the last decade. **Table 4** summarizes the status of the introduction of automated terminals, focusing on the level of automation. The symbols in the table indicate: ◎: mainstream status with many cases of introduction, ○: diffusion stage with several cases of introduction, and △: early stage with limited cases of introduction. In the case of marshaling yards and land-side container handling, remote control and automation are the basic systems. On the other hand, the manned operation is the mainstream for quay cranes, and full automation has been introduced only recently in a limited number of cases. In the case of horizontal transport within the premises, although there is a high degree of automation, various types of cargo handling machines have been introduced, and the level of automation differs greatly between ports.

In Japan, AGVs and remote-controlled ASCs were introduced at the south side container terminal of Tobishima Pier in the port of Nagoya in December 2005, which

Type	Activities	Typical cargo handling machine	Manned	Unmanned	
				Remote control	Automation
Waterside transport	Moving containers from ship to shore	STS (Ship To Shore Container Crane)/ QC (Quayside Conatiner Crane)	◎	○	△
Horizontal transport	Moving containers between the quayside and yard storage blocks	AGV (Automated Guided Vehicle), SC (Straddle Carrier), ShC (Shuttle Carrier), Chassis	◎	—	○
Marshaling yard	Moving containers at yard storage blocks	ASC (Automated Stacking Crane), ShC	—	○	◎
Landside transport	Moving containers from the terminal truck gate or intermodal railhead to the marshaling yard	ASC, ShC	—	◎	○

Source: Takahashi 2018 [7] and PEMA 2016 [14, 15].

Table 4.
The introduction of automated terminals with the level of automation.

is a relatively early stage in international perspective, but it is the only automated terminal in Japan at present. Currently, efforts are being made to promote the introduction of remote-controlled ASCs, mainly at strategic international container ports, and to improve the efficiency and optimization of terminal operations by using AI-based on container cargo information.

4. A case study of PI and blockchain technology for smart ports

In the following, a specific case study of a blockchain technology application, in a Logistics 4.0 Physical Internet environment, is explicated, as a representative system implementation for innovative, digital maritime logistics environments, with automated ships and terminals constituting flagship applications of Industry 4.0.

Three recent representative studies on the application of PI and BC in the supply chain are available [16–18]. Meyer et al. [16] proposed a conceptual framework for the exchange of value and physical assets in logistics networks that proposed a BC-based conceptual framework and provides a solution to the fundamental barrier of PI. As the main contribution, they identified barriers to transforming current logistics systems into PI networks through case studies. The key barriers included the creation of a network with equal participation, robustness of the framework, assurance of integrity and resilience, rewards in the operational process, and reliable data exchange. By further describing the key features of the technology, they discussed how the BC would address the barriers to PI adoption. They proposed Ethereum BC, implemented smart contracts based on the ERC721 standards[11], and evaluated the transport process in PIs. The authors conclude that BC technology can solve the barriers in PI because it enables a reliable and secure exchange of value in an untrustworthy environment. The authors propose a PoS based BC environment in order to save computational resources. In the case of small-scale PIs, the proposed solution already works, but the scalability[12] problem as a whole needs to be solved before PIs can be widely adopted.

Hassan et al. [17] presented a permitted BC architecture suitable for the integration of BC technology with PI. They discussed how to take advantage of the interoperability[13] between two permitted BCs. They demonstrated the applicability and practicality of the PI architecture to be built on top of a permitted BC and presented a case study of its application. The authors pointed out the scalability of both BC and PI networks as an issue to be solved.

Tan et al. [18] presented a framework of green logistics based on BC to realize sustainable logistics by integrating IoT and big data. The authors propose a framework with seven layers: physical layer, perception layer, network layer, blockchain layer, management layer, application layer, and user layer. The authors pointed out three issues: data storage and transmission, implementation cost, and risk. Then, for future research, the authors suggested to focus on the following: (1) developing a way to effectively connect the physical and perceptual layers to collect logistics data, and

[11] ERC721 is a common standard for smart contracts proposed by Ethereum. The feature of ERC721 is that nonfungible tokens (NFTs) can be handled in smart contracts. By using the ERC721 standard, the ownership and transaction history of NFTs will be able to be recorded on Ethereum BC.

[12] Scalability is the possibility of expanding the functionality of a system, even if it is small at first.

[13] Interoperability refers to the ability to collaborate and interoperability between different BC platforms.

(2) designing an incentive mechanism to encourage logistics companies to participate in the BC platform.

In contrast to the various advantages of BC, this technology requires a transformation of digital systems. First, existing processes need to be digitized. Currently, there are many tasks in logistic operations that are done by hand on paper or on computers that are not connected to a network. In order to effectively accumulate and utilize data in these tasks, it is necessary to digitize the tasks themselves or use AI (e.g., Optical Character Reader) services to digitize them.

Next, in order to work with platforms such as BC, existing systems need to have a mechanism to use APIs[14]. In the logistics field, many existing systems are still based on EDI[15], which supports only batch sending and receiving, while APIs support real-time sending and receiving. In the logistics sector, there are still many existing EDI-based systems; EDI supports only batch sending and receiving, while APIs support real-time sending and receiving, and the development cost is higher than APIs [3]. Making EDI-based core systems API compatible is an important task. The issue of standardization is important in the diffusion of APIs. At present, there is a bunch of standards at the level of international organizations, governments, and industries. Some of the standards conflict with each other. These standards need to be unified. Organizations like Digital Container Shipping Association (DCSA) help to expedite the process. DCSA aims to develop digital standards for the containership industry and has compiled and published electronic standards such as vessel schedules, port operations, and electronic B/Ls. The PoV should follow the standards and protocols published by DCSA. In addition, the API is an architectural style that can be easily manipulated and can flexibly respond to the unique standards of countries and industries, for example, 10-ft container, low floor chassis.

Munim et al. [19] identified the main challenges in the practical application of BC in the maritime sector as lack of standardization of data elements, lack of interoperability and scalability between systems, delay in legislation, lack of understanding of the technology, and lack of training facilities and materials. PiChain is facing the same challenges as it uses BC technology. In addition, it is necessary to solve the issues of attracting participating logistics companies and infrastructure development in the implementation of PI. The search for solutions to these issues remains a future task.

These previous studies pointed out the issues of scalability after conducting small-scale demonstrations. In this study, we propose a framework for building innovative Logistics 4.0 systems and applications to solve these issues.

4.1 Scope of application

We propose the following scope of application of BC technology in PI. PI contains three flows, namely physical (logistics) flow, information flow, and financial flow. BC technology is indispensable for two of the three flows: information flow and financial flow (**Figure 3**).

[14] API is an abbreviation for Application Programming Interface, which is a data exchange specification used by software components to exchange information with each other in real time.

[15] An abbreviation for Electronic Data Interchange, also known as "electronic data interchange," a technology that emerged in the 1970s and is mainly used for information interchange for electronic commerce between companies.

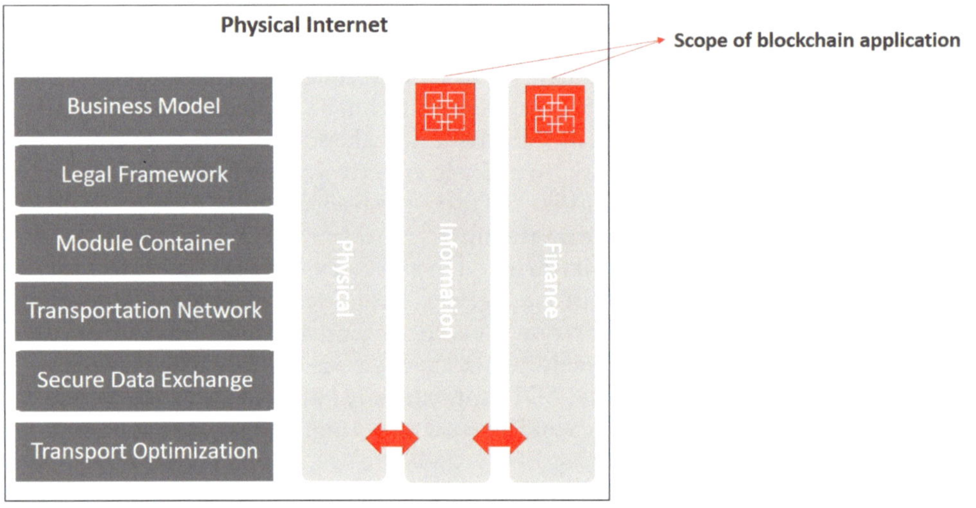

Figure 3.
The scope of BC technology application in PI.

4.2 Implementation framework

For implementation, this chapter proposes a new framework called PiChain, which consists of five components (**Figure 4**).

The first component is the PI that interconnects the maritime logistics networks. The second component includes networks such as LPWA that supports various types of IoT devices, and 5G and 6G that support cloud computing and edge computing. The third component consists of sensors, IoT devices, Internet of Robotic Things (IoRT), and drones. The fourth component includes big data for optimization with AI and visualization with business intelligence (BI). The top layer is the component that refers to the space optimization of business and operational processes implemented goals of logistics and sustainability goals (SDGs). All these components function on a decentralized platform that uses BCs to prevent data modification, which also support traceability and various types of payments.

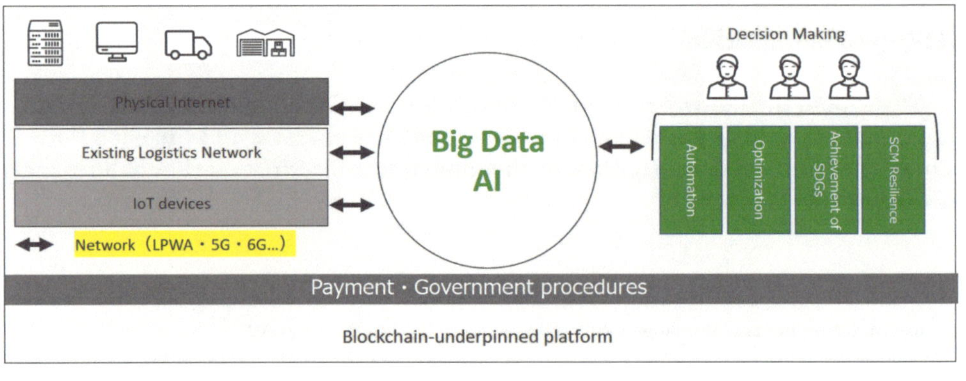

Figure 4.
Overview of the proposed framework "PiChain."

To give a better idea of how PiChain works, let us look at a few scenarios. In the future cargo transportation, upon booking information received, AI will automatically calculate the optimal transportation route and method constraints such as cargo destination, size, and weight using PI containers that match the size of the cargo. As soon as this information is finalized or updated, it is automatically sent to the shipper. In the shipper's internal system, AI uses the latest transportation information to optimize ordering, warehouse storage, and production planning. As soon as the consignee receives the shipment, the payment managed by BC's smart contract will be automatically executed.

4.3 Choosing a blockchain

To overcome the lack of scalability of BCs, as pointed out in previous studies, this study recommends the adoption of the Avalanche protocol (**Table 5**) proposed by Rocket 2019 [20].

The Avalanche protocol is one of the most promising platforms for BCs because of its scalability, ease of use, flexibility, and proper governance. Avalanche was initially built to serve the financial markets (cryptocurrency AVAX), but it is interoperable with both public and permitted BC. Therefore, it can be adopted by other industries in addition to finance. Avalanche is also capable of combining public and private BCs. Compared with the existing Classical and Nakamoto protocols, the BFT-based Avalanche protocol is very efficient and robust, and can also achieve high productivity and fast finality. While traditional protocols require any given node to communicate with all other nodes, the Avalanche protocol communicates with a small subset (validators), which dramatically reduces the latency to 1/3600 compared with Bitcoin (**Table 6**). As a result, Avalanche is able to achieve a performance of 7100 transactions per second, compared with 5 transactions per second for Bitcoin, the Nakamoto protocol equivalent.

We recommend a small-scale Proof of Value (PoV) to be executed. In the PoV, a small-scale PI network will be constructed by implementing the Avalanche protocol, which is small scale and scalable, in order to connect with the existing logistics

Protocol	Classic (1980)	Nakamoto (2008)	Avalanche (2019)
Typical applications	Byzantine General Problems	Bitcoin	AVAX
Robustness	✕	○	○
Low latency and quick finality[1]	○	✕	○
High processing capacity	○	✕	○
Lightweight	○	✕	○
Low power consumption	○	✕	○
51% attack resistance[2]	✕	✕	○
High scalability	✕	✕	○

[1]Finality means that the amount of money is certain to be obtained as expected. The Bank of Japan lists the following specific conditions for a finalized settlement: (1) The money received will not later be turned into scrap paper or disappear, and (2) the settlement made will never be reversed later.
[2]A 51% attack is the control of 51% (more than 50%) of the hash rate of the entire network by a malicious group or individual to perform fraudulent transactions.
Source: Prepared by the author based on Sirer 2020 [13].

Table 5.
Comparison of BC protocols.

Performance comparison	Bitcoin	AVAX
Latency	1	1/3600
Speed (transactions per second)	5	7100
Finality	Accomplished in 1 hour.	Accomplished in 1 second.
Number of simultaneous participants	About 20 people	millions of people

Source: Prepared by the authors based on Sirer 2020 [13].

Table 6.
Comparison of performance.

network and using BC technology, the collected big data will be analyzed for optimization, etc., using AI while ensuring its confidentiality. The results will be used for management decisions and environmental protection measures. This positive cycle will dramatically improve the efficiency of logistics and promote sustainable development. It will also be possible to measure and optimize the contribution of innovative technologies to the sustainable development of logistics and the SDGs. For example, it will be possible to quantify how much waste in loading and waiting for pickup is eliminated by the use of PI-containers, and how much congestion is eliminated by optimization at ports. Or how much truck driver time was saved by reducing waiting time, or how much CO_2 emissions were reduced, such measurements could be automatically recorded and measured on a reliable BC. The combination of Avalanche and PI in the logistic industry will drive logistics digitalization to a global scale.

4.4 Summary and future prospects

In this chapter, we have overviewed the international efforts for innovation in automation and digitalization for the realization of the Smart Port, including the development of technologies and demonstration experiments for their diffusion. It is necessary not only to automate cargo handling at the terminal, but also to share information in real time regarding pre-and post-processes, such as the arrival and departure of ships and the waiting status of vehicles, in cooperation with various IoT devices, and to prepare in advance based on predictive information using AI. It is expected to establish a de facto standard on a global scale by promoting the packaging of port handling machinery combining hardware and software. On the other hand, the international standardization for automated ships is being discussed internationally mainly by initiated by IMO as de jure standard. In addition, it will be necessary to share real-time information on the movements of ships using AIS and IoT and to make comprehensive efforts in cooperation with port infrastructures, such as coordinated operation with work vessels such as tugboats and refueling vessels, and automatic mooring at the wharf. In August 2020, MASSPorts, a framework for international collaboration on the operation of Maritime Autonomous Surface Ships (MASS) in ports, will be launched to establish guidelines for demonstration operations and to study interoperability in multiple ports around the world.

From the research and development stage to the full-scale deployment of new technologies, it is necessary to consider not only the individual optimization of ports and ships but also the overall optimization involving the ocean, ports, and the inland hinterland. As the need for mutual cooperation between ports and ships increases, new infrastructures, systems, laws and regulations, and international standardization need to be discussed. In addition, it is necessary to address not only the safety and cost aspects of installation and operation, but also cyber security, environmental aspects including renewable energy and electrification, and social acceptability. In order to enhance social acceptability, it is important to build a relationship of trust so that not only the port and maritime industries but also the general public can feel secure.

Furthermore, in this chapter, we have proposed PiChain, a framework for creating a sustainable, next-generation maritime logistics system, by applying PI to digitize maritime logistics networks and BC technology for secure information exchange to improve the overall efficiency of maritime logistics, at ports. The following three effects can be expected from the adoption of PiChain.

4.4.1 Strengthening supply chain resilience

Recently, there have been many disruptions in the supply chain due to unexpected circumstances such as bad weather, cyber-attacks, and port congestion. In particular, the covid-19 pandemic that began in early 2020 led to travel restrictions and border closures in some countries, which in turn caused disruptions in sea, land, and air logistics. The disruption of logistics also resulted in stagnant production in many countries. The framework proposed in this chapter, PiChain, is useful for supply chain management during emergencies and early recovery from disasters, as the BC-based platform provides real-time information and visualization of the entire delivery process, which in return enables quick response to unexpected delays. In addition, since PI containers can be freely combined or split, switching parts of cargo to alternative modes of transportation can be done flexibly when needed. Furthermore, the application of automated delivery methods, such as drones, will make it possible to deliver even in the middle of the night or in hazardous environments. In conclusion, PiChain can strengthen the resilience of the supply chain while managing a wide range of unknown risks.

In addition, cyber-attacks in the supply chain have been dramatically increasing in recent years. With risks increasing day by day, a high level of cybersecurity is vital for supply chain resilience. The PiChain framework uses BC technology to make the entire network highly resistant to cyber-attacks. Even in the event of being attacked, the stolen data are a hash value generated by BC, so it is difficult to recover the original data from the hash value, which significantly reduces the risk of information leakage. In addition, since the data are stored in a distributed manner in the cloud, it can be recovered quickly after an attack.

4.4.2 Port sustainability

Regarding the establishment of a sustainable supply chain within the framework of PiChain, the following three points can be summarized.

First, realizing the SDG Goals. Visualizing, measuring, and optimizing GHG emissions will help to minimize their negative impact on the environment. This will contribute to the realization of SDG Goal 13: Take urgent action to combat climate change and its impacts.

Second, improvement of working conditions. In the framework of PiChain, it is expected to improve the working conditions of workers. For example, AI-guided optimal delivery routes will shorten waiting time hence reducing stress for drivers. In addition, logistics workers will be able to enjoy the benefits of advanced visibility and perform their daily work in a more independent way. This will contribute to SDG Goal 8: Promote sustained, inclusive, and sustainable economic growth, full and productive employment, and decent work for all.

Third, improvement of service quality. Visible logistics management with PiChain will make just-in-time delivery easier. The deployment of drones will also make nighttime delivery possible. This will help improve the quality of logistic operations by enabling a quick response to any unforeseen circumstances that may arise.

4.4.3 Creating new business models

With the spread of innovative technologies, new business models will emerge. For example, the inspection at the yard when returning empty containers used to be done by human eyes. Now, using AI image recognition technology, AI can quickly analyze photos of containers automatically taken by surveillance cameras at the gate, and determine if the container is dirty or damaged with an accuracy of over 98%. This kind of service is already being offered in countries like China.

AI will be able to analyze the big data collected and accumulated from the IoT and other sources to realize end-to-end optimization and real-time visibility of the supply chain. New business models that provide niche services in the supply chain emerge continuously, benefiting from innovative technologies.

In addition, there will be businesses that provide training on technologies such as BC and AI. Not only corporate management but also frontline workers will acquire basic knowledge of the new technologies to work more comfortably and efficiently. Since such services are still few, demand will increase further and new businesses in this field are expected to grow considerably. With the digitization of operations and the creation of new business models, maritime logistics, and its various systems, including smart ports will evolve into the next generation, Industry 4.0 modus operandi.

5. Conclusion

As data-centric processes gain more momentum, shipping and port operations are transformed by meticulously embracing innovative business models and Industry 4.0 technologies. Reliable, secure, and efficient cross-collaboration maritime logistic processes are of paramount importance for the promotion of automated ports, as critical nodes in sustainable, digital supply chains.

A decentralized maritime logistics management system, such as a blockchain-based and IoT-aware system that is deployed over a Physical Internet reference architecture, can support and further advance the development of shipping digitalization and ports' automation. AI techniques and respective platforms can exploit real-time information on the movements of ships using AIS and IoT, also port infrastructures and machinery information, and data from vehicles and objects supporting the overall logistics flow, in road or air transport segments, respectively. In this chapter, we outline the technologies and provide a blueprint for building efficient, decentralized, scalable Logistics 4.0 systems, offering a prototype infrastructure model and immediate practice guidance to the next-generation shipping and port community.

Acknowledgements

This work was supported by JSPS KAKENHI Grant Number 21H01564.

DOI: http://dx.doi.org/10.5772/intechopen.102015

Author details

Enna Hirata[1]*, Daisuke Watanabe[2] and Maria Lambrou[3]

1 Kobe University, Kobe, Japan

2 Tokyo University of Marine Science and Technology, Tokyo, Japan

3 University of the Aegean, Chios, Greece

*Address all correspondence to: enna.hirata@platinum.kobe-u.ac.jp

References

[1] Lambrou M, Watanabe D, Iida J. Shipping digitalization management: Conceptualization, typology and antecedents. Journal of Shipping and Trade. 2019;**4**(1):1-17

[2] Morkunas VJ, Paschen J, Boon E. How blockchain technologies impact your business model. Business Horizons. 2019;**62**(3):295-306

[3] Hirata E. The potential of using blockchain technology in shipping and logistics industry. Journal of Logistics Shipping Economics. 2019;**53**:61-70

[4] Montreuil B. Toward a physical internet: Meeting the global logistics sustainability grand challenge. Logistics Research. 2011;**3**(2):71-87

[5] Heilig L, Voß S. Information systems in seaports: A categorization and overview. Information Technology and Management. 2017;**18**(3):179-201

[6] Asian Development Bank. Smart Ports in the Pacific; Asian Development Bank. Manila: Asian Development Bank; 2020

[7] Takahashi K. Trend analysis of automated container terminals in the world. Rep. Port Airpt. Res. Institute Sustainability Natl. Inst. Mar. Port Aviat. Technol. Yokosuka Jpn. 2018;**56**(4)

[8] Buck W, Gardeitchik J, van der Dejil A. Move Forward: Step By Step Towards A Digital Port. White Paper. Port of Rotterdam: Rotterdam, Netherlands; 2019. p. 2019

[9] United Nations. Digitalizing the Port Call Process, UNCTAD Transport and Trade Facilitation Series. Geneva: United Nations; No. 13. 2020

[10] International Maritime Organization. Autonomous shipping. Available from: https://www.imo.org/en/MediaCentre/HotTopics/Pages/Autonomous-shipping.aspx [Accessed 2021-07-17]

[11] Mitsubishi Research Institute: Class NK. FUTURE 2040-Unmanned Ships: The Future of Japan in 2040. Tokyo: Nippon Foundation; 2019

[12] Kutsuna K, Ando H, Kuwahara S, Nakamura S. Conceptual proposal of action planning system (APS) for manned autonomous ship maneuvering. The Japan Institute of Metals and Materials in English. 2019;**54**(2):88-92

[13] Sirer EG. Open and programmable finance with avalanche. In: Block Chain Jam 2020. 2020. Available from: https://cryptonews.com/videos/open-and-programmable-finance-with-avalanche.htm

[14] PEMA. Container Terminal Automation. Port Equipment Manufacturers Association. PEMA Information Paper. London: PEMA; 2016

[15] Class NK. Guidelines for Automated/Autonomous Operation on Ships (Version 1). Tokyo: Nippon Kaiji Kyokai; 2020

[16] Meyer T, Kuhn M, Hartmann E. Blockchain technology enabling the physical internet: A synergetic application framework. Computers and Industrial Engineering. 2019;**136**:5-17

[17] Hassan LAH, Mahmassani HS, Chen Y. Reinforcement learning framework for freight demand forecasting to support operational

planning decisions. Transportation Research Part E: Logistics and Transportation Review. 2020;**137**:101926

[18] Tan BQ, Wang F, Liu J, Kang K, Costa F. A blockchain-based framework for green logistics in supply chains. Sustainability. 2020;**12**(11):4656

[19] Munim ZH, Duru O, Hirata E. Rise, fall, and recovery of blockchains in the maritime technology space. Journal of Marine Science and Engineering. 2021;**9**(3):266

[20] Rocket T, Yin M, Sekniqi K, van Renesse R, Sirer EG. Scalable and Probabilistic Leaderless BFT Consensus through Metastability. ArXiv Prepr. ArXiv190608936 2019

Chapter 8

Enhancing the Resilience of Sustainable Supplier Management through Combination with Lean and Audit

Ping-Kuo Chen, Qiu-Rui He and Xiang Huang

Abstract

Industry 4.0 has positive effect on the enhancing of the resilience. However, if the resilience can be promoted by lean and auditing environment priority, after further combine with industry 4.0 environment, the resilience will become stronger. Even though, two research questions should be verified priority: How do manufacturers make good use of pull production and employee involvement under lean practices that can strengthen supplier management robustness and enhance the prevention ability of resilience? Why does the combination of lean practices with an audit mechanism strengthen the produce synergy to prevent and control opportunistic behaviour by suppliers? PLS and the Sobel test were applied to survey data from 231 Chinese manufacturers to test and verify research questions. Pull production and employee involvement can enhance responsible purchasing, emergency-response, manufacturing process coupling, and further strengthen supplier management robustness, further enhance the prevention ability of resilience in dealing with opportunistic behaviour. In addition, enhancing manufacturing process coupling has the indirect effect of strengthening emergency-response ability. The audit mechanism can control the dysfunctional behaviour of the supplier, further guiding cooperation with the practice of pull production and employee involvement; in addition, audits also trigger the supplier's trade-off mindset in terms of risk and profit maintenance.

Keywords: sustainable, supplier management, resilience, lean, audit, opportunistic behavior

1. Introduction

To deal with heavy competitive pressure, building a supply chain has become an important competitive strategy. Under the supply chain, the effective practice of using more operations between manufacturers and suppliers is critical to promote competitiveness and increase common economic profit; however, it also leads to increased pollution emissions. Considering social pressure, more manufacturers have adopted remedies to deal with pollution. However, if pollution emissions continue to increase, remedy costs are increased and lead to a reduction in common profits. Reducing remedy costs may cause conflict relative to social awareness.

To avoid this conflict, the development of sustainable supplier management is necessary. Sustainability is the concept of balancing the environmental, social, and economic profit cycles. To realize sustainability, resilience is a critical factor. Resilience is the capability of supply chains to prevent, respond, and recover from uncertainty risk [1, 2]. When they possess stronger resilience, manufacturers can strengthen environmental prevention, continue to detect potential problems caused by environmental pollution and recover from them in the shortest period, avoid large improvement costs, maintain economic profits, and meet green and satisfactory social requirements.

However, it is possible that profit motives will still drive suppliers to engage in opportunistic behavior and indirectly increase pollution emissions, further breaking sustainability. These opportunistic behaviors are hard to prevent and control even when there is awareness of opportunistic behavior, and pollution emissions usually become quite serious. Therefore, opportunistic behaviors are like uncertainty risks. If opportunistic behavior is hard to prevent when it appears, how to reduce and recover from the damage of opportunistic behavior in the shortest time is an important research issue.

To enhance the recovery ability of resilience, current theory indicates that information integration [3] and the preparation of redundancy resources [4] are two critical factors. When opportunistic behavior appears, a great information-sharing mechanism can adjust redundancy resources in the shortest period to recover from damage. Even so, redundancy resources, such as inventories, will increase long-term costs, and their preparation and adjustment also affect operational efficiency. Therefore, although redundancy resources reduce the damage level of opportunistic behavior and provide faster recovery, they also raise recovery costs and affect operational efficiency.

Based on the above, researchers, such as Spieske and Birkel [5], found that the development of the industry 4.0 environment has a positive effect on the improvement of resilience. It can integrate related information and further realize the supply chain visibility, help manufacturers and partners to avoid the preparation of redundancy resources, and raise a fast-responding ability. Therefore, it certainly has a positive effect on resilience ability raising. However, the industry 4.0 environment is hard to implement and establish. Based on the above, a lean environment should be established on a priority basis [6]; in addition, the lean environment should have a great auditing mechanism to ensure the lean practice. Even though, improvement of resilience admits of no delay. Therefore, if the improvement of resilience needs to await the finished development of the industry 4.0 environment, the development period will be vulnerable and is hard to control pollution emission. However, if the combination of lean and audit mechanisms has a positive effect to enhance the prevention ability of resilience, it can help the manufacturer to promote gradually the resilience. When the industry 4.0 environment is established, the resilience will become stronger. Even though, does the combination of lean and auditing have a positive effect on resilience?

Lean practices are used to eliminate redundant activities and achieve the maximization of operational efficiency through pull production, 5S, employee involvement, and total productive maintenance (TPM) [7]. Related research, such as that by

Spiegler et al. and Birkie [8, 9], has indicated that the elimination of redundancy activities goes against the recovery ability of resilience. However, according to a few successful cases, such as the Taiwan Semiconductor Manufacturing Company (TSMC) and Samsung Group, if manufacturers make good use of pull production and employee involvement under lean practices that can strengthen supplier management robustness and further enhance prevention resilience, then they are better able to prevent and control the appearance of opportunistic behavior and reduce recovery costs. If lean practices are combined with an audit mechanism, then synergy will occur and strengthen the prevention ability of resilience.

However, how do manufacturers make good use of pull production and employee involvement under lean practices that can strengthen supplier management robustness and enhance the ability of resilience to prevent and control opportunistic behavior? Why does the combination of lean practices with an audit mechanism strengthen the practice effect of pull production and employee involvement and even produce synergy to prevent and control opportunistic behavior by suppliers? The purpose of this study is to explore these research questions.

This chapter contributes to the operations management and sustainable development literature in two ways. First, our research results can guide managers in setting a suitable mechanism through a combination of lean practices and audits to enhance resilience and ensure sustainable supplier management within their organization, avoid the damage caused by opportunistic behavior of suppliers, achieve the goal of sustainability, and not rely on redundant resources. Second, understanding the role of audit in lean practices can guide manufacturers in knowing how to promote the audit mechanism.

2. Literature review and theoretical framework

2.1 Prevention and control of opportunistic behavior and resilience

The definition of sustainability in the supply chain is "the strategic, transparent integration and achievement of an organization's environmental, social and economic goals in the systematic co-ordination of key inter-organizational business processes for improving the long-term economic performance of the individual company and its supply chains" [10]. Sustainable supply chains also emphasize supplier management and promote the gradual development of sustainable supplier management [11].

To maintain sustainability, Rajesh and Ravi [12] believed that stronger resilience is necessary. Resilience can be defined as the ability of a system to prevent and recover from disruptions with negative effects and unpredictable risk events and return to a better situation [13–15]. Unpredictable risks are hard to avoid; however, compared with unpredictable natural risks, artificial risks are common. Of all unpredictable artificial risks, destructive opportunistic behavior by suppliers is the worst.

Opportunistic behavior by suppliers is not purposeful. The appearance of opportunistic behavior is usually profit-oriented, and suppliers worry about damage to their profits [16], which is a normal mindset. If we analyze a profit distribution based on the product selling price, the supplier's profit is just a small ratio of the selling price. Therefore, it is easy to trigger opportunistic behaviors that attempt to increase profits. These opportunistic behaviors may reduce production costs and increase profits; however, they also may indirectly increase pollution. Crucially, the probability of opportunistic behavior by suppliers is higher than other unpredictable risks and is hard to prevent. Therefore, researchers believe that manufacturers should enhance the recovery ability of resilience to reduce the damage level of opportunistic behavior. If prevention ability is increased, its efficiency is lower than that of its prevention ability and has no effect on the prevention and control of opportunistic behavior.

However, more manufacturers have indicated that enhancing the prevention ability of resilience has a substantial positive effect on the prevention and control of opportunistic behavior. If the prevention ability of resilience is increased, its efficiency is better than that of its recovery ability. Related studies, such as those by Pereira et al. and Brown and Badurdeen [17, 18], have also found that real-world enhancement of resilience is used to prevent and control opportunistic behavior. Therefore, enhancing the prevention ability of resilience is related to controlling opportunistic behavior. When the prevention ability of resilience is enhanced, opportunistic behavior by suppliers can be effectively prevented and controlled. Therefore, we developed the following hypothesis:

H1. When the prevention ability of resilience is enhanced, opportunistic behavior by suppliers can be prevented and controlled.

2.2 Lean and resilience

Lean is a business model that originated with Toyota Production Systems (TPS) that first came to be known in Western countries as "just-in-time" (JIT) manufacturing [19]. In the 1980s, researchers at the Massachusetts Institute of Technology coined the term "lean" to describe the simplicity of some car assembly plants, with Toyota being the best example [20]. Lean focuses on the elimination of everything that does not add value to the product and therefore is considered a "waste" of resources, such as overproduction, wait for time, transport, overprocessing, inventory, unnecessary motion, defects, and rework [21], to deliver quality products at a low cost with high productivity [22]. Studies, such as those by Kalyar et al. and Yu et al. [23, 24], argue that the practice of lean depends on related means or tools, including employees' involvement, pull production, elimination of waste, and 5S or total productive maintenance (TPM). Through lean, redundancy resources will be eliminated and reduce related costs and operational efficiency will also be promoted.

However, how can resilience prevention be enhanced through lean? The critical factor is supplier management robustness. A few successful cases indicate that promotion of the pull production process and driving employee involvement can enhance supplier management robustness. However, why do these two mechanisms have a positive effect on promoting supplier management robustness and further enhancing the prevention ability of resilience? We contemplate the following dynamics:

1. Enhancing responsible purchasing: Responsible purchasing means that every supplier needs to bear responsibility for tracking material quality, maintaining replenishment efficiency, and ensuring stable purchasing sourcing [25]. Lean elicits and avoids redundant production activities. When improving pull production, the supplier is required to bear the purchase responsibility to strengthen the purchasing process and avoid redundant production activities due to purchasing problems with raw material. When responsible purchasing is enhanced, supplier management robustness can be strengthened. Therefore,

according to Carvalho et al. and Azadegan et al. [26, 27], if any supplier exhibits an opportunistic behavior that could affect production efficiency and cause pollution to increase, it is easy to catch due to responsible purchasing. Thus, responsible purchasing becomes an inhibitor to prevent and control the appearance of opportunistic behavior. Based on the above, responsible purchasing has a positive effect on the prevention ability of resilience [28].

2. Enhancing emergency-response ability: Emergency-response ability means that manufacturers or suppliers can respond immediately or even control for damage before it is caused [29]. Lean thinking encourages all employees of manufacturers and suppliers to continually become involved [30, 31] in promoting pull production. To ensure that continuous involvement produces a positive effect, employees need to be trained. Training improves employees' ability to respond to emergencies. Sabadka [32] indicated that when adopting a training programme to promote employee involvement, the emergency-response ability of employees will increase. When a supplier exhibits opportunistic behavior, any employee from a manufacturer or another supplier can be immediately aware of the behavior and respond, even controlling damage before it is caused [33]. Based on the above, enhancing emergency-response ability is deemed to strengthen supplier management robustness and further enhance the prevention ability of resilience [34, 35].

3. Enhancing manufacturing process coupling: Manufacturing process coupling is defined as deployed with manufacturers' and suppliers' processes [36]. According to Ugochukwu et al. [37], to avoid inventory and overproduction and raw material waste and improve just-in-time results, pull production pushes the accumulation of inventory control in the different manufacturing process levels and production process linking suppliers and manufacturers to enhance production efficiency. Therefore, the coupling of the manufacturing process between manufacturers and suppliers is enhanced and shows a closer linkage [38]. At that time, production operations between manufacturers and suppliers will be a staggered arrangement, which will enhance supplier management robustness [39]. However, enhancing manufacturing process coupling may have an indirect positive effect on resilience. The process between manufacturers and suppliers is complex; if that process can become strongly coupled, it can be deemed that manufacturers expand their control power to the supplier. Manufacturers can deeply understand any situation from suppliers, shorten the time to respond to immediate related problems from suppliers, and further control the response to those problems [40], which is similar to promoting the positive effect of emergency-response ability on enhancing the prevention ability of resilience [41, 42].

Based on the above, three hypotheses are developed to explore our first research question.

H2a: Establishing responsible purchasing has a positive effect on enhancing the prevention ability of resilience.

H2b: Enhancing emergency-response ability has a positive effect on enhancing the prevention ability of resilience.

H2c: Enhancing manufacturing process coupling has a positive effect on enhancing emergency-response ability.

2.3 Synergy of combination with audit

According to the Oxford dictionary, an audit is defined as a systematic review or assessment [43]. In the past, the concept of an audit has usually been applied in the quality management field, and its purpose is to self-assess to allow continuous improvement to further ensure that the system, process, or product satisfies requirements or criteria [44]. Recently, the concept of audit mechanisms has also been implemented in green improvement. When an audit mechanism is applied to the green improvement field, its purpose is to measure the performance of pollution-prevention activities [45, 46].

With the practice of lean proven to have a positive effect on green environmental improvements, an increasing number of studies, such as those by de Freitas et al. and Leong et al. [47, 48], have found that combining audits can produce synergy to promote green environmental development. Audits can help manufacturers assess and monitor lean processes, avoid any redundant activities causing pollution emissions, and further prevent and control pollution. The audit process can be divided into two phases, including the development of prevention standards or criteria and follow-up and assessment [49]. The development of prevention standards is beforehand work, and suppliers or partners are required to follow. Then, under lean practices, follow-up suppliers or partners follow the standards or criteria. In addition, manufacturers play the role of leader auditors to assess whether these suppliers and partners attend to and obey these standards or criteria. When these two phases are combined with lean, it is similar to the monitoring process of lean practice efficiency in green environmental improvement [50].

Pull production and employee involvement are two important mechanisms in lean practice. This study believes that these two mechanisms can promote supplier management robustness and further enhance resilience to prevent and control opportunistic behavior by suppliers to avoid sustainable disruptions. According to the experiences of a few successful cases, if lean is combined with audits, it can produce positive synergy to strengthen the practice of pull production and employee involvement and have a positive effect on enhancing the prevention ability of resilience. However, why these effects occur requires an understanding of the following dynamics:

1. Development of standards and criteria to control dysfunctional behavior. Dysfunctional behavior is a resistance phenomenon [51, 52] that derives from a conflict of interest. The appearance of opportunistic behavior is based on profit orientation. Pull production and employee involvement can enhance manufacturing process coupling, responsible purchasing, and emergency-response ability to restrain these opportunistic behaviors. However, though they can be restrained, these factors are hard to control further. According to Feld [53], designing the standards and criteria of audits is based on real demand and decisions about the environment. Through these standards and criteria, suppliers will be able to understand their opportunistic behaviors that cause risk and could lead to serious damage which makes it difficult for these suppliers to obtain more profit. Therefore, this strategy can control their dysfunctional behavior. When dysfunctional behavior is controlled, it can ensure the enhancement of manufacturing process coupling, responsibility purchasing, and emergency-response ability to produce better effects [54–56], further strengthening resilience to prevent and control opportunistic behavior. Based on the above, we develop the following three hypotheses to explore.

H3a: Control of dysfunctional behavior through the development of standards and criteria will strengthen responsible purchasing.
H3b: Control of dysfunctional behavior through the development of standards and criteria will strengthen emergency-response ability.
H3c: Control of dysfunctional behavior through the development of standards and criteria will strengthen manufacturing process coupling.

2. Follow-up and assessment will trigger a trade-off. Although the purpose of follow-up and assessment is to establish a process to help and guide suppliers to follow related standards and criteria to cooperate in improving pull production and employee involvement, follow-up and assessment processes trigger supplier trade-off [57, 58]. Specifically, under the follow-up and assessment process, manufacturers have the responsibility to help suppliers to understand that they will encounter related risks and lose related benefits. As a reminder of the previous discussion, the appearance of opportunistic behavior comes from a concern about losing profit and not bearing related costs. Therefore, the process of follow-up and assessment is a chance to communicate thoroughly with suppliers about delivery risks and strengthen cooperative intentions to maintain suppliers' benefits [59]. Based on the above, audits will trigger a trade-off in risks and benefits that will guide suppliers to self-control opportunistic behavior and heighten their intention to cooperate in enhancing supplier management robustness [57, 60, 61]. Trade-off enhances the control effect of dysfunctional behavior. Therefore, we develop the following three hypotheses to explore.

H4a: Triggering of a trade-off has a mediating effect on the control of dysfunctional behavior and the enhancement of responsible purchasing.
H4b: Triggering of a trade-off has a mediating effect on the control of dysfunctional behavior and the enhancement of emergency-response ability.
H4c: Triggering of a trade-off has a mediating effect on the control of dysfunctional behavior and the enhancement of manufacturing process coupling.

2.4 Theoretical framework

According to the related literature review and hypotheses development, this study develops the theoretical framework shown in **Figure 1**. In line with **Figure 1**, this study further tests the path relationships amongst the prevention ability of resilience, prevention and control of opportunistic behavior, enhancement of manufacturing process coupling, the establishment of a responsible purchasing process, emergency-response ability training, control of dysfunctional behavior, and triggering of a trade-off. Through the verification of our theoretical framework, we can explore and explain our research questions.

3. Materials and methods

3.1 Questionnaire, operationalization and variables of the constructs, data collection, and sample profile

To test our research hypotheses and further explore our theoretical framework, this study utilizes survey-based empirical data from Chinese manufacturers. As part

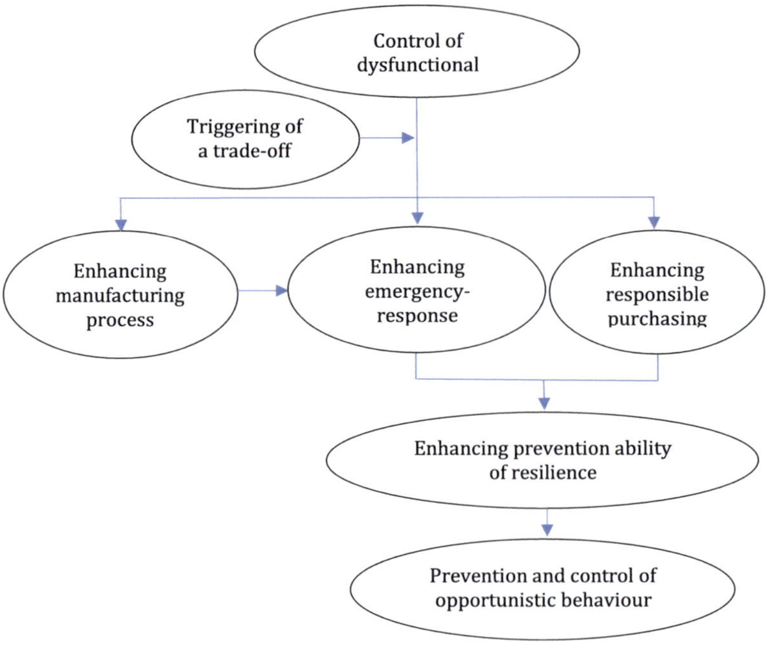

Figure 1.
Theoretical framework.

of a broader research project, a cross-sectional survey instrument was first designed. In line with the theoretical framework described in **Figure 1**, the questionnaire encompasses seven constructs, including enhancing the prevention ability of resilience, prevention and control of opportunistic behavior, manufacturing process coupling, responsible purchasing processes, and emergency-response ability; controlling dysfunctional behavior; triggering trade-off. According to related studies, we defined the operationalization of each construct and its related variables. These variables became the items or questions in the questionnaire, as shown in **Table 1**.

Based on the questionnaire, we attempted to collect related empirical data. Questionnaires were sent to 373 manufacturing companies in China. We received 231 valid responses, for a response rate of 61.93%. To characterize the profile of the companies in the sample, we investigated three characteristics—enterprise size, product type, and age of implementation of lean and audit for the promotion of supplier management robustness and resilience. According to aggregated results, the characteristics of the respondents are shown in **Table 2**.

3.2 Method

Partial least squares (PLS) analysis is a convenient method for estimating path relationship models with latent variables while including mediation effects. Because the theoretical framework of this study involves many path relationships and mediation effects, PLS is adopted as the main method to test our theoretical framework and hypotheses.

In PLS analysis, bootstrapping is used to test the statistical significance of the hypothesized relationships. The bootstrapping procedure entails generating 5000

Constructs	Variables	Operationalization	Citation source
1. Through pull production, will the following indices be enhanced significantly and further promote manufacturing process coupling between your company and suppliers?			
Enhancing of manufacturing process coupling (M)	M1. Efficiency of VMI and Kanban system	Manufacturing process coupling is deployed with suppliers' processes through pull production	[36, 62]
	M2. Efficiency of manufacturing information integration		
	M3. Efficiency of production modules integration between manufacturers and suppliers		
2. When improving pull production, will the following indices be enhanced significantly and further promote the supplier's responsible purchasing?			
Enhancing of responsible purchasing (P)	P1. Enhancing of purchasing quality of raw material P2. Every supplier has stable purchasing sourcing P3. Every supplier can achieve stable replenishment P4. Every supplier can provide stable inventory planning	Supplier bears the responsibility to track material quality, maintain replenishment, and ensure stable sourcing	[63, 64]
3. Through the promotion of employee involvement, will the following indices be enhanced significantly and further promote your company's emergency-response ability?			
Enhancing of emergency-response ability (E)	E1. Enhanced forecasting of the damage path when a supplier exhibits opportunistic behavior	Emergency-response ability means that manufacturers can respond immediately and even control damage before it is caused	[65, 66]
	E2. Your company can immediately assess the possible damage level and balk early when a supplier exhibits unusual behavior		
	E3. Your company can immediately identify possible damage sourcing and balk early when a supplier exhibits unusual behavior		
	E4. Your company can immediately adjust production operations to reduce the effects when a supplier exhibits unusual behavior		
4. Can opportunistic behavior by suppliers be prevented and controlled by observing the following situation?			
Prevention and control of opportunistic behavior (C)	C1. Realizing that a supplier's promised cooperation is usually late	Manufacturers can observe which situation to prevent and control the supplier's opportunistic behavior	[67]
	C2. Observing whether a supplier breaches the agreed-upon cooperation to maximize its own benefit		
	C3. Observing whether a supplier takes advantage of accidents to make compromises		
5. Which capability should be enhanced if a company hopes to obtain greater prevention ability of resilience?			

Constructs	Variables	Operationalization	Citation source
Enhancing the prevention ability of resilience (R)	R1. Enhancing process monitoring capability R2. Possessing the capability to detect unusual behavior in the pre-crisis stage R3. Enhancing the early response capability to any possible accidents	Resilience can be defined as the ability of a system to prevent and recover from disruptions with negative effects and unpredictable risk events and return to a better situation	[65, 66, 68]
6. Under the audit process, develop and require that the supplier abides by standards and criteria that ensure and control for supplier behavior that is necessary for lean practice. However, how does the development of standards and criteria control the certainty of supplier cooperation with lean practice?			
Control of dysfunctional behavior (D)	D1. Control of resistance to cooperation D2. Control of intention to cooperate D3. Control of cooperation cognition	Try to control the resistance phenomenon and raise cooperation intention, cognition, and awareness	[69]
7. Under the audit process, follow up and assess whether the supplier follows the standards and criteria related to cooperating with a lean practice that is important at a given stage. However, how can the follow-up and assessment enhance the certainty that the supplier will cooperate with lean practice?			
Triggering of a trade-off (T)	T1. Supplier begins to think of the risk of opportunistic behavior T2. Supplier is aware that opportunistic behavior will lead to unstable profits T3. Supplier understands that opportunistic behavior is undesirable if it hopes to increase its profits through stable cooperation	Trigger the trade-off in risk and benefit and guide supplier to self-control the opportunistic behavior	[8, 17]

Table 1.
Questionnaire content, operationalization, variables of each construct, and citation source.

subsamples of randomly selected cases with replacement. Under the analysis process, the path coefficients are generated for each randomly selected subsample, and the t-value is calculated for every coefficient. According to the calculation results, the path coefficient and t-value are statistically significant and applied to evaluate the research hypotheses. As the analysis tool, we used SmartPLS 3.0.

In addition to PLS, we also used the Sobel test to verify the mediating effect. According to Hayes [70], a large sample may cause an error in evaluating the mediation effect when PLS is used for testing. However, the Sobel test can overcome this problem. For verification, Preacher and Leonardelli developed a free tool to perform the Sobel test. The test results verify the mediating effect. The tool is provided on the lab website of Preacher and Leonardelli.

However, to first test the theoretical framework and hypotheses with PLS, the validity and reliability of the constructs should be tested. To measure validity and reliability, factor loadings, composite reliability (CR), average variance extracted (AVE), and discriminant validity are the main indices. Regarding the requirements of the indices, the factor loadings should exceed 0.4 [71]; the CR and AVE should exceed 0.7 and 0.5 [72]. An exception is that if AVE is lower than 0.5 but higher than 0.36 and CR is above 0.7, then the situation can be accepted [73]. Discriminant validity is

Characteristics	Profiles
Enterprise size (number of employees)	Up to 100 = 4.33% Between 101 and 300 = 28.57% Between 301 and 500 = 30.3% Between 501 and 1000 = 24.68% Above 1000 = 12.12%
Type of product	Manufacture of Smart Grid and Intelligent Electrical Apparatus = 23.81% Manufacture of fabricated metal products, except machinery and equipment = 21.21% Manufacture of computer, electronic and optical products = 14.72% Manufacture of electrical equipment = 3.46% Manufacture of motor vehicles, trailers, and semi-trailers = 5.63% Manufacture of other components = 22.08% Others = 9.09%
Age of implementation of lean and audit	Under 1 year = 6.06% 1 year to 3 years = 37.23% 3 years to 5 years = 28.14% 5 years to 7 years = 14.29% Over 7 years = 14.29%

Table 2.
Sample profiles.

adopted to measure whether each construct can be discriminated from others' constructs. Therefore, the correlation between the constructs should be tested. If the correlation value is lower than 0.7, then every construct can be discriminated [73].

Finally, the model's goodness of fit should be measured. Regarding goodness of fit, the standardized root-mean-square residual (SRMR) is used as the main index. The SRMR was initially proposed for use in combination with CB-SEM, but it has also been extended to PLS. The SRMR is reported to be an approximate measure of model goodness of fit and has been widely adopted for this purpose. Thus, SRMR is adopted to measure the model's goodness of fit.

4. Test results

4.1 Construct measures

Before testing the hypotheses, we test the validity and reliability of the constructs and discriminant validity. According to **Table 3**, all the factor loadings exceed 0.4. Therefore, the factor loadings satisfied the requirement. Regarding CR, according to **Table 3**, all the CR values exceed 0.7. Regarding AVE, the AVE values for the prevention and control of opportunistic behavior and triggering of a trade-off are higher than 0.5 and satisfy the measurement requirements. However, the values of enhancing manufacturing process coupling, responsible purchasing, emergency-response ability, and the prevention ability of resilience, as well as controlling dysfunctional behavior, are less than 0.5 but higher than 0.36. As noted by Fornell and Larcker [73], this situation may still be considered acceptable. Next, we test for discriminant validity. According to **Table 4**, the correlation values between constructs are lower than 0.7, and the test results satisfy the requirements.

Constructs	Variables	Factoring loading	CR	AVE
Enhancing of manufacturing process coupling (M)	M1	.532	.707	.448
	M2	.681		
	M3	.785		
Enhancing of responsible purchasing (P)	P1	.570	.739	.414
	P2	.612		
	P3	.717		
	P4	.673		
Enhancing of emergency-response ability (E)	E1	.681	.732	.410
	E2	.618		
	E3	.658		
	E4	.616		
Prevention and control of opportunistic behavior (C)	C1	.805	.824	.610
	C2	.769		
	C3	.769		
Enhancing of prevention ability of resilience (R)	R1	.749	.719	.462
	R2	.652		
	R3	.634		
Control of dysfunctional behavior (D)	D1	.579	.704	.429
	D2	.797		
	D3	.570		
Triggering of a trade-off (T)	T1	.798	.783	.547
	T2	.686		
	T3	.733		

Table 3.
Construct measures assessment: composite reliability and convergent validity.

	Mean	SD	(M)	(P)	(E)	(C)	(R)	(D)
(M)	3.945	.549						
(P)	3.930	.551	.402					
(E)	3.986	.513	.338	.332				
(C)	3.856	.785	.539	.409	.489			
(R)	4.196	.482	.405	.268	.467	.473		
(D)	4.003	.531	.278	.182	.409	.297	.487	
(T)	4.133	.589	.454	.358	.406	.412	.521	.437

Table 4.
Discriminant validity (correlation).

4.2 Estimation of the theoretical framework

The PLS analysis test results are shown in **Table 5**. This table shows the path coefficients, results of the t-statistics value, and an explanation of the construct variances. In terms of the construct variances, we find that each of the endogenous variables is adequate, explaining 20% of the variance for enhancing manufacturing

	Hypotheses	Path coefficient	t-value	Results
H1	Enhancing of responsible purchasing ➔ Enhancing of prevention ability of resilience	.487	9.354**	Supported
H2a	Enhancing of emergency-response ability ➔ Enhancing of prevention ability of resilience	.310	4.206**	Supported
H2b	Enhancing of manufacturing process coupling ➔ Enhancing of emergency-response ability	.321	4.377**	Supported
H2c	Control of dysfunctional behavior ➔ Enhancing of responsible purchasing	.195	3.230**	Supported
H3a	Control of dysfunctional behavior ➔ Enhancing of emergency-response ability	.193	2.690**	Supported
H3b	Control of dysfunctional behavior ➔ Enhancing of manufacturing process coupling	.385	6.097**	Supported
H3c	Control of dysfunctional behavior ➔ Triggering of a trade-off	.301	4.450**	Supported
H4a	Triggering of a trade-off ➔ Enhancing of responsible purchasing	.454	7.892**	Supported
	Control of dysfunctional behavior ➔ Triggering of a trade-off	.318	3.446**	
H4b	Triggering of a trade-off ➔ Enhancing of emergency-response ability	.454	7.892**	Supported
	Control of dysfunctional behavior ➔ Triggering of a trade-off	.168	2.093*	
H4c	Triggering of a trade-off ➔ Enhancing of manufacturing process coupling	.454	7.892**	Supported
	Enhancing of responsible purchasing ➔ Enhancing of prevention ability of resilience	.221	3.145**	
Variance explained in the endogenous variables				
	Enhancing of manufacturing process coupling		R^2 = .200	
	Enhancing of responsible purchasing		R^2 = .194	
	Enhancing of emergency-response ability		R^2 = .356	
	Enhancing of prevention ability of resilience		R^2 = .297	
	Prevention and control of opportunistic behavior		R^2 = .237	
	Triggering of a trade-off		R^2 = .206	
Model fit				
	SRMR	.087		

*p < .05.
**p < .01.

Table 5.
PLS structural model results.

process coupling, 19.4% of the variance for enhancing responsible purchasing, 35.6% of the variance for enhancing emergency-response ability, 29.7% of the variance for enhancing the prevention ability of resilience, 23.7% of the variance for preventing and controlling opportunistic behavior, and 20.6% of the variance for triggering trade-off.

Regarding the test results of the hypotheses, the path coefficient for the relationship between the enhancement of resilience and the prevention and control of opportunistic behavior is 0.487 ($p < .01$); thus, enhancing the prevention ability of resilience has a positive effect on the prevention and control of opportunistic behavior, which supports H1. The path coefficient for the relationship between enhancing responsible purchasing and enhancing the prevention ability of resilience is 0.310 ($p < .01$); thus, enhancing responsible purchasing has a positive effect on enhancing the prevention ability of resilience, which supports H2a. H2b is supported because the path coefficient is 0.321 ($p < .01$); thus, enhancing emergency-response ability has a positive effect on enhancing the prevention ability of resilience. The path coefficient for the relationship between enhancing manufacturing process coupling and enhancing emergency-response ability is 0.195 ($p < .01$); thus, enhancing manufacturing process coupling has a positive effect on enhancing emergency-response ability, which supports H2c.

The path coefficients for the relationship between the control of dysfunctional behavior, enhancement of responsible purchasing, enhancement of emergency-response ability, and enhancement of manufacturing process coupling are 0.193 ($p < .01$), 0.385 ($p < .01$), and 0.301 ($p < .01$); thus, the control of dysfunctional behavior has a positive effect on enhancing responsible purchasing, enhancing emergency-response ability, and enhancing manufacturing process coupling, which supports H3a, H3b, and H3c. The path coefficient for the relationship between the control of dysfunctional behavior and the triggering of a trade-off is 0.454 ($p < .01$), the path coefficients for the relationship between the triggering of a trade-off and the

Input:			Test statistic:	Std. Error:	p-value:
a	0.454	Sobel test:	48.19392924	0.00299565	0
b	0.318	Aroian test:	48.19254578	0.00299573	0
s_a	0.00375	Goodman test:	48.19531282	0.00299556	0
s_b	0.006053	Reset all	Calculate		

Mediating effect of the triggering of a trade-off in the relationship between control of dysfunctional behavior and enhancing of responsible purchasing. The Sobel test result is 48.194 ($p < .01$).

Input:			Test statistic:	Std. Error:	p-value:
a	0.454	Sobel test:	30.86061235	0.0024715	0
b	0.168	Aroian test:	30.85962805	0.00247158	0
s_a	0.00375	Goodman test:	30.86159675	0.00247142	0
s_b	0.005264	Reset all	Calculate		

Mediating effect of the triggering of a trade-off in the relationship between the control of dysfunctional behavior and enhancing of emergency-response ability. The Sobel test result is 30.861 ($p < .01$).

Input:			Test statistic:	Std. Error:	p-value:
a	0.454	Sobel test:	44.60555141	0.00224936	0
b	0.221	Aroian test:	44.60423639	0.00224943	0
s_a	0.00375	Goodman test:	44.60686655	0.00224929	0
s_b	0.004606	Reset all	Calculate		

Mediating effect of the triggering of a trade-off in the relationship between the control of dysfunctional behavior and enhancing of manufacturing process coupling. The Sobel test result is 44.606 ($p < .01$).

Table 6.
Sobel test results.

enhancing of responsible purchasing with enhancing emergency-response ability and enhancing manufacturing process coupling are 0.318 ($p < .01$), 0.168 ($p < .05$), and 0.221 ($p < .01$), respectively; thus, we find that the triggering of a trade-off has mediating effects on the relationships between controlling dysfunctional behavior and enhancing responsible purchasing, enhancing emergency-response ability, and enhancing manufacturing process coupling, which supports H4a, H4b, and H4c, respectively. In terms of measuring model fit, the SRMR is the main index used. According to the test, the SRMR is 0.087, and the model fit can be accepted.

This study also adopts the Sobel test to verify mediating effects, and the test results are shown in **Table 6**. According to **Table 6**, the test results of the p-value for hypotheses H4a, H4b, and H4c are lower than 0.01, which means that the mediating effect of the triggering of a trade-off exists and has a positive effect on the relationships between the control of dysfunctional behavior, enhancing of responsible purchasing, enhancing of emergency-response ability, and enhancing of manufacturing process coupling.

5. Discussion

This section discusses the test results and answers further research questions. The first question is, how do manufacturers make good use of pull production and employee involvement under lean practices that can strengthen supplier management robustness and enhance the ability of resilience to prevent and control opportunistic behavior by suppliers? Our test results indicate that because the good use of pull production and employee involvement under lean practices enhances responsible purchasing and emergency-response ability to promote supplier management robustness, this practice has a positive effect on enhancing the prevention ability of resilience and further proves and controls opportunistic behavior by suppliers. Specifically, enhancing responsible purchasing is much like attributing responsibility. If a supplier exhibits opportunistic behavior based on a profit orientation, its purchasing efficiency will appear unusual and its purchasing quality will decrease, which will indirectly cause an increase in pollution. Due to the attribution of responsibility, each supplier has its own responsible purchase sourcing and needs to bear responsibility for its raw material quality; as a result, manufacturers can quickly become aware of opportunistic behavior by suppliers, which produces a warning effect and restrains any intention of opportunistic behavior. This is just like strengthening supplier management robustness and can be deemed that the prevention ability of resilience is enhanced.

The enhancement of emergency-response ability is based on the promotion of employee involvement. To ensure that lean practices are followed, lean usually encourages employee involvement. To promote involvement efficiency, manufacturers usually design related training programmes. In addition to employees from manufacturers, employees from related suppliers also need to be trained. Through effective training, employees from manufacturers and suppliers can come to possess rich knowledge and cognition not only to improve lean practices and their response-ability but also to increase them [74]. A few researchers, such as Minh et al. [75], have found that increasing response-ability has a positive effect on supplier management. Therefore, when a supplier exhibits opportunistic behavior, employees of manufacturers and other suppliers can adopt emergency responses and further control. Therefore, it can be deemed that supplier management robustness is strengthened and has a positive effect on enhancing the prevention ability of resilience.

Pull production also enhances manufacturing process coupling. When a complex process between manufacturers and suppliers is an effective coupling, it has a positive effect on the promotion of emergency-response ability. More employees of manufacturers or other suppliers will have the chance to intervene in the manufacturing process. Therefore, when any supplier exhibits unusual behavior, employees of manufacturers or other suppliers become aware of this behavior faster and can thus prevent or control it more quickly. Based on the above, manufacturing process coupling can be deemed to have a positive effect on strengthening supplier management robustness and indirectly enhancing the prevention ability of resilience. Therefore, manufacturers make good use of pull production and employee involvement under lean practices that can strengthen supplier management robustness and enhance resilience to prevent and control opportunistic behavior.

The second research question is why does the combination of lean practice with an audit mechanism strengthen the practice effect of pull production and employee involvement and produce synergy to strengthen the prevention ability of resilience and further control opportunistic behavior by suppliers? Developing related standards and criteria and improving follow-up/assessment are two important aspects of the audit process. These standards and criteria are guidelines that guide suppliers to cooperate with the practices of pull production and employee involvement. When suppliers fully follow these guidelines, their emergency-response ability, responsible purchasing, and manufacturing process coupling will be enhanced. The development of these standards and criteria is based on real situational demands. However, before requiring suppliers to follow these guidelines, manufacturers as auditors have the responsibility to explain these standards and criteria and help suppliers to understand efficiency and how they can maintain profits by following these standards and criteria to improve pull production and employee involvement [76]. Actually, the appearance of opportunistic behavior is based on profit orientation. For the appearance of opportunistic behavior, the supplier must exhibit some dysfunctional behavior during the cooperation process. If suppliers can understand the positive efficiency of these standards and criteria and ensure that their profits can be maintained, these standards and criteria can control suppliers' dysfunctional behavior and further eliminate opportunistic behavior [77].

However, to ensure that these suppliers can fully follow these standards and criteria, manufacturers usually play the role of auditors in follow-up and assessment. Under the follow-up and assessment process, manufacturers have the responsibility to communicate with suppliers and help them to understand the risk of opportunistic behavior and the potential damage to profits. In the real world, considerations of profit maintenance certainly trigger a trade-off mindset in terms of risk and profit. According to Bahr and Sweeney [78], this is a powerful influence that guides suppliers to follow the standards and criteria that improve pull production and employee involvement and eliminate opportunistic behavior. Based on the above, this is why combining audit mechanisms with lean practices can strengthen the practice of pull production and employee involvement and enhance the preventive ability of resilience to deal with opportunistic behavior by suppliers.

6. Conclusion

To enhance the prevention ability of resilience to deal with opportunistic behaviors by suppliers and further maintain effective sustainability, this study explored two research questions: How do manufacturers make good use of pull production and employee involvement under lean practices that can strengthen supplier management robustness and enhance the prevention ability of resilience to deal with opportunistic behavior? Why does the combination of lean with an audit mechanism strengthen the practice effect of pull production and employee involvement and even produce synergy to prevent and control opportunistic behavior by suppliers?

According to the test results, effective practice of pull production and employee involvement can enhance responsible purchasing, emergency-response ability, and manufacturing process coupling and further strengthen supplier management robustness, which enhances the prevention ability of resilience to deal with opportunistic behavior. In addition, enhancing manufacturing process coupling has an indirect effect, strengthening emergency-response ability and further enhancing the prevention ability of resilience. The audit mechanism can control the dysfunctional behavior of the supplier, further guiding cooperation with the practice of pull production and employee involvement; in addition, audits trigger the supplier's trade-off mindset in terms of risk and profit maintenance. Based on the prior discussion, this trade-off mindset can enhance the ability of resilience to prevent and control opportunistic behavior.

Regarding the academic implications of this study, although some conflict exists between lean and resilience, our research proved that if manufacturers make good use of pull production and employee involvement when implementing lean, it can enhance manufacturing process coupling, responsible purchasing, and emergency-response ability; strengthen supplier management robustness; further enhance the ability of resilience to prevent and control opportunistic behavior. Therefore, our research results provide a new vision and expand research knowledge on the relationship between lean and resilience. In terms of practical implications, our research results can help manufacturers to understand the importance of the practice of pull production and employee involvement under lean practices and guide manufacturers to think about how to establish an effective audit process and environment to strengthen the practice efficiency of pull production and employee involvement to enhance the prevention ability of resilience to deal with opportunistic behavior by suppliers.

Although our research results provide many valuable suggestions, there are a few limitations. First, although the research results explained how the practice of pull production and employee involvement under lean practices can enhance resilience to maintain sustainable supplier management, how to effectively practice these two mechanisms has not been explored. In addition, the research results clarified why the combination of lean and audits can produce synergy for enacting resilience; however, a method to design an effective audit process is also lacking. Future research can explore these two limitations in greater depth.

Acknowledgements

This study was supported by the National Natural Science Foundation of China (NSFC, Grant no. 71872131) and STU Scientific Research Initiation Grant (SRIG, Grant no. 20007).

Conflict of interest

The authors declare no conflict of interest.

Author details

Ping-Kuo Chen*, Qiu-Rui He and Xiang Huang
Shantou University, Shantou City, China

*Address all correspondence to: a1104100@ms23.hinet.net

References

[1] Ponomarov SY, Holcomb MC. Understanding the concept of supply chain resilience. The International Journal of Logistics Management. 2009; **20**:124-143. DOI: 10.1108/0957409091 0954873

[2] Day JM. Fostering emergent resilience: The complex adaptive supply network of disaster relief. International Journal of Production Research. 2014;**52**: 1970-1988. DOI: 10.1080/ 00207543.2013.787496

[3] Dubey R, Gunasekaran A, Childe SJ, Papadopoulos T, Blome C, Luo Z. Antecedents of resilient supply chains: An empirical study. IEEE Transactions on Engineering Management. 2017;**66**: 8-19. DOI: 10.1109/TEM.2017.2723042

[4] Tan WJ, Zhang AN, Cai W. A graph-based model to measure structural redundancy for supply chain resilience. International Journal of Production Research. 2019;**57**:6385-6404. DOI: 10.1080/00207543.2019.1566666

[5] Spieske A, Birkel H. Improving supply chain resilience through industry 4.0: A systematic literature review under the impressions of the COVID-19 pandemic. Computers & Industrial Engineering. 2021;**158**:107452. DOI: 10.1016/j.cie.2021.107452

[6] Umar M, Khan SAR, Yusliza MY, Ali S, Yu Z. Industry 4.0 and green supply chain practices: An empirical study. International Journal of Productivity and Performance Management. 2021;**71**(3):814-832. DOI: 10.1108/IJPPM-12-2020-0633

[7] Ruiz-Benítez R, López C, Real JC. The lean and resilient management of the supply chain and its impact on performance. International Journal of Production Economics. 2018;**203**: 190-202. DOI: 10.1016/j.ijpe.2018. 06.009

[8] Spiegler VL, Naim MM, Wikner J. A control engineering approach to the assessment of supply chain resilience. International Journal of Production Research. 2012;**50**:6162-6187. DOI: 10.1080/00207543.2012.710764

[9] Birkie SE. Operational resilience and lean: In search of synergies and trade-offs. Journal of Manufacturing Technology Management. 2016;**27**: 185-207. DOI: 10.1108/JMTM-07-2015-0054

[10] Carter CR, Rogers DS. A framework of sustainable supply chain management: Moving toward new theory. International Journal of Physical Distribution & Logistics Management. 2008;**38**:360-387. DOI: 10.1108/ 09600030810882816

[11] Brandenburg M, Rebs T. Sustainable supply chain management: A modeling perspective. Annals of Operations Research. 2015;**229**:213-252. DOI: 10.1007/s10479-015-1853-1

[12] Rajesh R, Ravi V. Supplier selection in resilient supply chains: A grey relational analysis approach. Journal of Cleaner Production. 2015;**86**:343-359. DOI: 10.1016/j.jclepro.2014.08.054

[13] Gouda SK, Saranga H. Sustainable supply chains for supply chain sustainability: Impact of sustainability efforts on supply chain risk. International Journal of Production Research. 2018;**56**:5820-5835. DOI: 10.1080/00207543.2018.1456695

[14] Ye F, Hou G, Li Y, Fu S. Managing bioethanol supply chain resiliency: A

risk-sharing model to mitigate yield uncertainty risk. Industrial Management & Data Systems. 2018;**118**:1510-1527. DOI: 10.1108/IMDS-09-2017-0429

[15] Chen Y, Chen IJ. Mixed sustainability motives, mixed results: The role of compliance and commitment in sustainable supply chain practices. Supply Chain Management: An International Journal. 2019;**24**:622-636. DOI: 10.1108/SCM-10-2018-0363

[16] Lui SS, Ngo HY. Drivers and outcomes of long-term orientation in cooperative relationships. British Journal of Management. 2012;**23**:80-95. DOI: 10.1111/j.1467-8551.2010.00719.x

[17] Pereira CR, Christopher M, Da Silva AL. Achieving supply chain resilience: The role of procurement. Supply Chain Management: An International Journal. 2014;**19**:626-642. DOI: 10.1108/SCM-09-2013-0346

[18] Brown A, Badurdeen F. Increased supply chain resilience through consideration of disruption impact severity in the supplier segmentation process. In: IIE Annual Conference; December 2015; Parramatta. Gogia: Institute of Industrial and Systems Engineers (IISE); 2015. p. 1815

[19] Sugimori Y, Kusunoki K, Cho F, Uchikawa S. Toyota production system and kanban system materialization of just-in-time and respect-for-human system. The International Journal of Production Research. 1977;**15**: 553-564. DOI: 10.1080/002075477089 43149

[20] Womack JP, Jones DT, Roos D. The Machine That Changed the World. New York: Rawson Associates; 1990

[21] Toyota OT. Production System: Beyond Large-Scale Production. Portland: Productivity Press; 1988. DOI: 10.4324/9780429273018

[22] Franchetti M, Bedal K, Ulloa J, Grodek S. Lean and green: Industrial engineering methods are natural stepping stones to green engineering. Industrial Engineer. 2009;**41**:24-30

[23] Kalyar MN, Shafique I, Abid A. Role of lean manufacturing and environmental management practices in eliciting environmental and financial performance: The contingent effect of institutional pressures. Environmental Science and Pollution Research. 2019;**26**: 24967-24978. DOI: 10.1007/s11356-019-05729-3

[24] Yu W, Chavez R, Feng M, Wong CY, Fynes B. Green human resource management and environmental cooperation: An ability-motivation-opportunity and contingency perspective. International Journal of Production Economics. 2020;**219**: 224-235. DOI: 10.1016/j.ijpe.2019.06.013

[25] Sanders A, Elangeswaran C, Wulfsberg JP. Industry 4.0 implies lean manufacturing: Research activities in industry 4.0 function as enablers for lean manufacturing. Journal of Industrial Engineering and Management (JIEM). 2016;**9**:811-833. DOI: 10.3926/jiem.1940

[26] Carvalho H, Maleki M, Cruz-Machado V. The links between supply chain disturbances and resilience strategies. International Journal of Agile Systems and Management. 2012;**5**: 203-234. DOI: 10.1504/IJASM.2012.047653

[27] Azadegan A, Patel PC, Zangoueinezhad A, Linderman K. The effect of environmental complexity and environmental dynamism on lean practices. Journal of Operations

Management. 2013;**31**:193-212. DOI: 10.1016/j.jom.2013.03.002

[28] Laasch O, Gherardi S. Delineating and reconnecting responsible management, learning, and education (RMLE): A research agenda through a social practices lens. In: Academy of Management Annual Meeting; August 2019; Boston, New York, USA: Academy of Management (AOM); 2019

[29] Lilien L, Gupta A, Yang Z. Opportunistic resource utilization networks—A new paradigm for specialized ad hoc networks. Computers & Electrical Engineering. 2010;**36**: 328-340. DOI: 10.1016/j.compeleceng.2009.03.010

[30] Bruun P, Mefford RN. Lean production and the Internet. International Journal of Production Economics. 2004;**89**:247-260. DOI: 10.1016/j.ijpe.2003.10.007

[31] Bon AT, Kee TS. Implementation of Lean manufacturing for productivity improvement in Malaysia. In: International Conference on Industrial Engineering and Operations Management (IEOM); March 2015; Dubai. New York: IEEE; 2015. pp. 1-6

[32] Sabadka D. Innovation lean principles in automotive green manufacturing. Acta Logistica. 2014;**1**:23-27

[33] Holden RJ. Lean thinking in emergency departments: A critical review. Annals of Emergency Medicine. 2011;**57**:265-278. DOI: 10.1016/j.annemergmed.2010.08.001

[34] Wilson G. Six Sigma and the Product Development Cycle. London: Routledge; 2005. DOI: 10.4324/9780080493084

[35] Das K. Integrating resilience in a supply chain planning model. International Journal of Quality & Reliability Management. 2018;**35**: 570-595. DOI: 10.1108/IJQRM-08-2016-0136

[36] Golini R, Kalchschmidt M. Managing inventories in global sourcing contexts: A contingency perspective. International Journal of Production Economics. 2015; **165**:64-78. DOI: 10.1016/j.ijpe.2015.03.022

[37] Ugochukwu P, Engström J, Langstrand J. Lean in the supply chain: A literature review. Management and Production Engineering Review. 2012;**3**: 87-96

[38] Pakdil F, Leonard KM. Implementing and sustaining lean processes: The dilemma of societal culture effects. International Journal of Production Research. 2017;**55**:700-717. DOI: 10.1080/00207543.2016.1200761

[39] Azevedo SG, Carvalho H, Cruz-Machado V. LARG index: A benchmarking tool for improving the leanness, agility, resilience and greenness of the automotive supply chain. Benchmarking: An International Journal. 2016;**23**:1472-1499. DOI: 10.1108/BIJ-07-2014-0072

[40] Guo S, Li T, Zhou K. An improved case retrieval method for the production manufacturing process of aluminum electrolysis. In: International Conference on Industrial Informatics-Computing Technology, Intelligent Technology, Industrial Information Integration (ICIICII); December 2017; China. New York: IEEE; 2017. pp. 16-20

[41] Narasimhan R, Swink M, Kim SW. Disentangling leanness and agility: An empirical investigation. Journal of Operations Management. 2006;**24**: 440-457. DOI: 10.1016/j.jom.2005.11.011

[42] Scarlat RO, Cisneros AT, Koutchesfahani T, Hong R, Peterson PF. Preliminary safety analysis of a PBMR supplying process heat to a co-located ethylene production plant. Nuclear Engineering and Design. 2012;**251**:53-59. DOI: 10.1016/j.nucengdes.2011.10.069

[43] Charalambous CP. Surgical Audit. In: Charalambos PC, editor. Career Skills for Surgeons. Cham: Springer; 2017. pp. 197-211

[44] Garza-Reyes JA. A systematic approach to diagnose the current status of quality management systems and business processes. Business Process Management Journal. 2018;**24**:216-233. DOI: 10.1108/BPMJ-12-2016-0248

[45] Bhupendra KV, Sangle S. Pollution prevention strategy: A study of Indian firms. Journal of Cleaner Production. 2016;**133**:795-802. DOI: 10.1016/j.jclepro.2016.05.169

[46] Shohihah I, Djamhuri A, Purwanti L. Determinants of internal audit effectiveness and implication on corruption prevention in the religious ministry. Wacana Journal of Social and Humanity Studies. 2018;**21**

[47] de Freitas JG, Costa HG, Ferraz FT. Impacts of Lean Six Sigma over organizational sustainability: A survey study. Journal of Cleaner roduction. 2017;**156**:262-275. DOI: 10.1016/j.jclepro.2017.04.054

[48] Leong WD, Lam HL, Ng WPQ, Lim CH, Tan CP, Ponnambalam SG. Lean and green manufacturing—A review on its applications and impacts. Process Integration and Optimization for Sustainability. 2019;**3**:5-23. DOI: 10.1007/s41660-019-00082-x

[49] Stephenson M, Mcarthur A, Giles K, Lockwood C, Aromataris E, Pearson A. Prevention of falls in acute hospital settings: A multi-site audit and best practice implementation project. International Journal for Quality in Health Care. 2016;**28**:92-98. DOI: 10.1093/intqhc/mzv113

[50] Dieste M, Panizzolo R. The effect of lean practices on environmental performance: An empirical study. In: Alves AC, Kahlen FJ, Flumerfelt S, Siriban-Manalang AB, editors. Lean Engineering for Global Development. Cham: Springer; 2019. pp. 225-258. DOI: 10.1007/978-3-030-13515-7_8

[51] Franklin S. Sexism as a means of reproduction: Some reflections on the politics of academic practice. New Formations. 2015;**86**:14-33. DOI: 10.3898/NEWF.86.01.2015

[52] Yushak MS, Dollah R, Bakar NA. The adoption of lean principles to reduce resistance to change in transforming a shipyard. Journal of Business Management and Accounting. 2016;**6**:105-121

[53] Feld WM. Lean Manufacturing: Tools, Techniques, and How to Use Them. Boca Raton: CRC Press; 2000. DOI: 10.1201/9781420025538

[54] Price K, Weaver J, Tribbett SB, Carpenter C. Using the lean process to achieve skin-to-skin after cesarean births. Journal of Obstetric, Gynecologic, & Neonatal Nursing. 2015;**44**:S16-S17. DOI: 10.1111/1552-6909.12682

[55] Ferri LM, Pedrini M. Socially and environmentally responsible purchasing: Comparing the impacts on buying firm's financial performance, competitiveness and risk. Journal of Cleaner Production. 2018;**174**:880-888. DOI: 10.1016/j.jclepro.2017.11.035

[56] Sahoo S. Assessing lean implementation and benefits within

Indian automotive component manufacturing SMEs. Benchmarking: An International Journal. 2020;**27**: 1042-1084. DOI: 10.1108/BIJ-07-2019-0299

[57] Gonzalez-Padron TL. Ethics in the supply chain: Follow-up processes to audit results. Journal of Marketing Channels. 2016;**23**:22-33. DOI: 10.1080/1046669X.2016.1147341

[58] Demartini C, Trucco S. Integrated Reporting and Audit Quality. Cham: Springer; 2017

[59] Setyaningrum D, Kuntadi C. The effects of competence, independence, audit work, and communication on the effectiveness of internal audit. Journal of Economics, Business, & Accountancy Ventura. 2019;**22**:39-47. DOI: 10.14414/jebav.v22i1.879

[60] de Campos JGF, de Mello AM. Transaction costs in environmental purchasing: Analysis through two case studies. Journal of Operations and Supply Chain Management. 2017;**10**: 87-102. DOI: 10.12660/joscmv10n1p87-102

[61] Akhavan RM, Beckmann M. A configuration of sustainable sourcing and supply management strategies. Journal of Purchasing and Supply Management. 2017;**23**:137-151. DOI: 10.1016/j.pursup.2016.07.006

[62] Cagliano R, Caniato F, Spina G. The linkage between supply chain integration and manufacturing improvement programmes. International Journal of Operations & Production Management. 2006;**26**:282-299. DOI: 10.1108/01443570610646201

[63] Wagner B, Svensson G. Sustainable supply chain practices: Research propositions for the future. International Journal of Logistics Economics and Globalisation. 2010;**2**:176-186. DOI: 10.1504/IJLEG.2010.032432

[64] van Weele A, van Tubergen K. Responsible purchasing: Moving from compliance to value creation in supplier relationships. In: Bouchery Y, Corbett CJ, Fransoo JC, Tan T, editors. Sustainable Supply Chains. Cham: Spriger; 2017. pp. 257-278

[65] Scholten K, Scott PS, Fynes B. Mitigation processes–antecedents for building supply chain resilience. Supply Chain Management: An International Journal. 2014;**19**:211-228. DOI: 10.1108/SCM-06-2013-0191

[66] Tieman M. Halal risk management: Combining robustness and resilience. Journal of Islamic Marketing. 2017;**8**: 461-475. DOI: 10.1108/JIMA-06-2015-0041

[67] Wang Z, Ye F, Tan KH. Effects of managerial ties and trust on supply chain information sharing and supplier opportunism. International Journal of Production Research. 2014;**52**: 7046-7061. DOI: 10.1080/00207543.2014.932931

[68] Chowdhury MMH, Quaddus M. Supply chain readiness, response and recovery for resilience. Supply Chain Management: An International Journal. 2016;**21**:709-731. DOI: 10.1108/SCM-12-2015-0463

[69] Sharma SK, Bhat A. An empirical investigation of the contribution of supply chain design characteristics on supply chain risks in Indian automobile industry. International Journal of Business Continuity and Risk Management. 2012;**3**:117-135. DOI: 10.1504/IJBCRM.2012.047063

[70] Hayes AF. Beyond Baron and Kenny: Statistical mediation analysis in the new

millennium. Communication Monographs. 2009;**76**:408-420. DOI: 10.1080/03637750903310360

[71] Hasan B, Ali J. An empirical examination of factors affecting group effectiveness in information systems projects. Decision Sciences Journal of Innovative Education. 2007;**5**:229-243. DOI: 10.1111/j.1540-4609.2007.00139.x

[72] Hair JF Jr, Hult GTM, Ringle C, Sarstedt M. A Primer on Partial Least Squares Structural Equation Modeling (PLS-SEM). 2nd ed. UK: Sage publications; 2016

[73] Fornell C, Larcker DF. Evaluating structural equation models with unobservable variables and measurement error. Journal of Marketing Research. 1981;**18**:39-50. DOI: 10.1177%2F002224378101800104

[74] Vijayan J, Radharamanant T, Sridharant R. Sea lion with enhanced exploration phase for optimization of polynomial fitness with SEM in lean technology. Evolutionary Intelligence. 2020:1-18. DOI: 10.1007/s12065-020-00370-3

[75] Minh KS, Zailani S, Iranmanesh M, Heidari S. Do lean manufacturing practices have negative impact on job satisfaction? International Journal of Lean Six Sigma. 2019;**10**:257-274. DOI: 10.1108/IJLSS-11-2016-0072

[76] El-Rajabi MT, Gunasekaran A. The accuracy of earnings forecasts disclosed in the prospectuses of newly formed public companies in Jordan. Managerial Auditing Journal. 2006;**21**:117-131. DOI: 10.1108/02686900610639275

[77] Yadlapalli A, Rahman S, Gunasekaran A. Socially responsible governance mechanisms for manufacturing firms in apparel supply chains. International Journal of Production Economics. 2018;**196**: 135-149. DOI: 10.1016/j.ijpe.2017.11.016

[78] Bahr W, Sweeney E. Environmental sustainability in the follow-up and evaluation stage of logistics services purchasing: Perspectives from UK shippers and 3PLs. Sustainability. 2019; **11**:2460. DOI: 10.3390/su11092460

Chapter 9

Production Systems Performance Optimization through Human/ Machine Collaboration

Paul-Eric Dossou, Valentin Verdier and Alan Ogor

Abstract

The growth of enterprises is a constant source of research and development of new technologies. Indeed, to stand out from the competition and optimize their production, companies are moving toward the centralization of information and the implementation of machines. This dynamic requires a significant investment in terms of organization and research. Industry 4.0 is therefore at the heart of this reflection, as shown in the literature. It brings together many technologies, such as Artificial Intelligence (AI), the Internet of Things (IoT), and Big Data. This chapter focuses on company performance optimization through a sustainable Industry 4.0 framework involving methodologies such as lean manufacturing and DMAIC, new technologies as robotics, in addition to social, societal, and environmental transformations. This chapter will present robotic displacement solutions adapted to the industrial environment for improving production systems performance. Solutions for human-machine interaction problems such as human-machine interface or flexibility 4.0 will be shown.

Keywords: Industry 4.0, performance optimization, robotics, artificial intelligence, big data, human-machine collaboration, internet of things (IoTs)

1. Introduction

Faced with increasing competition, companies must develop new ways of optimizing their production, and this involves the use of new technologies such as robotics, artificial intelligence, internet of things, big data analytics. Even if these technology implementations in large companies have shown their efficiency for increasing the company supply chain performance, most SMEs are not willing to exploit them. Some of the reasons for these breaks are the technologies costs, human fear, employees' knowledge or education on technologies, and resistance to change. For instance, the problem of artificial intelligence or robot acceptability in companies could be pointed out.

The robotic implementation requires the writing of very precise specifications to answer the problems of the company. Robotic solutions are not well known by all companies, and some of them have difficulty visualizing the benefits of this technology. One of the major obstacles is the lack of data on the capabilities of robots to perform generic tasks in certain industrial fields.

Industry 4.0 is expanding with new technology enhancements. Numerous Industry 4.0 concept frameworks exist in the literature such as presented in [1]. The digital and technological transformation of the company is based on dimensions such as a horizontal integration, used to transform the physical production system (robot, internet of things, cyber-physical systems) and processes, or a vertical integration for structuring, and managing data and decisions that would be taken for increasing the company performance. Despite the positive impact of these concepts on the company performance, the integration of robotics, IoT, or artificial intelligence in SMEs transformation is confidential in France. However, technologies such as autonomous guided vehicles (AIV) could be used to transport loads in their production systems or within their warehouses, and cobots to perform daily tasks on fixed stations. Indeed, these frameworks do not obtain the membership of SMEs and it is necessary to find solutions to transform them technologically, digitally, and to optimize them. This chapter presents a framework that exploits sustainability as the kernel of the transformation in order to take into account social, societal, and environmental aspects, combined with new technologies for defining levers of transformation and increasing the company performance. The main objective of the new framework is to transform digitally and sustainably the SMEs for increasing their performance by using new technologies for aiding operators in their daily tasks and facilitating operational information management (between operators, machines, robots, and the information system).

This chapter focuses on solutions of human/machine collaboration for optimizing the company production system. It describes new Industry 4.0 concepts for improving the production processes through the implementation of new technologies such as AIV, cobots, IoT, information systems, and decision-aided tool. These solutions will contribute to the company's digital transformation. The objective of this chapter is to show different solutions, allowing the improvement of logistics within the framework of Industry 4.0.

After a literature review of organizational methodologies, Industry 4.0, robotic collaboration, and big data analytics, the sustainable Industry 4.0 framework will be presented, and the associated human/machine collaboration concepts will be shown. Use cases based on an electronics card company will be exposed.

2. Literature review

The digital transformation for increasing the company performance requires the focus on theories and concepts that could be exploited for improving the enterprise. Indeed, organizational and management methodologies are essential, but Industry 4.0 concepts, robotic collaboration concepts, and big data analytics could also be used in this transformation. Some of these theories and concepts are presented in the following part in order to choose those that are adapted to the sustainable Industry 4.0 framework and the intelligent tool for supporting the company transformation.

2.1 Organizational methodologies

The improvement of the company production system requires to exploit the adequate methodology. Numerous methodologies are used in companies for increasing their performance such as GRAI Methodology [2], CIMOSA [3], or PERA [4] for structuring the global company, lean manufacturing, DMAIC (Define, Measure,

Analyze, Improve, Control) method, design of experiments for focusing on the production system, and solving specific problems. The performance criteria mostly used are quality, cost, and delivery time (QCD).

Based on the theory of systems, GRAI Methodology, contrary to CIMOSA (technological aspects) and PERA (human aspects), focuses on all the company aspects: decisional, informational, and physical systems. Five models (physical, functional, process, informational, and decisional) have to be used for transforming a company and improving its performance. This methodology is adapted to the objective to integrate Industry 4.0 concepts in SMEs but a zoom on the physical system is necessary to increase the efficiency of the company transformation. Indeed, lean manufacturing methodology is the most exploited because of its objective to structure the supply chain organization around customer demand satisfaction in terms of quality, cost, and delivery time.

The concept of lean manufacturing has been firstly described in [5] and applied in Toyota Company. Lean manufacturing is a methodology used for reducing seven wastes such as transportation, overproduction, motion, waiting, defects, inventory, over-processing. Lean principles allow optimizing the company efficiency. As exposed in [6], "sustainable manufacturing and lean practices focus on creating an intelligent network system that improves productivity, quality, and customer orientation, while eliminating waste." Many tools could be used in the frame of lean manufacturing methodology implementation such as Value Stream Mapping (VSM), Single Minute Exchange of Die (SMED), Failure Mode Effects Analysis (FMEA), 5s, Total Productive Maintenance (TPM), Kaizen, Kanban.

As explained in [7] lean manufacturing not only contributes to optimize added value for satisfying customer expectations but also increases environmental benefits. Indeed, SMEs could not improve their performance by ignoring the actual environmental context. In addition, in the use of lean manufacturing, the cadence of the production line that is called takt time could be considered by mistake (bad application of lean concepts) as nonsocial and nonsocietal. For instance, if the takt time is not well defined, it could create stress for operators because of their desire to succeed. Indeed, the positive impact is defined in the company through the elimination of waste time and non-added value, giving operators more value time for well finishing their tasks. The use of lean tools such as SMED, for reducing the external operations, allows to implement tools near machines optimizing by this organization the ergonomics and the useless moving.

This continuous improvement method integrates physical and informational flows in an industry with aiming at the identification and elimination of wastages that affect lead time, material cost, and quality of products [8, 9]. But for a SME the digital transformation of its processes needs to solve specific problems (use cases) for ensuring the feasibility and efficiency of solutions that will be implemented. Both DMAIC and DOE are able to manage these specific cases (use cases).

Six sigma is a method based on DMAIC (Define, Measure, Analyze, Improve, Control) principles. Six sigma allows to improve the quality of the production system and not only the product quality. DMAIC is used as a problem-solving method for increasing the quality level in the company.

Then, a combination of GRAI methodology, lean manufacturing DMAIC, and DOE methods will allow to define an efficient and well-adapted framework for Industry 4.0 concepts implementation in SMEs. The following part details the concepts of Industry 4.0 and the necessity to integrate sustainability in the digital transformation approach.

2.2 Industry 4.0

Industry 4.0 concepts use a multitude of technologies to improve company performance. They are involved in logistics, production, data management, and communication between systems. These technologies meet the modernization needs of businesses. Several technologies and tools must be taken into account to integrate the concepts of the industry of the future such as the verticality of production systems, the horizontality of the integration of production chains, the optimization of the value chain, and the use of disruptive technologies. These technologies are cyber-physical systems (CPS), internet of things (IoTs), human/machine interface (HMI), cloud computing, big data, artificial intelligence, advanced robotics, immersive (augmented or virtual) reality, simulation, and cybersecurity [1]. All of these technologies have enabled great advances in the company's digital transformation. For instance, a usual application of these technologies could consist in the exploitation of sensors for collecting information on production lines, big data system for capitalizing these data in a server for analyzing them, and for taking good decisions. Then, according to the production processes and by using these data, operators could interact in the production environment with collaborative or mobile robots. Cyber-physical system stations could be deployed to control all the production systems by integrating programmable logic controllers with different inputs and outputs and various communication modules such as IO-Link modules or Ethernet interfaces.

As presented in [10, 11], based on lean manufacturing, Industry 4.0 could make the company "processes smart by enabling digitalization, modern information-sharing technologies, smart machines, which, in amalgamation, help in fast, effective, and efficient decision-making".

2.2.1 Robotics in Industry 4.0 concepts

Autonomous intelligent vehicles (AIV) are used in warehouses for transporting products. In addition to problems of flow management and optimization, specific problems could be presented such as the management of the robot autonomy or prioritization. They could be exploited for transporting raw materials or final products from production lines to storage and vice versa. Indeed, these mobile robots are equipped with internal tracking and embedded system. They are able to move in warehouses to carry stocks of products. The robots transport their material to the exact location at a specific time [12]. They are able to move in a fleet and to recognize each other [13]. Moreover, they are not separated from traditional operators and move in a common environment. They have a camera and/or laser system to prevent possible collisions. Then, the problem of safety could be pointed out and different safety systems could be integrated into the robot for insuring the production system efficiency. If the robots detect a force, they could stop and activate their safety. They are also able to open doors that are connected to cyber-physical systems. Thanks to this, logistics are smoother, and productivity is increased. All these transport times, which are no longer provided by man, allow him to work on other issues. Development robots allow workers to concentrate on creativity, productivity, and other dynamic processes, which lay the basis for growth and prosperity [12].

Cobots are collaborative robots able to interact with humans. Cobots are used to support operators on repetitive or specific tasks. In [14], the top-3 reasons to choose to implement cobots (operational efficiency, innovation, and ergonomics) have been repeated and the automation of production lines with cobots has been promoted with the use of lean manufacturing methods. The cobots are affiliated with the methods of Lean Manufacturing as they promote the automation of production lines [14].

Cobots have cameras to effectively visualize their environment and adapt accordingly. They are able to recognize and identify shapes, bar codes, QR codes or even colors. Some of them are used for quality control thanks to their high precision. Vision has become the key to Industry 4.0. Cobots are lightweight and easy to configure, unlike conventional robots [12]. Cobots are less costly than their counterparts and can yield more stable effects [12]. On top of that, they have a safety system that physically blocks them when they detect a collision. They are able to switch from a collaborative mode to a cooperative mode. In addition, cobots can work with each other. They are able to communicate *via* the network dedicated to them.

2.2.2 Internet of things

Industry 4.0 is a concept-driven by IoT, allowing interconnection between objects, equipment, and computers. Robots can be controlled remotely by a central computer using logical programming. Human intervention is then no longer necessary. It is only used for maintenance or recalibration. The classic IoT also includes the internet of robotic things (IoRT). The robots are also equipped with inputs and outputs to control external systems. The data and values used by the robots *via* their sensors are stored in databases in real-time. They can then be operated by external systems. The combination of local computational power and IoT has turned ordinary sensors into intelligent sensors such that the measured data are calculated locally in a sensor module in a complex manner [15]. Robotics and the internet of things have been motivated by several ambitions that are all interconnected. IoT focuses on ubiquitous sensing, control, and recording services, while robotic societies concentrate on development, engagement, and autonomous behavior [12]. The combination of the two technologies makes it possible to limit errors on production lines and increase their efficiency.

All the sensors (cameras, force sensors, etc.) present on the robots allow the inspection to be carried out and participate in quality controls. The IoT is revolutionizing not only production methods but also maintenance strategies [16]. They must be able to exploit robot data in order to prevent possible problems [16]. New skills are expected for operators in the industry of the future. This concept of Operator 4.0 aims to present the transition of the Human-CPS interaction toward a Human-Automate symbiosis for a balance within the production chain [16]. IoT focuses on services promoting pervasive sensing, surveillance, and recording and the emphasis on processing, engagement, and independent activity in robotic societies [17].

As presented in [18–20], IoT "refers to intelligent physical and virtual objects which are integrated in a global (or local company) network, which have identities, and which communicate between themselves or with other internet-enabled devices."

In [21], IoT is defined as a technological concept that utilizes sensors, microcontrollers, and other embedded terminal devices through which real-time data can be collected from manufacturing machinery and facilities.

2.2.3 3D printing

3D printing is an important technology in the concept of Industry 4.0. It is used for rapid prototyping of mechanical parts. The accuracy and quality of the prints are high enough to make tools for robotics. It is possible to produce different parts whether they are rigid (support) or flexible to adapt to needs [17]. In particular, companies are developing grippers for their robot arms using this technology. Robotic-enabled 3D printing represents a more sustainable manufacturing method [12]. Thanks to 3D printing, companies are making reliable mechanical implementations to deploy new use cases. The flexibility of this technology encourages them to constantly develop their robotic solutions.

2.2.4 Cyber-physical systems

Robotics allows better optimization of variable productions and therefore better economic performance. Automatons and computers allow robots to evolve and be smarter. Application flexibility allows computers to optimize production according to schedule demand or markets [12]. CPS is defined in [22] as a "system that integrates computation, communication, and control." It uses sensors for obtaining data, which will be capitalized and analyzed with computing devices and a decision-aided system for taking good decisions concerning the physical system. CPS contributes to improve productivity by remotely controlling physical machinesinputs and outputs. This concept is used to qualify sensors in production lines.

CPS is described in [23, 24] as physical and engineered systems whose operations are monitored, controlled, coordinated, and integrated by a computing and communicating core. The concept of a cyber-physical system is presented in [25] as based on emerging technologies such as additive manufacturing, advanced robotics, augmented and virtual reality, big data, cloud computing, and the internet of things.

As explained in [26], lean manufacturing and Industry 4.0 could be combined for transforming a manufacturing system into a Cyber-Physical Production system (CPPS) with advanced productivity capabilities.

As noted in [27, 28], the "successful integration of SMEs into Industry 4.0 is a relevant social challenge and thus, specific policies and programs should be designed accordingly.

2.2.5 Big data analytics

With the implementation of the CPS, big data are obtained from the physical and informational systems and need to be analyzed for taking good decisions in the company. The objective is to increase the company's performance.

Big data correspond to the collection of massive data from various sources. These data are structured, non-structured, or semi-structured but must be analyzed and exploited to taking decisions. A typology of data sources has been proposed in [29]:

- Manufacturing resource data including real-time performance data of smart devices, collected through the industrial Internet of Things and production data

- Manufacturing systems and computer data aid data (product design, order configuration, material allocation, production planning, business management, etc.)

- Internet data issued from open Web sites (social services sites, e-commerce platforms, social networking platforms).

Seven features have been defined in [30] for characterizing big data: volume, variety, velocity, veracity, value, variability, and volatility. As explained in [31] the level of production standardization, operation network, and service precision could be substantially revamped by using big data analytics. In industrial and manufacturing systems, big data promote enterprises to accurately perceive changes in the system and facilitate scientific analysis and decision making for optimizing the production process, reducing cost, and improving operational efficiency [32]. Two main paradigms could be used for big data analytics:

- Model-driven approaches focus on how the physical system works, rely on a deep understanding of the system or process, and can benefit from scientifically established relationships [33]

- Data-driven approaches are based on the correlation between system status parameters and the target estimated by carious artificial intelligent models [34].

These data contribute to the elaboration and the efficiency of an intelligent manufacturing system in a company. The intelligence of the production systems is based on their ability to accumulate and analyze big data [34]. This analysis can improve customer service, enhance product quality, and create more value in the enterprise as expected by SMEs. Indeed, technological problems have to be solved in this case such as data quality management, data security and privacy protection, the generality of the conceptual framework in actual production, data integration processing in industrial manufacturing systems, and accessing primary manufacturing data. Then, the intelligent system (including the big data analytics) that will be proposed needs to integrate these aspects.

All the concepts of Industry 4.0 that have been presented above are required for digitally transforming the company but their efficient utilization in SMEs needs to focus on the brakes on Industry 4.0 implementation in SMEs and to find levers for accelerating their use in the SME performance improvement. Indeed, sustainability, including social and societal dimensions such as the place of the human in the future production process (human/robot collaboration), but also environmental demands (people expectations, the earth preservation, and official rules), appears as the parameter to integrate for obtaining the membership to Industry 4.0 philosophy.

2.3 The context of the robotic collaboration

Robots have revolutionized the manufacturing process of companies. They have enhanced the automation of systems and the execution of repetitive tasks at low prices [12]. The potential of robots is great, and the resulting applications are numerous. In addition, some robots use AI to improve their performance. They are able to learn from their environment and from their experience. Several working methods have been established so that human and machine can collaborate.

Human-robot collaborative systems are presented in [35] as a solution with a shared workspace, which mixes the dexterity and cognitive faculties of human operators and the accuracy, in addition to the repeatability skills of robots.

The coexisting mode results in the distinct separation of workspaces between human and machine, no interaction is possible in this configuration. The advantage is that the robots can operate in difficult conditions for humans (e.g., high temperature, risk of intoxication.) The cooperation mode is manifested by the work of human and machine in the same space of work on different objects or tasks. Finally, the collaborative mode results in the simultaneous work of human and machine on common objects or tasks.

Unlike operators, robots are not distracted, and they work without interruption and have a low error rate thanks to their precision and repeatability. Robots are able to predict their maintenance. To do this, they collect data throughout the production lines.

If robots are destined to perform fast and dangerous gestures, safety zones are set up to limit access. Operators are not left out of this technology, because they are able to control them *via* portable systems such as computers, tablets, or even phones. They thus ensure the supervision of the robots. These increasingly intelligent robots, in cases where human intervention is difficult, may be able to make decisions based on their visions, productions, or knowledge of the state of the production line.

A detailed risks analysis has to be done by exploiting the safety guidelines and standard documents such as:

- The type-A standard ISO 12100 focused on the machinery risk assessment [36]

- The type-C standards ISO 10218 parts 1 and 2 for the general safety requirements for industrial robots and integrated robots systems [37]

- The technical specification ISO TS 15066 for the safety requirements destined to collaborative operations [38]

- The technical report ISO TR 20218-1 for the main safety measures for the design and integration of end-effectors used robot systems and collaborative operations [39].

Contrary to the classical robot, collaborative robots (cobots) are contained with intuitive interfaces that support human operators in the physical workload of manufacturing tasks [40]. In addition to the safety required for ensuring the good production and the optimization of the manufacturing system, the human-cobot collaboration needs the elaboration of an interface

- For making robots, cobots, and IoTs managed by the operators without additional knowledge in robots programming or IoT utilization,

- and for facilitating the operator decision-making.

They are no barriers between cobots and human operators, but safety mechanisms to prevent harming humans are endowed [41]. They also provide solutions to ergonomics problems, by being alternative solutions to awkward postures and repetitive movements [42].

Robot programming also needs the user to be familiar, but operators in SMEs have no knowledge about the programing language. However, they have to be informed about the physical and computational action the robot can carry out [43]. Then, a new programming environment called CAPIRCI has been developed. It allows non-technical users to create typical programs executable by COBOTTA, the collaborative robot by DENSO WAVE Ltd.

This chapter proposes to exploit the idea of this programing interface, for developing an interface that aims for operators to manage with button the new technology tools integrated in the production manufacturing such as robots, cobots, mobile robots, IoTs, and also to take good decisions.

Social, societal and environmental aspects have been integrated in the Industry 4.0 concepts implementation and allow to obtain a human-centered manufacturing, more resilient and sustainable, that has been defined by the European commission as the Industry 5.0.

The concepts and methodology developed in this chapter are based on this objective. The idea in this c contrary to the proposition presented in [44] as the "automation of complex business and production processes with the help of artificial intelligence (AI), while employees undertake monitoring activities instead of being actively involved in those processes" is to let the operators in processes at the center of the digital transformation.

3. Concepts and methodology

The Industry 4.0 concept implementation in SMEs requires the use of sustainability as the kernel of the company's digital transformation. This c proposes the use of GRAI methodology in combination with lean manufacturing, DMAIC, and Design of Experiments for elaborating a sustainable framework for this transformation in order to improve the company performance [45]. The framework allows to improve the company supply chain through three axes (**Figure 1**).

- The physical transformation is destined to transform the SME by implementing lean manufacturing concepts but also by using DMAIC and Design of Experiments methods for solving use cases (problems) in the internal and external logistics process of the company. The integration of robots, cobots, mobile robots, IoTs, and other tools is realized at this level.

- The decisional transformation is used for structuring the company decisions in short, middle, and long terms by exploiting GRAI methodology.

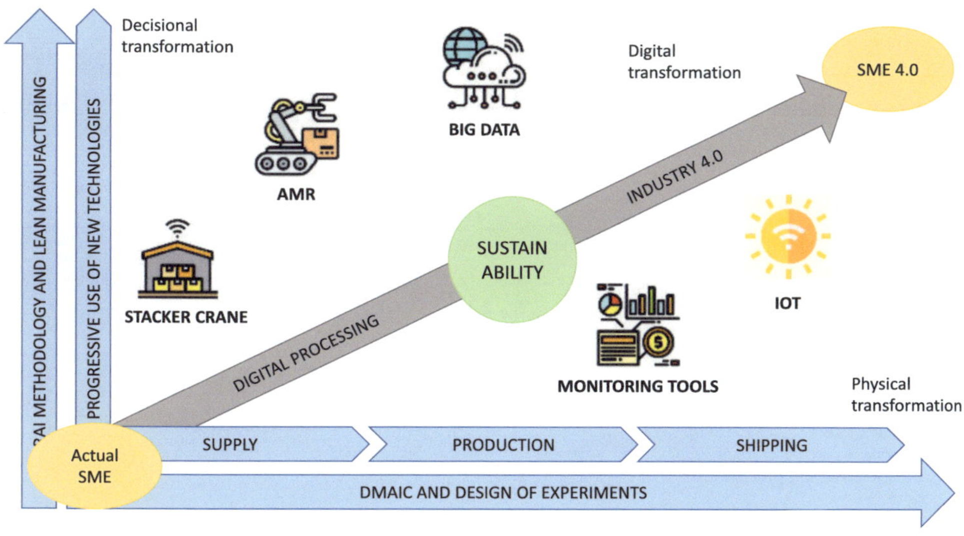

Figure 1.
Framework for sustainable Industry 4.0 concept implementation.

- And the informational transformation involving the integration of an information system such as ERP, MES, WMS in the company for improving its performance, but also the exploitation of an intelligent manufacturing system including the decision aided module, the human-machine interface, and the cyber-physical system adapted to the company being transformed.

The sustainable digital transformation is supported by intelligent manufacturing and logistics human-machine collaboration (HMC) system (**Figure 2**). The objective is to facilitate the collaboration between the physical new technologies (robots, cobots, mobile robots, IoTs), the information system, and the operators but also contribute to the production processes optimization. It will allow the operators to be at the center of the production process in terms of ergonomics, production management, and flexibility.

The software tool is composed of the following:

- An information system interface that manages data between the company information system, the production managers, the production system, and the operators. Information will come from the production system through the cyber-physical system containing the IoTs and will be integrated into the information system. And in the other direction, information and production orders and constraints will come from the information system for the manufacturing system (operators, machines, IoTs).

- A management module that contains big data (reference data, input and output data, and results of a problem or task) and an analytics module.

- A human-machine interface (HMI) allows the operator to manage machines, robots, production tasks, and decisions that he will have to take.

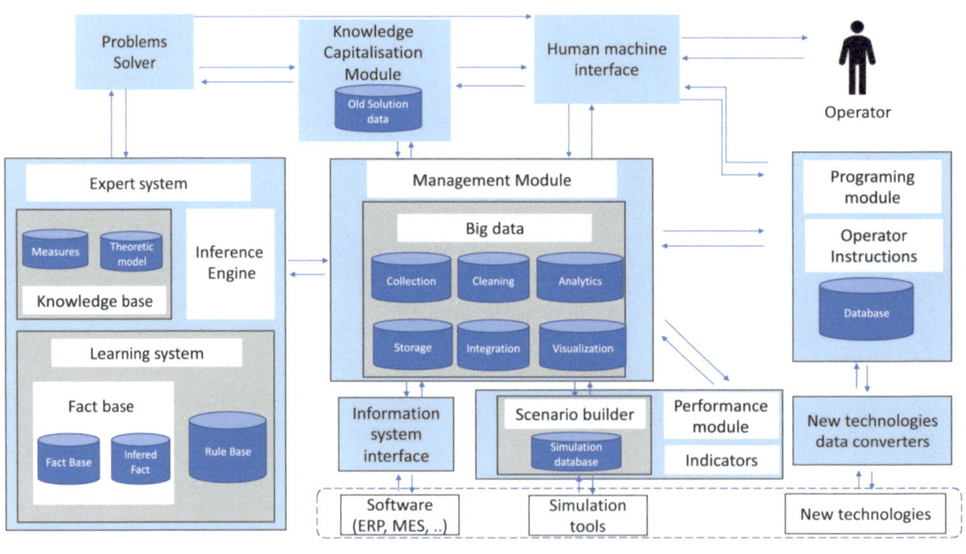

Figure 2.
Architecture of the intelligent manufacturing and logistics HMC system.

- A performance module is a decision-aided module that contains a dashboard for showing the operator, information on the system performance (robot machine, process, and operator), and support him for taking a good decision. This module also contains a digital twin (simulator) for showing the operator the impact of his decision before validation.

- A programming module that allows the acquisition of instructions coming from machines or robot tools (or going to them) that will be exploited by operators.

- An instruction transcriber treats the program or instructions from operators to machines or from machines to operators.

- An expert system that contains a knowledge base, an inference engine, and a learning system that allows to manage the problem to solve (use cases).

- A problem-solving module that is used for transcribing the operator difficulties into an adequate format for being analyzed and solved.

- A capitalization module that is used for recording operator instructions or problem results in order to reuse them for a new use case.

In addition to the framework and the intelligent manufacturing HMC system, a sustainable flexibility 4.0 approach has been defined for optimizing the use of the manufacturing resources (technical and human). The following part is destined to this flexibility.

4. Sustainable flexibility 4.0

4.1 Sustainable flexibility 4.0 tool

The sustainable flexibility 4.0 is based on the use of production management techniques such as scheduling, theory of constraints, operational research algorithms, and artificial intelligence for defining for optimizing the exploitation of cobots, robots, machines, mobile robots, and IoTs, of the logistics and manufacturing system (**Figure 3**). It involves the optimal use of technical resources, the good management of operational tasks by operators, and the optimization of human resources. As in the previous software tool, sustainability is the kernel of flexibility optimization. It implies the flexibility of organization around the operators.

4.2 Sustainable flexibility 4.0 approach

The general approach for using the sustainable flexibility 4.0 in a company is described as follow (**Figure 4**).

- Validation of the company processes optimization with lean manufacturing principles

- Elaboration of the first organization of the production system

- Integration of the first production orders for the resources (human and technical)

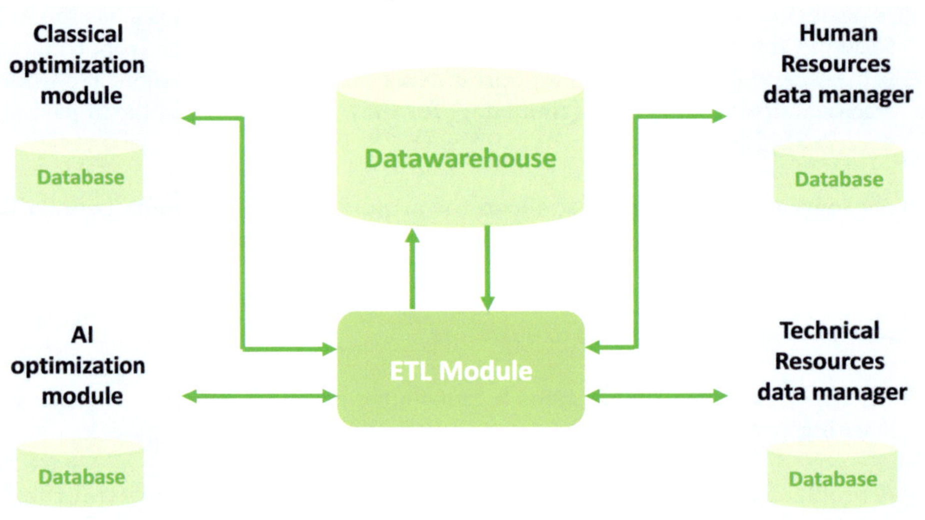

Figure 3.
Architecture of the sustainable flexibility 4.0 tool.

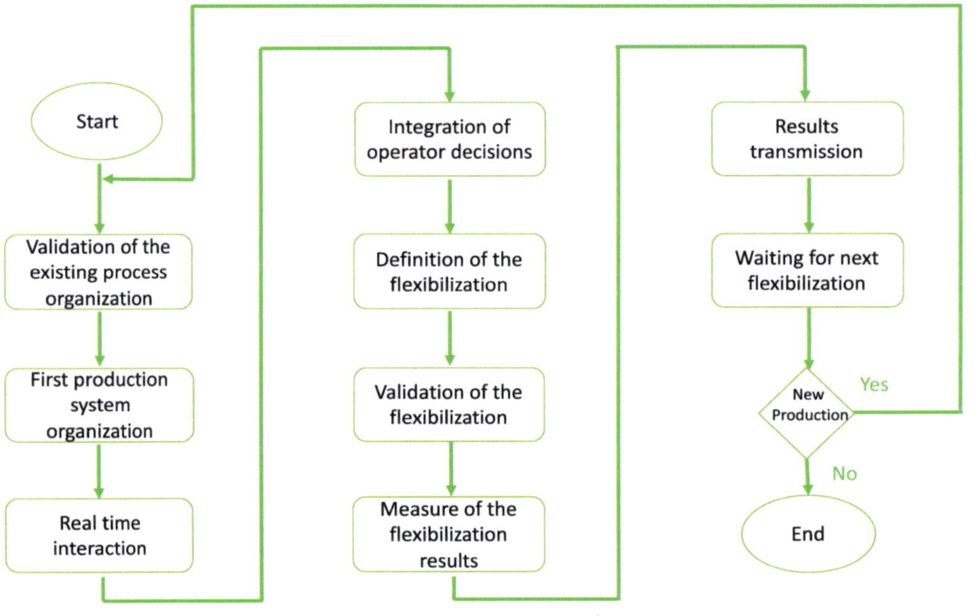

Figure 4.
Sustainable flexibility approach.

- Real-time interaction with the information system for managing the flexibility according to the production manager orders and the customer demand

- Integration of the operator decisions for technical and human flexibilization in collaboration with the intelligent tool

- Definition of the flexibilization to apply
- Validation of the flexibility in real time
- Measure of the flexibilization results
- Transmission through the intelligent module of the results to the operator and the information system (for production managers)
- Waiting for the next flexibilization.

5. Use case

Indeed, the framework has been used with success on SME for defining the steps the company of the digital transformation as presented in [42]. This part presents use cases that have been solved in this company. The company is an electronic card production enterprise and would like to transform digitally itself for being more competitive. The objective of the company was to be able to transfer the cobot from one production line to the other in less than 6mn for increasing the company's global performance. Indeed, the same cobot will produce an electronic card near the operator and at the end of this production will be integrated into the packaging process.

5.1 Cobots utilization optimization

Industry 4.0 concepts allow to review the operating methods of traditional industry. Operators are giving way to robots and cobots which today are mainly developed to perform specific tasks on fixed workstations. **The challenge of Industry 4.0 is to make production more flexible.** It is, therefore, necessary to improve fixed robots by making them mobile and adaptive then, production lines will be more flexible and smarter. The solution was to allow mobile robots to be able to take cobots from a station to another without human intervention to optimize production time. But the validation of the moving has to be done by operators. The development of a fully autonomous production line leads in particular to new problems of stability and precision for cobots. A mobile robotic system including mobile support and a fixed cobot has been elaborated. In the development of this solution, it was necessary to take into account the precision of the robot and thus adapt its movements. It was also important to solve the problem of cobot calibration when it arrives at the new production line. Subsequently, it was essential to ensure stability for the proper functioning of the robot, especially during high-speed actions or moving. It was also important to solve the problem of power (electric and pneumatic). Indeed, a cobot on a fixed station can be easily powered *via* a wired mains socket. For a robot moving, it is not simple. It was necessary to find alternatives that overcome these power supply problems.

For solving the use case, a cobot has been used. All the interconnected sensors allow the cobots to learn about their environment and decide on the tasks to be carried out based on the information received. Parts of the transporting system and connections have been elaborated by exploiting 3D printing as suggested in Industry 4.0 context. An AIV has been used to transport the robotic system from one station to the other. The problem of connection between the robotic system and the mobile robot had to be solved. Indeed, this solution has been implemented in the company and has shown its effectiveness in allowing the transport of cobots to their workstations, eliminating a task that would be repetitive and tiring for operators.

The challenge of the robotic solutions described in this chapter is to be able to use a cobot at the fixed origin on several workstations. The movement of the cobot needs to be deepened. One possibility of movement is the attachment of a cobot on an inter-station trolley. This system allows it to move between different fixed positions. In this chapter, the choice was made on the solution of the inter-station trolley due to its adaptability to the company industrial environment and its easiness to be transported by an AIV.

5.2 Technical solutions for moving the cobot

5.2.1 Proposition 1

The movement of the inter-station trolley is ensured by the AIV. The important aspects to consider are the fixation and the stability of the cobot on its workstation. Jacks represent a possibility of fixing the inter-station trolley to the ground when the latter is placed in front of a workstation. Four jacks are positioned on either side of the carriage. They each have a force of 90 kg. A mechanical part makes up the fixing mechanism. It allows a large contact surface with the ground. In addition, the jacks are actuated by the automaton controlling the entire production chain. The digital outputs control the analog outputs of the system. When the jack system is actuated, the trolley wheels are raised and the trolley is then secured to the ground. The advantage of this solution is that the fixed stations are not mechanically modified. The inter-station trolley is able to ensure its own stability. However, due to the low weight of the trolley, mostly made of aluminum profiles, the stability is not sufficient. The forces applied to the carriage when it is fixed to the ground cause a partial tilting of the structure. In addition, this solution is dependent on the flatness of the ground.

5.2.2 Proposition 2

Another alternative is the implementation of an electromagnets system to ensure the stability of the inter-station trolley. Electromagnets are used to lock access in many establishments. They guarantee high safety due to their holding force of 272 kg in the case studied. The electromagnets are positioned on the inter-station carriage and the metal plates on the fixed station. To ensure the mechanical insertion of the system, 3D printing supports have been created. These are installed on the aluminum profiles making up the workstation and the trolley. To complete the device, an obstacle sensor is installed on the inter-station trolley so that the electromagnets are activated at a short distance from the fixed station. When the electromagnets are activated, they are then brought into contact with the metal plates. The two parts are then locked together and ensure the attachment between the inter-station carriage and the fixed station. The advantages of this solution are the ease of installation and the low cost. The stability is higher than that with the jacks system. However, this device is sensitive to shear forces. This weakness can cause the inter-station cart to stall when the cobot is performing its tasks at the workstation.

5.2.3 Proposition 3

The fastening solution chosen for the company is the Vero-S system from Shunk enterprise. This device is made up of tightening modules and positioning pullers. Each clamping module has a tensile force of 8000 N. The operating principle is as follows: the clamping modules are normally closed by slides. An air pressure of 5.10^5 to 6.10^5 Pa is sent to the clamping modules to release the slides. The positioning zippers then fit into the clamping modules; then the slides close with the air purge. The air supply is controlled by solenoid valves, directly linked to the cyber-physical systems of the production line. To use this system, two clamping modules are positioned on the fixed station and two pull tabs on the inter-station carriage. When the AIV approaches the truck in front of the workstation, the Vero-S system is activated and allows a strong fixation and stability between the two structures. This solution responds to all types of exerted forces. In addition, the Vero-S system allows locking in three dimensions which makes it possible to prevent shifts in flatness between the base of the robot and the fixed station, in particular in the Z direction not allowing it to be checked mechanically. On the other hand, the calibration of the cobot will be able to correct it.

5.3 Power transmission

Once the cobot is locked to the fixed and stable position, it must be powered. For the SME study, the cobot used is a techman TM5 700 developed by Omron, and it can carry maximum payloads of 6 kg for a reach of 0.700 m. The power supply required by the techman is 240 V AC and has a maximum charge current of 14 amps. The cobot is placed on a trolley, the choice of a power supply battery allowing a cobot function is possible but greatly weighs down the trolley and could hinder its movement. In this study, the choice fell on the use of electrical modules (initially a mains socket) arranged on the trolley and on the fixed station using 3D printed support. The brackets have been adjusted so that the electrical modules are connected only when the fastening system is in place and no operator can receive a discharge. The modules located on the fixed station are supplied by the mains. The system works well and allows power to the cobot. To go further the main plugs have been replaced by more advanced electrical modules composed of 19 power supply passages, which allowed to power the cobot but also to supply the cobot. Other components of the truck (example: solenoid valve), have been implemented, in order to transmit information via the inputs and outputs of the cobot.

The cobot is able to use pneumatic grippers, so it is necessary to think of a system similar to the electrical modules that allow air transmission. By using pneumatic modules fixed on the trolley and the stationary station using 3D printed support, they connect when the fastening system is in place.

6. Conclusions

In this chapter, a new framework sustainable Industry 4.0 concepts implementation has been presented. Then, an intelligent logistics and manufacturing human-machine collaboration system has been exposed. An approach for implementing sustainable flexibility 4.0 in SMEs has been explained and the supporting tool shown. A focus has been made in the flexibility technical problems that have been presented through a use case of an electronic card production company. This chapter exposes the interests for SMEs of robotic mobility and human-machine collaboration in a sustainable Industry 4.0 context and the new technological challenges that are issued from flexibility deployment. The adaptability of systems is a major issue in the context of the industry of the future. The concepts and solutions provided in this chapter illustrate new possibilities for logistics and manufacturing optimization. These improvements make the workstations of the production lines autonomous by putting the operator as the operational manager of the workstations (including IoTs, cobot, and mobile robot management). Operators are then less exposed to repetitive and stressful tasks. In addition, this flexibility helps to reduce development costs by increasing the versatility of cobots. Finally, the solutions presented in this chapter contribute to the digitalization of companies and strengthen the field of use of new technologies and humans at the heart of the industry.

Acknowledgements

Icam, site of Grand Paris Sud has contributed actively to this research. A demonstrator including cobots, mobile robots, IoTs, and technical tools has been financed by Icam and is being implemented for realizing the project.

Author details

Paul-Eric Dossou[1,2]*, Valentin Verdier[1] and Alan Ogor[1]

1 Icam, Lieusaint, France

2 University of Gustave Eiffel, AME, SPLOTT, Marne-La-Vallée, France

*Address all correspondence to: paul-eric.dossou@icam.fr

References

[1] Elbestawi MO, Centea D, Singh I, Wanyama T. SEPT learning factory for industry 4.0 education and applied research. Procedia Manufacturing. 2018;**23**:249-254. DOI: 10.1016/j.promfg.2018.04.025

[2] Doumeingts G, Ducq Y, Vallespir B, Kleinhans S. Production management and enterprise modelling. Computers in Industry. 2000;**42**:245-263

[3] Jorysz HR, Vernadat FB. CIM-OSA, part 1: Total enterprise modelling and the function view. International Journal of Computer Integrated Manufacturing. 1990;**3 and 4**:144-156

[4] Williams TJ. The Purdue enterprise reference architechture. Computers in Industry. 1994;**24**(2):141-158

[5] Bassi L. Industry 4.0: Hope, hype or revolution? In: 2017 IEEE 3rd International Forum on Research and Technologies for Society and Industry (RTSI). Italy: IEEE; 2017. pp. 1-6

[6] Sievers F, Reil H, Rimbeck M, Stumpf-Wollersheim J, Leyer M. Empowering employees in industrial organizations with IoT in their daily operations. Computers in Industry. 2021;**129**:103445

[7] Fonseca LM. Industry 4.0 and the digital society: Concepts, dimensions and envisioned benefits. In: Proceedings of the International Conference on Business Excellence. Vol. 12. Bucharest, Romania: Sciendo; 2018. pp. 386-397

[8] Pagliosa M, Tortorella G, Ferreira JCE. Industry 4.0 and lean manufacturing. Industry 4.0 and Lean Manufacturing: A systematic literature review and future research directions. Journal of Manufacturing Technology Management. 2021;**32**(30):543-569. DOI: 10.1108/JMTM-12-2018-0446

[9] Ohno T. Toyota Production System: Beyond Large Scale Production. Cambridge, MA: Productivity Press; 1988

[10] Guleria P, Pathania A, Sharma S, Sa JC. Lean six-sigma implementation in an automobile axle manufacturing industry: A case study. Materials Today: Proceedings. Available online 9 october 2021. DOI: 10.1016/j.matpr.2021.09.177

[11] Jimenez G, Santos G, Sa JC, Ricardo S, Pulido J, Pizarro A, et al. Improvement of productivity and Quality in the value chain through lean manufacturing—a case study. Procedia manufacturing. 2019;**41**:882-889

[12] Javaid M, Haleem A, Pratap Singh R, Suman R. Substantial capabilities of robotics in enhancing industry 4.0 implementation. Cognitive Robotics. 2021;**1**:58-75. DOI: 10.1016/j.cogr.2021.06.001

[13] Lynch L, McGuinness F, Clifford J, Rao M, Walsh J, Toal D, et al. Integration of autonomous intelligent vehicles into manufacturing environments: Challenges. Procedia Manufacturing. 2019;**38**:1683-1690. DOI: 10.1016/j.promfg.2020.01.115

[14] Quenehen A, Pocachard J, Klement N. Process optimization using collaborative robots—comparative case study. IFAC-PapersOnLine. 2019;**52**:60-65. DOI: 10.1016/j.ifacol.2019.11.131

[15] Javaid M, Haleem A, Pratap Singh R, Suman R. Significance of sensors for industry 4.0: Roles, capabilities, and

applications. Sensors International. 2021;**2**:100110. DOI: 10.1016/j.sintl.2021.100110

[16] Gallo T, Santolamazza A. Industry 4.0 and human factor: How is technology changing the role of the maintenance operator? Procedia Computer Science. 2021;**180**:388-393. DOI: 10.1016/j.procs.2021.01.364

[17] Keneth ES, Kamyshny A, Totaro M, Beccai L, Magdassi S. 3D Printing Materials for Soft Robotics. Advanced Materials. 2020;**33**:2003387. DOI: 10.1002/adma.202003387

[18] Brous P, Jansen M, Herder P. The dual effects of the Internet of Things (IoT): A systematic review of the benefits and risks of IoT adoption by organizations. International Journal of Information Management. 2020;**51**:1-17. DOI: 10.1016/j.ijinfomgt.2019.05.008

[19] Sundmaeker H, Guillemin P, Fries P, Woelfflé S. Vision and Challenges for Realizing the Internet of things. Brussels: European Commission; 2010

[20] Schimitt T, Wolf C, Taro Lennerfors T, Okwir S. Beyond "Leanear" production: A multilevel approach for achieving circularity in a lean manufacturing context. Journal of Cleaner Production. 2021;**318**(2021):128531

[21] Ammar M, Haleem A, Javaid M, Bahl S, Verma AS. Implementing industry technologies in self-healing materials and digitally managing the quality manufacturing. Materials Today: Proceedings. Available online 5 october 2021. DOI: 10.1016/j.matpr.2021.09.248

[22] Anisoke A, Alafropatis K, Garza-Reyes JA, Kumar A, Luthra S, Rocha-Lona L. Lean manufacturing and internet of things—A synergetic or antagonist relationship? Computers in Industry. 2021;**129**:103464

[23] Rüttimann BG, Stöckli MT. Lean manufacturing and industry 4.0—twins, partners or contenders? A due clarification regarding the supposed clash two production systems. Journal of Service Science and Management. 2016;**9**:485-500

[24] Rajkumar R, Lee I, Sha L, Stankovic J. Cyber-physical systems: The next computing revolution. Published in Design Automation Conference. IEEE. 26 july 2010. pp. 731-736. DOI: 10.1145/1837274.1837461. https://ieeexplore.ieee.org/document/5523280

[25] Marinelli M, Deshmukh AA, Janardhanan M, Nielsen I. Lean manufacturing and industry 4.0 combinative application: Practices and perceived benefits. IFAC PapersOnLine. 2021;**54**(1):288-293

[26] Muller JM, Voigt KI. Sustainable industrial value creation in SMES; A comparison between industry 4.0 and made in China 2025. International Journal of Precision Engineering and Manufacturing-Green Technology. 2018;**5**(5):659-670. DOI: 10.1007/s40684-018-0056-z

[27] Estensoro M, Larrea M, Müller JM, Sisti E. A resource-based view on SMEs regarding the transition to more sophisticated stages of industry 4.0. European Management Journal. Available online 13 october 2021. DOI: 10.1016/j.emj.2021.10.001

[28] Sarbu M. The impact of industry 4.0 on innovation performance: Insights from German manufacturing and service firms. Technovation. Available online 21 november 2021. DOI: 10.1016/j.technovation.2021.102415

[29] Chen M, Yang J, Zhou J. 5G-smart diabetes: Personalized diabetes diagnosis with healthcare big data clouds. IEEE Communications Magazine. 2018;**56**(4):16-23

[30] Wolfert S, Ge L, Verdouw C, Bogaardt MJ. Big data in smart farming—A review. Agricultural Systems. 2017;**153**:69-80

[31] Wang J, Xu C, Zhang J, Zhong R. Big data analytics for intelligent manufacturing systems: A review. Journal of Manufacturing Systems. Available online 5 march 2021. DOI: 10.1016/j.jmsy.2021.03.005

[32] Belhadi A, Zkik K, Cherrafi A, Yusof S, El Fezazi S. Understanding big data analytics fr manufacturing processes: Insights from literature review and multiple case studies. Computers & Industrial Engineering. 2019;**137**:106099

[33] Benosman M. Model-based vs data driven adaptive control: An overview. International Journal of Adapt Control Process. 2018;**32**(5):753-776. DOI: 10.1002/acs.2862

[34] Geiger C, Sarakakis G. Data-driven design for reliability. In: Proceedings—Annual Reliability and Maintainability Symposium. Association for Computing Machinery digital library. 2016. DOI: 10.1109/RAMS.2016.7448023

[35] Li C, Chen Y, Shang Y. A review of industrial big data for decision making in intelligent manufacturing. Engineering Science and Technology, an International Journal. Available online 01 June 2021. DOI: 10.1016/j.jestch.2021.06.001

[36] International Organization for Standardization. Safety of Machinery-General Principles for Design-Risk Assessment and Risk Reduction (ISO 12100:2010). 2010. Available from: https://www.iso.org/standard/51528.html

[37] International Organization for Standardization. Robots and Robotic Devices—Safety Requirements for Industrial Robots. 2011. Part 1: Robots (ISO 10218-1:2011). Available from: https://www.iso.org/standard/51330.html and Part 2: Robot Systems and Integration (ISO 10218-2:2011). Available from: https://www.iso.org/standard/41571.html

[38] International Organization for Standardization. ISO TS 15066—Robots and Robotic Devices—Collaborative Robots (ISO/TS 15066:2016). 2016. Available from: https://www.iso.org/standard/62996.html

[39] International Organization for Standardization. Robotics—Safety Design for Industrial Robot Systems—Part 1: End-Effectors (ISO/TR 20218:2018). 2018. Available from: https://www.iso.org/standard/69488.html

[40] Segura P, Lobato-Calleros O, Ramirez-Serrano A, Soria I. Human-robot collaborative systems: Structural components for current manufacturing applications. Advances in Industrial and Manufacturing Engineering. 2021;**3**:100060

[41] Parra PS, Calleros OL, Ramiez-Serrano A. Human-robot collaboration systems: Components and applications. Int. Conf. Control, Dynamic Syst., Robot. 2020

[42] Villani V, Pini F, Leali F, Secchi C. Survey on human-robot collaboration in industrial settings: Safety, intuitives interfaces and applications. Mechatronics. 2018;**55**:248-266. DOI: 10.1016/j.mechatronics.2018.02.009

[43] Realvasquez-Vargas A, Arredondo-Soto KC, Garcia-Alcarraz JL, Marquez-Lobato BY, Cruz-Garcia J. Introduction and configuration of a collaborative

robot in an assembly task as a means to decrease occupational risks and increase efficiency in a manufacturing company. Robotics and Computer-Integrated Manufacturing. 2019;**57**:315-328. DOI: 10.1016/j.rcim.2018.12.015

[44] Fogli D, Gargioni L, Guida G, Tampalini F. A hybrid approach to user-oriented programming of collaborative robots. Robotics and Computer-Integrated Manufacturing. 2022;**73**:102234

[45] Dossou PE. Development of a new framework for implementing industry 4.0 in companies. Manufacturing. 2019;**38**:573-580. DOI: 10.1016/j.promfg. 2020.01.072

Chapter 10

Supply Chain: A Modeling-Based Approach for Cyber-Physical Systems

Ágota Bányai

Abstract

Within the frame of this chapter, the author focuses on the distribution processes of green supply chain solutions and describes a potential mathematical model, taking environmental aspects into consideration. The first part of the chapter includes a systematic literature review. Based on the identified research gap, a new mathematical model is described, which makes it possible to describe last-mile logistics processes from an environmental point of view. The functional model of the distribution system includes the potential of Industry 4.0 technologies, which makes it possible to gather real-time information from the distribution process and use real-time status information for a sophisticated design and operation. The mathematical model of this approach defines an NP-hard optimization problem; therefore, heuristic optimization algorithm is supposed to solve the design and operation tasks of the green distribution problem. As the computational results show, cyber-physical systems increase the performance of green supply chain solutions and have a great impact on operational cost. As the numerical example shows, the integrated approach resulted in a 5.3% cost reduction in transportation operations.

Keywords: green supply chain, green distribution, industry 4.0 technologies, heuristic optimization, greenhouse gas emission, energy efficiency

1. Introduction

In recent years, a rising number of production and service companies work only with suppliers that adhere to environmental standards and regulatory policies, which are drivers for sustainable supply chain operations. These standards and regulatory policies can be classified into nine groups: pollution bans, technology standards, performance standards, emission trading policies, taxes, subsidies, information policies, eco-labels, and sustainable procurement policies [1]. Sustainable supply chain solutions and sustainable distribution solutions are influenced by all of these policies and related fields.

The definitions define that sustainable distribution refers to the macroeconomic allocation of objects (final products). Microeconomic aspects should also be taken into consideration because green distribution is influenced by business decisions, while economic and financial policies are represented by macroeconomics. Green distribution includes a wide range of operations, including transportation, warehousing, loading and unloading, packaging and labeling, custom services, and marketing. This wide range of logistics-related operations must be performed as green as possible. Today, the new technologies of the fourth industrial revolution make it possible to gather information from large complex systems in the form of real-time failure data and status information, and use them for more sophisticated decision-making. Within the frame of this chapter, an optimization-based approach for the optimal design and operation of green distribution is described. The significance of a problem is based on the fact that the application of Industry 4.0 technologies and the transformation of conventional supply chain solutions into a cyber-physical system can increase availability, flexibility, efficiency, sustainability, and transparency. The research question of this work is the validation of the impact of cyber-physical solutions on green supply chains.

This paper is organized as follows: Section 2 presents a systematic literature review, which summarizes the research background of distribution processes in the green supply chain from a descriptive and content analysis point of view. Section 3 describes the model framework of green distribution processes, including both, the functional and the mathematical models. The model is focusing on the sustainability-related aspects, including energy consumption, greenhouse gas emissions, and energy costs. Section 4 discusses the numerical analysis of the defined optimization model and validates the expected impact of cyber-physical solutions on green supply chains. Conclusions, future research directions, limitations, and managerial impacts are discussed in Section 5.

2. Systematic literature review

Within the frame of this systematic literature review, the following questions will be answered: What is the current state of the knowledge in the field of distribution in green supply chain solutions? Which methodologies can be used for the optimization of design and operation of green distribution systems? Which influencing factors are important from the environmental impact point of view? What are the main research gaps and limitations?

2.1 Methodology of systematic literature review

The systematic literature review can be divided into three main parts. The first part is the descriptive analysis, which focuses on the statistical analysis and numerical description of search results in Scopus. The second phase is the content analysis, where based on the results of the descriptive analysis the research topics and the scientific results are described and evaluated. The third part summarizes the results of descriptive and content analysis and focuses on the current state of knowledge, current research results, and research gaps (**Figure 1**).

The process of the systematic literature review includes the following main phases: (1) definition of search questions based on the available search fields in Scopus; (2) search process; (3) inclusion and exclusion process, where only journal articles were added from the different types of source types and non-English articles were excluded from the search results; (4) descriptive (statistical and numerical) analysis; (5)

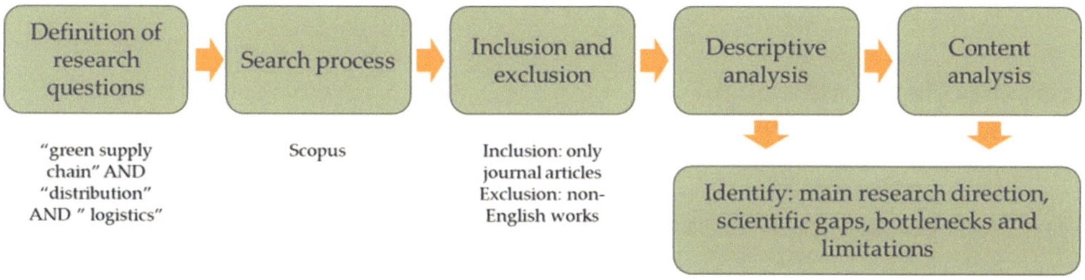

Figure 1.
Process of the systematic literature review.

content analysis, where the topics and research results are identified; (6) definition of consequences, identification of main research directions, research gaps, and bottlenecks.

2.2 Descriptive analysis

Within the frame of the descriptive and content analysis the following search was used in the Scopus: (TITLE-ABS-KEY ("green supply chain") AND TITLE-ABS-KEY (distribution) AND TITLE-ABS-KEY (logistics)) AND (LIMIT-TO (DOCTYPE, "ar")). The following numerical analysis is based on the results of this search. Initially, as a result of this search, 50 articles were identified and analyzed. The search was conducted in March 2022; therefore, new articles may have been published since then.

Figure 2 shows the distribution of published articles based on the search results in Scopus. As **Figure 2** shows, more than 50% of the articles were published in the last 5 years, and this fact shows the increased importance of green supply-chain-focused researches.

Figure 3 shows the classification of the published articles and research work by the nationality of the authors. As **Figure 3** shows, authors from Europe, Asia, and America are working on research topics focusing on green supply chain design and operation. From a global economic perspective, it is an important fact, that this research field is becoming increasingly important not only in developed countries but also in developing countries.

Figure 4 demonstrates the distribution of articles by subject area in Scopus. It can be concluded, that the green distribution-related researches are multidisciplinary

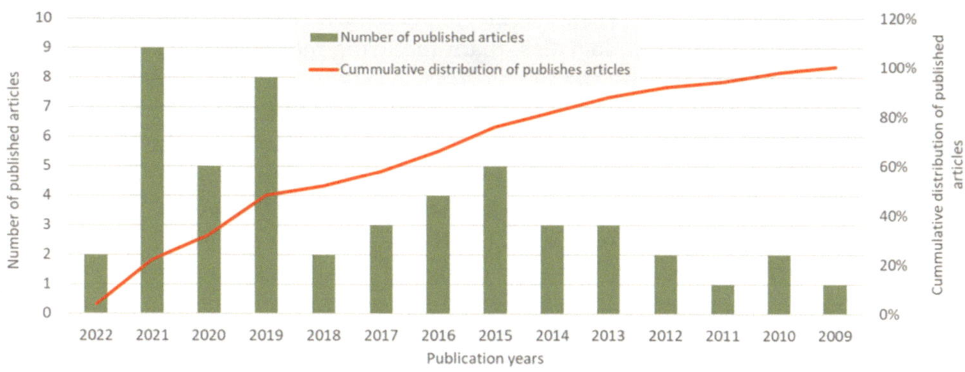

Figure 2.
Classification of articles by year of publication based on search results in Scopus.

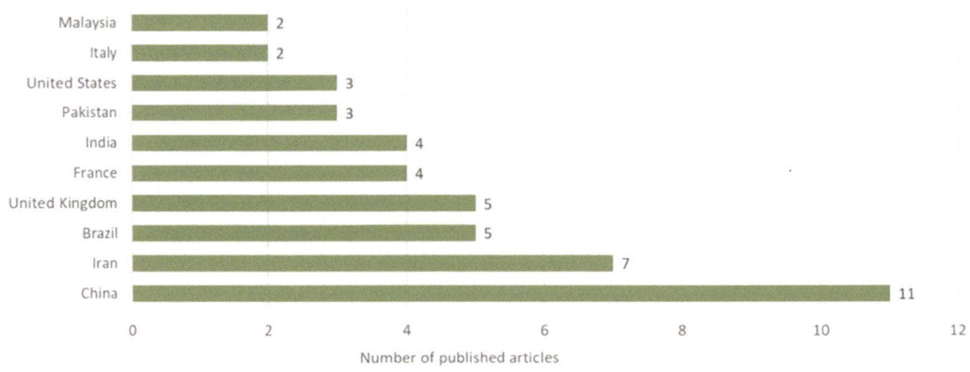

Figure 3.
Classification of articles by the nationality of the authors based on search results in Scopus.

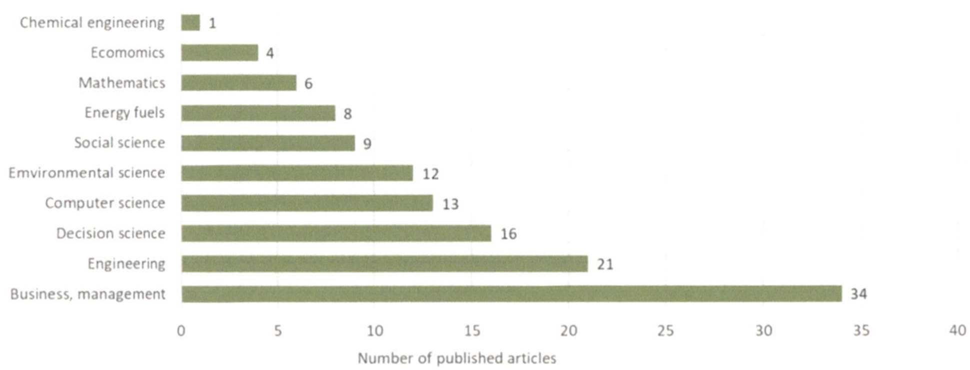

Figure 4.
Distribution of articles by Scopus keywords in the field of green distribution-related research.

researches, where a wide range of science fields is required to solve technological, logistics, human resource management, economic, and ecological problems including business and management, engineering, decision sciences, telecommunication and computer sciences, environmental sciences, social sciences, mathematics and optimization, chemical engineering and materials science. These topics are covered by journals in the following fields: sustainability, operational research, industrial engineering, management research, logistics, manufacturing technologies, mathematics, and transportation business.

An internationally accepted measure of the quality of scientific works is the independent citation. **Figure 5** shows the ten most cited articles based on the results of the Scopus search and the distribution of the independent citations. The *h-index*, which is the largest number *h* of published articles having at least *h* independent citations is in the case of green distribution research is 20. This h-index seems to be acceptable in the field of technology, engineering, and environmental researches, because in the case of other sciences, such as physics, space sciences, clinical medicine, and genetics, there are more papers, more scientists, and more citations.

Figure 6 demonstrates the distribution of green supply chain-related articles by open access types. Gold open access includes journals published only in open access. In the case of hybrid gold open access, the authors can choose the open access

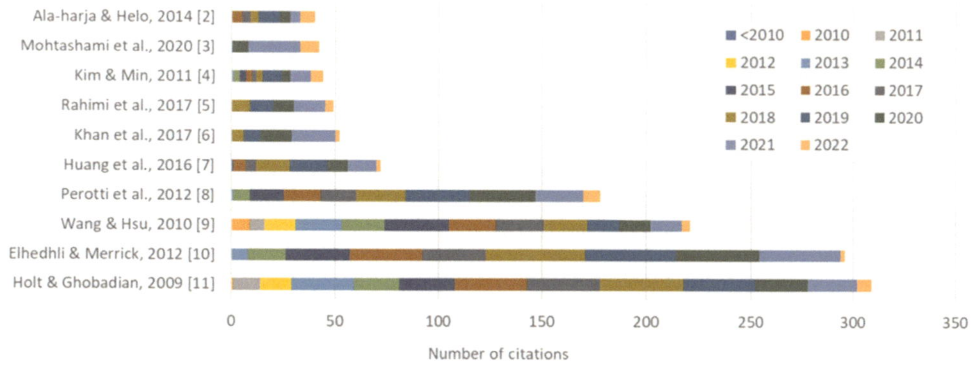

Figure 5.
Yearly distribution of independent citation of the ten most cited articles in the field of green supply chain-related research [2–11].

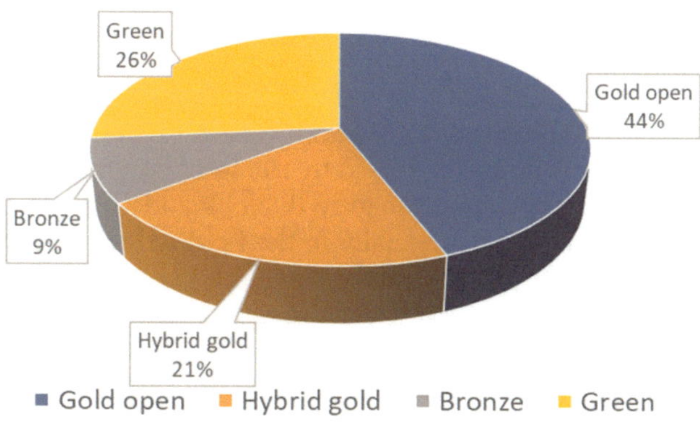

Figure 6.
Distribution of green supply chain article from availability (open access) point of view.

publication. In the case of green open access, the published articles are available in different repositories. In the case of bronze open access, the publisher offers temporally or permanently unlimited free access to the articles. 34 of the analyzed 51 articles are available online, which is an acceptable proportion.

Figure 7 demonstrates the distribution of the keywords mostly used by the authors of green distribution design-related articles. The analysis of keywords shows, that they can be clustered in the following way: environmental aspects (greenhouse gas emission, CO emission, carbon, climate change, sustainability, carbon footprint); optimization (linear programming, decision making, genetic algorithm, fuzzy models, algorithms, knapsack problems, factor analysis, numerical models, dynamic programming, comparative analysis, game theory); and logistics (distribution of goods, facility location problems, coordination management, network design, transportation, vehicles, chain to chain competition).

The use of keywords e-tailers and e-commerce distribution shows, that the environmental impact is important not for physical distribution but also in the case of e-business and e-commerce solutions, where the design and operation of eco-friendly operation focus on eco-friendly packaging, reusable plastics, purchasing carbon offsets, and reducing shipping distances.

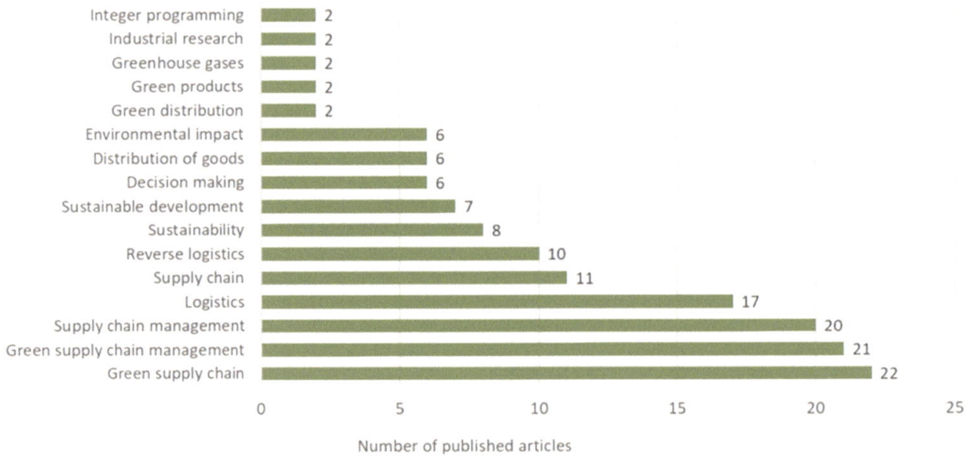

Figure 7.
Distribution of used keywords of green distribution-related articles based on the results of Scopus search.

2.3 Content analysis

The importance of the optimization of supply chain processes and the technological and logistics resources is underlined also by the fact, that logistics-induced greenhouse gas emissions caused by economic growth block and obstruct the greening process of supply chain solutions, especially in the field of last-mile logistics [12].

The product development process can be integrated with green purchasing, green manufacturing, green distribution, and green reverse logistics, which are an essential part of the green supply chain. This integration can lead to decreased environmental impact in all stages of the supply chain [13]. The product development environment can be also integrated with the forward and reverse flow of the supply chain in the circular economy including production, distribution, and customers in the forward direction and collection, disassembly, recycling, and disposal in the reverse direction to improve the greening process of supply chain solutions [14]. The products and the behavior of consumers can also influence the performance and environmental impact of distribution processes. From product development and labeling point of view, studies show, that consumers prefer green-labeled products and green distribution labels, especially in the case of tier1, tier 2, and tier 3 consumers [15].

Different models are used to demonstrate the impact of green distribution on the environmental impact of the green supply chain. The path analysis is a useful method to analyze this impact and to justify, that the participants of the green supply chain including suppliers, manufacturers, and service providers must focus on the facilities and operation-related policies to increase the performance of those variables [16].

The Nash and Stackelberg game is also a suitable method to analyze the impact of policies and regulations on the equilibrium strategies from sustainability of competitive forward and reverse supply chains focusing on financial aspects and greening [17]. A survey with 43 items was tested using partial least squares structural equation modeling to identify the most common practices facilitating environmental collaboration. The study shows that internal environmental management, eco-design, and green marketing play an important role in the greening process of supply chains, while no substantial impact was identified between green human resources, green information, and systems technology [18].

Network analysis can be used to perform a wide range of design tasks for green distribution processes including facility location and routing. These design tasks are essential to creating a sustainable and green distribution system, where the optimal location of distribution centers has a great impact on the energy efficiency and greenhouse gas emission of transportation processes [19, 20]. The greening process can be influenced both on the managerial and operational levels [21].

The risk evaluation plays an important role in the operation of green distribution networks because in an uncertain environment the performance of the distribution processes can be influenced by the results of forecasting and super positioning of customers' demands and other system parameters. This importance of risk evaluation is discussed in the case of agricultural products in a cold chain logistics solution, where the perspective of the ecological economy is taken into consideration [22] and it is shown, that the logistics mechanism of distribution processes can be improved by permanent improvement and supervision of logistics intermodal mechanism. Fuzzy models are also used to solve design and operation problems of green distribution problems in an uncertain environment [23].

The coordinated optimization of the complex system of green distribution networks shows a suitable way to take a wide range of influencing factors into consideration while optimizing the green supply chain because the complex model of the green supply chain defines different layers such as a layer of distributors, producers, and customers, and the coordinated optimization model plays the parameters and influencing factors of these players of the distribution network into consideration [24].

The analysis of action mechanism of cross-border supply chain solutions shows, that in the case of large geographical area the establishment of green supply chain models for green distribution has remarkable importance for the implementation and development of the green supply chain [25].

The design and operation of green distribution systems can be also described as an optimization problem of inventory routing problems, where the bi-objective optimization of both inventory costs and fuel consumption using mixed-integer linear programming can lead to an efficient green distribution [26]. Another approach focuses on a stochastic model, which takes profit, service level, and environmental impact as green criteria into consideration [5]. This is a new way of solving inventory routing problems because in recent decades these problems were focused only on economic performance and service level, shortages, delivery delays, and environmental footprint were not considered.

Investigations focusing on the relationships between proactive environmental strategy, green supply chain solutions, and performances of logistics providers show, that the environmental impact can be positively influenced by eco-efficiency and eco-branding through green distribution, inventory management, and reverse processes [27, 28].

Research results show, that e-tailers, third party service providers, and consumers have a great impact on the greening process of distribution, therefore it is important to involve all of these players in the optimization process of distribution networks and build a close communication between them [29], and strengthen green supply chain coordination system [30].

Cities as major population centers represent supply chain solutions with a high density of distribution operations, therefore in urban regions, the greening of last-mile logistics operations is especially important, especially from the health of residents' point of view [31]. Another approach to greening distribution processes in the field of urban planning focuses on the assessment of the impact of the urban intelligent transportation system on the success of the green supply chain management system. The study validated the hypothesis that an urban intelligent transportation system, knowledge of manufacturers, and business processes have a great positive impact on the success of green supply chain management (green distribution) in the case of agricultural products [32].

The interconnection and hyperconnection of supply chains represent a special problem for supply chain management because transferring products between the centers of different supply chains can cause waiting queues and high environmental pollution. Research focusing on the design of forward and reverse logistics of hyperconnected supply chains shows, that the integrated optimization of queuing problems and transportation networks can lead to the reduction of environmental impact [3]. Other integrated approaches for the optimization of distribution processes focus on the multi-echelon location routing problem, where genetic algorithm and dynamic island model-based heuristics is used to minimize the energy costs associated with transportation [33]. Using a mixed-integer programming model to solve a large-scale integrated location-routing problem with genetic algorithm and particle swarm heuristics, it is possible to optimize the number and location of cross-docking facilities in green distribution processes [34].

The application of just-in-time philosophy can improve the efficiency of both manufacturing systems and whole supply chains. As research results in the case of return vehicle supply chains show, the just-in-time model can support the greening processes of conventional solutions to improve environmental awareness and reduce environmental impact of distribution processes [35].

The practices of green supply chain management influence not only the environmental effect of distribution processes, but they have a great impact on organizational performance. The study based on the results of questionnaire-related research describes a theoretical model, which explains the analytical relationships between green supply chain processes and organizational performance [36].

Enhancing stock efficiency and environmental sustainability goals in direct distribution logistic networks can be improved using lean management and green management principles within logistics to reduce the environmental impact of distribution processes [37].

The partner selection process is also an important influencing factor for green supply chain solutions, as in the case of the optimization of a reverse logistics network the results of integrated fuzzy-artificial immune optimization heuristics-based solutions show [38].

The success of green distribution processes is also based on emission measuring operations and estimation of carbon footprint including capturing, calculation, and management of emissions across the transportation and distribution network [39, 40]. The performance evaluation can be based on logistics performance indicators and environmental performance indicators, and these can be integrated into a green logistics performance indicator [4]. Benchmarking is also a suitable tool to support evaluation and process improvement in green distribution networks [11].

For the solution of green supply-chain-related optimization problems, a wide range of integrated optimization and process improvement methods can be used: game theory [7], spanning-tree based genetic algorithm [9], Lagrangian heuristics [10], path analysis [16], integrated CPU-GPU heuristic inspired on variable neighborhood search [41], fuzzy genetic algorithm [42], simulation [43], analytical hierarchy process [44], decision making trial and evaluation laboratory for the identification of cause-effect chain components of distribution systems [45, 46]. Other heuristic algorithms, such as quantum particle swarm optimization are also suitable for the solution of multi-objective optimization of multi-echelon supply chain and distribution, where a wide range of constraints can be considered including capacity, production cost, transportation and material handling cost, greenhouse gas emissions, and time window [47].

Several scenarios and case studies related to the design and operation of green supply chain and green distribution were assessed and evaluated to compare the effects of technology, logistics, human resources, and policies on the efficiency, reliability, and availability of environmental impact of green supply chain solutions. The most important fields of case studies are from general distribution processes [6, 48], but valuable case studies were published in the field of food industry [2], air conditioner manufacturers [7], third party logistics providers [8], motorcycle industry [17], healthcare [28], direct distribution logistic networks [37], electronic equipment and instruments manufacturing companies [38], distribution of fruits and vegetables [49], automotive industry [50], power networks [51], agri-food supply chain [52] and disrupted supply chain solutions in the pandemic era [53]. The methodological framework and main research directions of green distribution networks, including methods, objective functions, case studies and special conditions, and constraints are shown in **Figure 8**.

2.4 Consequences and identification of research gaps

The consequences based on the above described systematic literature review, including descriptive and content analysis, can be summarized as follows:

- Sustainable distribution is not only influenced by both technological and logistics parameters, but also by product development also has a great impact on the environmental impact of distribution processes.

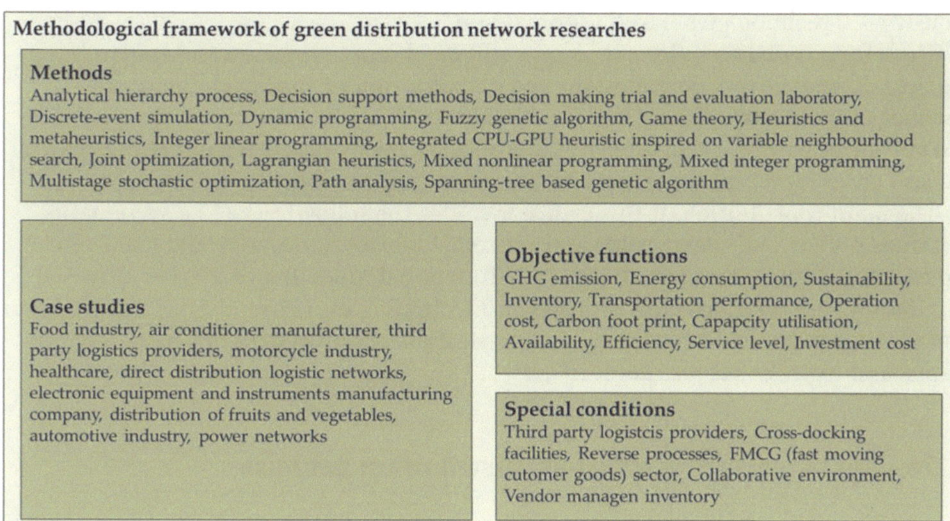

Figure 8.
Methodological framework and main research directions of green distribution networks, including methods, objective functions, case studies, and special conditions and constraints.

- Competitive distribution becomes more and more important in the case of disrupted supply chains, where environmental impact plays an important role.

- The risk evaluation has a great impact on the financial and environmental impact of distribution systems, especially in the case of an uncertain environment.

- Consumers influence the environmental impact of distribution networks and their greening process.

- Direct distribution systems can be transformed into multi-echelon distribution networks to decrease the environmental effect and improve cost efficiency.

- Emission measuring operations and estimation of carbon footprint including capturing, calculation, and management of emissions across the transportation and distribution network are key success factors for green distribution.

- Green distribution networks represent NP-hard optimization problems, where integrated heuristic solution algorithms are used to find the solutions to multi-objective problems.

As a research gap, it can be concluded that the analyzed articles are focusing on the analysis and optimization of conventional supply chain and distribution networks and only a few of them discuss the potentials of cyber-physical systems, interconnected and hyperconnected networks.

The increasing number of publications indicates the importance and scientific potential of research on green distribution systems. The articles that addressed the design and operation of green distribution systems are based on conventional supply chain environment, but few of the articles have aimed to research the potentials of Industry 4.0 technologies-based optimization.

Therefore, Industry 4.0 technologies still need more attention and research in the field of integration, cooperation, and globalization of supply chains and distribution networks. Accordingly, the main focus of this research is the modeling and optimization of a cyber-physical distribution network, where not only financial but also environmental aspects are taken into consideration.

The main contribution of this article includes the followings: (1) a systematic literature review with descriptive and content analyses to describe the main research directions and identify research gaps; (2) functional modeling of a cyber-physical distribution network based on Industry 4.0 technologies; (3) mathematical model to find the best parameters for the cyber-physical distribution network from environmental and logistics aspects point of view.

3. Description of a cyber-physical distribution network

Within the frame of this section, the functional and mathematical model of a cyber-physical distribution system is described. The functional model focuses on the transformation of conventional distribution systems into a cyber-physical distribution using Industry 4.0 technologies, while the mathematical model includes "green" objective functions, such as minimization of energy consumption and greenhouse gas emission, and related constraints (time, capacity, and energy).

3.1 Functional model of a cyber-physical distribution network

In conventional distribution systems operating in parallel, the low level of cooperation means that many optimization options are not feasible. This not only reduces the efficiency of distribution systems but also increases their environmental impact. To address this, available Industry 4.0 technologies can be used to transform independent distribution systems operating in parallel into a cyber-physical distribution network, where the integration of individual distribution systems can be achieved, resulting in coordination that can greatly improve system performance and at the same time achieve a much more environmental friendly network operation (**Figure 9**).

The transformation of a traditional distribution network into a cyber-physical system may require the use of the following technologies:

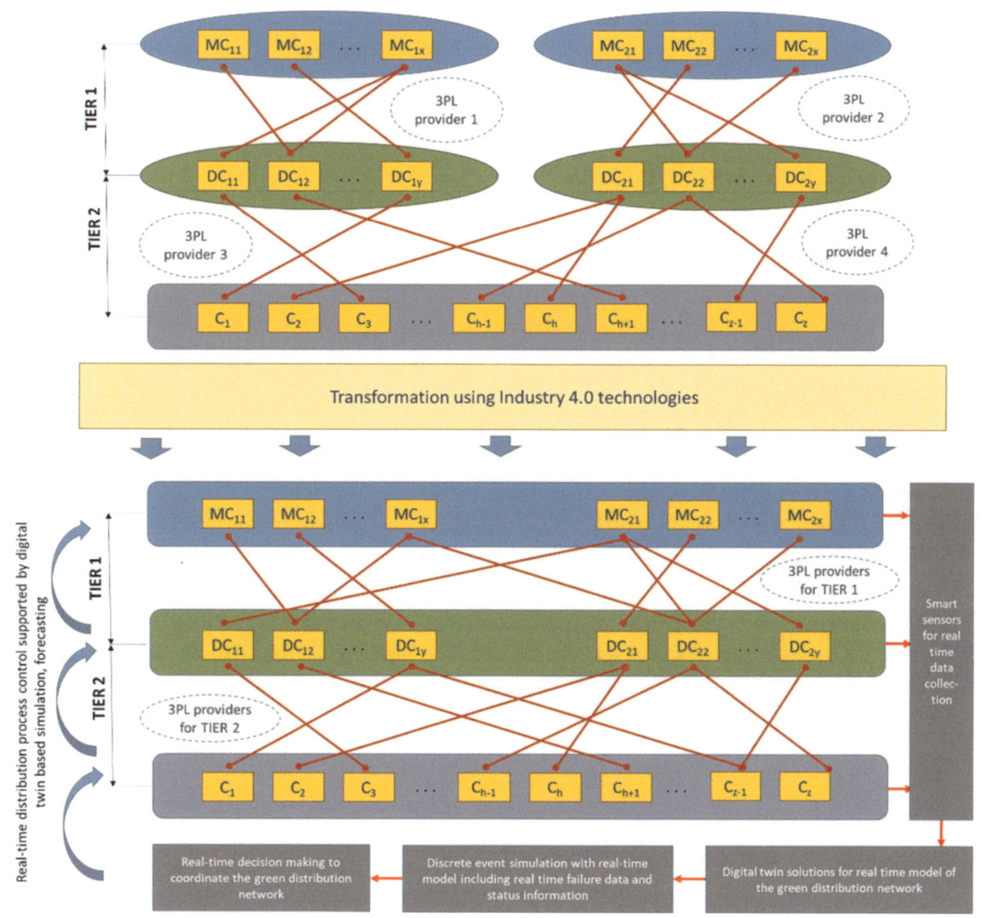

Figure 9.
Transformation of conventional distribution systems into a cyber-physical distribution network using Industry 4.0 technologies including smart sensors, edge computing, digital twinning, discrete event simulation, and real-time data-based decision making.

- smart sensors: using smart sensors we can gather real-time data from the resources and processes of the distribution network, including real-time failure data and status information;
- edge computing: using this distributed computing paradigm, we can bring computation and data storage operations closer to the sources of data sources, which is important in the case of large geographical areas, such as a distribution network;
- edge node: this layer is the connection between smart sensors of the physical system and the distribution cloud; edge node includes the tasks of IoT management, offline data analysis, and storage;
- digital twin: using different digital twin solutions it is possible to create real-time models of the distribution network; digital twin integrates data from multiple sources, from field sensors to ERPs of the players in the distribution network (manufacturers, distribution centers, and third-party logistics providers);
- discrete event simulation: with a real-time model including real-time failure data and status information more sophisticated forecasting can be made, which is an essential condition for the optimal coordination of technological, logistics, and human resources; the results of real-time discrete event simulation are required for the decision-making process.

3.2 Mathematical models of distribution networks

Within the frame of this section, the mathematical models of a conventional and cyber-physical distribution network are described. The mathematical models are focusing on energy efficiency-related "green" objective functions, including energy consumption and greenhouse gas emission as the most important influencing factors of environmental impact. The mathematical model includes time, capacity, and energy-related constraints.

3.2.1 Mathematical model of a conventional distribution network

The objective function of the optimization problem is either the energy consumption or the real or virtual greenhouse gas emission. The energy consumption as objective function can be defined as follows in the case of conventional distribution:

$$EC^{CONV} = \sum_{a=1}^{a_{max}} EC_a^{MD} + \sum_{a=1}^{a_{max}} EC_a^{DC} \rightarrow min \, . \tag{1}$$

where EC^{CONV} is the energy consumption of the conventional distribution system, EC_a^{MD} is the energy consumption between the manufacturer cluster a and distribution cluster a, EC_a^{DC} is the energy consumption between the distribution cluster a and the consumers, a_{max} is the number of independent distribution networks.

The energy consumption between the manufacturer cluster a and the distribution cluster a can be defined as follows:

$$EC_{a}^{MD} = \sum_{\alpha=1}^{\alpha_{maxa}} \varepsilon_{v_{\alpha a}}\left(q_{v_{\alpha a}}\right) \bullet l_{\alpha a}^{opt}(\Theta_{\alpha a}) \tag{2}$$

where $v_{\alpha a}$ is the transportation vehicle assigned to route α of distribution system a in Tier1 between manufacturers and distribution centers, α_{maxa} is the number of distribution routes for distribution system a in Tier1 between manufacturers and distribution centers, ε_{v_α} is the energy consumption of transportation vehicle $v_{\alpha a}$ assigned to route α of distribution system a in Tier1 between manufacturers and distribution centers, $l_{\alpha a}^{opt}$ is the length of the optimal distribution route α of distribution system a in Tier1 between manufacturers and distribution centers, which is a function of the $\Theta_{\alpha a}$ set of distribution centers assigned to route α of distribution system a in Tier1 between manufacturers and distribution centers, and $q_{v_{\alpha a}}$ is the current capacity of transportation vehicle assigned to route α of distribution system a in Tier1 between manufacturers and distribution centers.

The energy consumption between the distribution cluster a and consumers assigned to distribution center a can be defined as follows:

$$EC_{a}^{DC} = \sum_{\beta=1}^{\beta_{maxa}} \varepsilon_{v_{\beta a}}\left(q_{v_{\beta a}}\right) \bullet l_{\beta a}^{opt}(\Theta_{\beta a}) \tag{3}$$

where $v_{\beta a}$ is transportation vehicle assigned to route β of distribution system a in Tier2 between distribution centers and consumers, β_{maxa} is the number of distribution routes for distribution system a in Tier2 between distribution centers and consumers, $\varepsilon_{v_{\beta a}}$ is the energy consumption of transportation vehicle $v_{\beta a}$ assigned to route β of distribution system a in Tier2 between distribution centers and consumers, $l_{\beta a}^{opt}$ is the length of the optimal distribution route β of distribution system a in Tier2 distribution centers and consumers, which is a function of the $\Theta_{\beta a}$ set of distribution centers assigned to route β of distribution system a in Tier2 between distribution centers and consumers, and $q_{v_{\beta a}}$ is the current capacity of transportation vehicle assigned to route β of distribution system a in Tier2 between distribution centers and consumers.

The second objective function is the greenhouse gas emission, which can be defined for the following GHGs: carbon dioxide, methane, nitrous oxide, and fluorinated gases. The GHG emission can be defined in the following way for the different GHGs in the case of conventional distribution:

$$EM_{MGHG}^{CONV} = \sum_{a=1}^{a_{max}} EM_{MGHG}^{MDa} + \sum_{a=1}^{a_{max}} EM_{MGHG}^{DCa} \rightarrow min\,. \tag{4}$$

where EM_{MGHG}^{CONV} is the *GHG* emission of the conventional distribution system, EM_{MGHG}^{MDa} is the GHG emission of the vehicle assigned to the distribution operations between the manufacturer cluster a and distribution cluster a, EM_{MGHG}^{DCa} is the GHG emission of vehicles assigned to distribution operations between the distribution cluster a and the consumers, and $MGHG = [CO_2, SO_2, CO, HC, NO_x, PM]$ is the matrix of greenhouse gases to be taken into consideration.

The emission between the manufacturer cluster a and the distribution cluster a can be defined as follows:

$$EM_{MGHG}^{MDa} = \sum_{\alpha=1}^{\alpha_{maxa}} \vartheta_{MGHG}^{TIER1,v_{\alpha a}} \bullet \varepsilon_{v_{\alpha a}}\left(q_{v_{\alpha a}}\right) \bullet l_{\alpha a}^{opt}(\Theta_{\alpha a}) \tag{5}$$

where $\vartheta_{MGHG}^{TIER1,v_{\alpha a}}$ is the specific GHG emission in the case of transportation vehicle assigned to route α of distribution system a in Tier1 between manufacturers and distribution centers.

The emission between the distribution cluster a and consumers assigned to distribution center a can be defined as follows:

$$EM_{MGHG}^{DCa} = \sum_{\beta=1}^{\beta_{maxa}} \vartheta_{MGHG}^{TIER2,v_{\beta a}} \bullet \varepsilon_{v_{\beta a}}\left(q_{v_{\beta a}}\right) \bullet l_{\beta a}^{opt}(\Theta_{\beta a}) \tag{6}$$

where $\vartheta_{MGHG}^{TIER2,v_{\beta a}}$ is the specific GHG emission in the case of transportation vehicle assigned to route β of distribution system a in Tier2 between distribution centers and consumers.

As constraints, we can take the following into consideration: capacity of vehicles, capacity of loading and unloading equipment, capacity of distribution centers, time window for manufacturer, time window for customers, time window for 3PL providers in Tier1, time window for 3PL providers in Tier2, and available energy for electric vehicles.

Constraint 1a: We can define the upper limit of the loading capacity of transportation vehicles. It is not allowed to exceed this upper limit of loading capacity while assigning distribution tasks to the routes and scheduling the delivery tasks:

$$\forall \alpha, a : \ C_{v_{\alpha a}} \geq \sum_{i=1}^{i_{max}} q_i \in \Psi_{\alpha a} \tag{7}$$

where $C_{v_{\alpha a}}$ is the upper limit of loading capacity of the transportation vehicle assigned to route α of distribution system a, i_{max} is the upper limit of customers' demands, q_i is the volume or weight (capacity unit) of customers' demand i, $\Psi_{\alpha a}$ is the set of customers' demands assigned to route α of distribution system a.

Constraint 2a: We can define the upper limit of the material-handling capacity of loading and unloading equipment. It is not allowed to exceed this upper limit of material handling capacity while assigning distribution tasks to the routes and scheduling the delivery tasks:

$$\forall \alpha, a : \ C_{z_{\alpha a}} \geq \sum_{i=1}^{i_{max}} z_i\left(q_i \in \Psi_{\alpha a}\right) \tag{8}$$

where $C_{z_{\alpha a}}$ is the upper limit of the material-handling capacity of the loading and unloading equipment assigned to delivery tasks of route α of distribution system a, z_i is the required material handling capacity of customers demand i.

Constraint 3a: We can define the upper limit of the storage capacity of distribution centers. It is not allowed to exceed this upper limit by assigning manufacturers to distribution centers and distribution centers to customers:

$$\forall a : \ CW_a \geq \sum_{i=1}^{i_{max}} \sum_{\alpha=1}^{\alpha_{max}} q_{i\alpha} \in \Psi_{\alpha a} \tag{9}$$

where CW_a is the storage capacity of the distribution center of distribution system a, $q_{i\alpha}$ is the customers' demand i assigned to route α of distribution system a.

Constraint 4a: We can define a time window for the potential manufacturing process for each demand of customers. It is not allowed to exceed this lower and upper limit while assigning customers' demands to manufacturers and scheduling them:

$$\forall i, a: \quad \tau_{ia}^{MINm} \leq \tau_{ia}^{m} \leq \tau_{ia}^{MAXm} \tag{10}$$

where τ_{ia}^{MINm} is the lower limit of the time window for the manufacturing process for customers' demand i at the manufacturer of the distribution system a, τ_{ia}^{MAXm} is the upper limit of the time window for the manufacturing process for customers' demand i at the manufacturer of the distribution system a, τ_{ia}^{m} is the scheduled manufacturing time for customers' demand i at the manufacturer of the distribution system a.

Constraint 5a: We can define a time window for the customers' demands. The manufactured products must be delivered within this predefined time window to the customers and it is not allowed to exceed this time window:

$$\forall i, a: \quad \tau_{ia}^{MINcd} \leq \tau_{ia}^{cd} \leq \tau_{ia}^{MAXcd} \tag{11}$$

where τ_{ia}^{MINcd} is the lower limit of the time window for delivering the manufactured product to customer i in the distribution system a, τ_{ia}^{MAXcd} is the upper limit of the time window for delivering the manufactured product to customer i in the distribution system a, τ_{ia}^{cd} is the scheduled delivery of manufactured product to customer i in the distribution system a.

Constraint 6a: The material handling operations can be performed by third-party logistics providers in the case of Tier1 and Tier 2. We can define an available time window of these 3PL providers and it is not allowed to exceed this time window while assigning and scheduling material handling tasks performed by the 3PL providers:

$$\forall i, a, \mu: \quad \tau_{ia\mu}^{MIN3PL} \leq \tau_{ia\mu}^{3PL} \leq \tau_{ia\mu}^{MAX3PL} \tag{12}$$

where $\tau_{ia\mu}^{MIN3PL}$ is the lower limit of the time window of availability of third-party logistics provider for customers' demand i in distribution system a in Tier μ, $\tau_{ia\mu}^{MAX3PL}$ is the upper limit of the time window of availability of third-party logistics provider for customers' demand i in distribution system a in Tier μ, $\tau_{ia\mu}^{3PL}$ is the scheduled logistics service for customers' demand i in distribution system a in Tier μ.

Constraint 7a: As a sustainability and energy efficiency-related constraint, we can define the available energy of transportation vehicles and other material handling equipment. For example, in the case of electric vehicles we can define the available capacity of batteries or the required reloading time:

$$\forall a, \alpha: \quad \varepsilon_{v_{\alpha a}}\left(q_{v_{\alpha a}} \in \Psi_{\alpha a}\right) \bullet l_{\alpha a}^{opt}(\Theta_{\alpha a}) \leq E_{v_{\alpha a}}^{max} \tag{13}$$

where $E_{v_{\alpha a}}^{max}$ is the upper limit of available energy (capacity of a battery in the case of electric vehicles).

3.2.2 Mathematical model of a cyber-physical distribution network

In the case of a cyber-physical distribution system, where Industry 4.0 technologies make it possible to integrate the operation of the different distribution system within and between tiers the energy consumption can be computed in the following way:

$$EC^{CYB} = EC^{MD} + EC^{DC} \rightarrow min\,. \tag{14}$$

where EC^{CYB} is the energy consumption of the cyber-physical distribution system, which integrates all individual separated distribution systems of the conventional solution, EC^{MD} is the energy consumption between manufacturers and distribution clusters, EC^{DC} is the energy consumption between the distribution centers and consumers.

The energy consumption between manufacturers and distribution centers in Tier 1 can be defined as follows:

$$EC^{MD} = \sum_{\alpha=1}^{\alpha_{max}} \varepsilon_{v_\alpha}\left(q_{v_\alpha}\right) \bullet l_\alpha^{opt}(\Theta_\alpha) \tag{15}$$

where v_α is the transportation vehicle assigned to route α in Tier1 between manufacturers and distribution centers, α_{max} is the total number of distribution routes for Tier1 between manufacturers and distribution centers, ε_{v_α} is the energy consumption of transportation vehicle v_α assigned to route α in Tier1 between manufacturers and distribution centers, l_α^{opt} is the length of the optimal distribution route α in Tier1 between manufacturers and distribution centers, which is a function of the Θ_α set of distribution centers assigned to route α in Tier1 between manufacturers and distribution centers, and q_{v_α} is the current capacity of transportation vehicles assigned to route α in Tier1 between manufacturers and distribution centers.

The energy consumption between the distribution centers and consumers in Tier2 can be defined as follows:

$$EC^{DC} = \sum_{\beta=1}^{\beta_{max}} \varepsilon_{v_\beta}\left(q_{v_\beta}\right) \bullet l_\beta^{opt}(\Theta_\beta) \tag{16}$$

where v_β is the transportation vehicle assigned to route β in Tier2 between distribution centers and consumers, β_{max} is the number of distribution routes in Tier2 between distribution centers and consumers, ε_{v_β} is the energy consumption of transportation vehicle v_β assigned to route β in Tier2 between distribution centers and consumers, l_β^{opt} is the length of the optimal distribution route β in Tier2 between distribution centers and consumers, which is a function of the Θ_β set of distribution centers assigned to route β in Tier2 between distribution centers and consumers, and q_{v_β} is the current capacity of transportation vehicles assigned to route β in Tier2 between distribution centers and consumers.

The transformation of the conventional distribution system into cyber-physical distribution is suitable from energy consumption point of view, if

$$\sum_{a=1}^{a_{max}} EC_a^{MD} + \sum_{a=1}^{a_{max}} EC_a^{DC} \gg EC^{MD} + EC^{DC} \tag{17}$$

In the case of a cyber-physical distribution system, the emission of greenhouse gases can be computed in the following way:

$$EM_{MGHG}^{CYB} = EM^{MD} + EM^{DC} \rightarrow min\,. \tag{18}$$

where EM_{MGHG}^{CYB} is the GHG emission of the cyber-physical distribution system, which integrates all individual separated distribution systems of the conventional solution, EM^{MD} is the GHG emission between manufacturers and distribution clusters, EM^{DC} is the GHG emission between the distribution centers and consumers.

The GHG emission between manufacturers and distribution centers in Tier 1 can be defined as follows:

$$EM_{MGHG}^{MD} = \sum_{\alpha=1}^{\alpha_{maxa}} \vartheta_{MGHG}^{TIER1,v_\alpha} \bullet \varepsilon_{v_\alpha}\left(q_{v_\alpha}\right) \bullet l_\alpha^{opt}(\Theta_\alpha) \tag{19}$$

where $\vartheta_{MGHG}^{TIER1,v_\alpha}$ is the specific GHG emission in the case of transportation vehicles assigned to route α in Tier1 between manufacturers and distribution centers.

The emission between the distribution centers and consumers in Tier2 can be defined as follows:

$$EM_{MGHG}^{DC} = \sum_{\beta=1}^{\beta_{maxa}} \vartheta_{MGHG}^{TIER2,v_\beta} \bullet \varepsilon_{v_\beta}\left(q_{v_\beta}\right) \bullet l_\beta^{opt}(\Theta_\beta) \tag{20}$$

where $\vartheta_{MGHG}^{TIER2,v_\beta}$ is the specific GHG emission in the case of transportation vehicles assigned to route β in Tier2 between distribution centers and consumers.

The transformation of the conventional distribution system into cyber-physical distribution is suitable from GHG emission point of view, if

$$\sum_{a=1}^{a_{max}} EM_{MGHG}^{MDa} + \sum_{a=1}^{a_{max}} EM_{MGHG}^{DCa} \gg EM_{MGHG}^{MD} + EM_{MGHG}^{DC} \tag{21}$$

As constraints, we can take the following into consideration: capacity of vehicles, capacity of loading and unloading equipment, capacity of distribution centers, time window for manufacturer, time window for customers, time window for 3PL providers in Tier1, time window for 3PL providers for Tier2, available energy for electric vehicles.

Constraint 1b: We can define the upper limit of the loading capacity of transportation vehicles. It is not allowed to exceed this upper limit of loading capacity while assigning distribution tasks to the routes and scheduling the delivery tasks. The difference between the constraints *1a* and *1b* is that, while in the case of a conventional distribution network, customer demand can only be assigned to the transport vehicles within the given distribution network, in the case of a cyber-physical distribution system, any customer demand can be assigned to any transportation vehicle:

$$\forall\alpha: \; C_{v_\alpha} \geq \sum_{i=1}^{i_{max}} q_i \in \Psi_\alpha \tag{22}$$

where Ψ_α is the set of customers' demands assigned to route α in the cyber-physical distribution network.

Constraint 2b: We can define the upper limit of the material handling capacity of loading and unloading equipment. It is not allowed to exceed this upper limit of material-handling capacity while assigning distribution tasks to the routes and scheduling the delivery tasks. The difference between the constraints *2a* and *2b* is that, while in the case of a conventional distribution network, customer demand can only be assigned to the transport vehicles and related material handling equipment (loading and unloading equipment, packaging machines, labeling) within the given distribution network, in the case of a cyber-physical distribution system, any customer demand can be assigned to any material handling equipment:

$$\forall \alpha, a: \ C_{z_\alpha} \geq \sum_{i=1}^{i_{max}} z_i \left(q_i \in \Psi_\alpha\right) \tag{23}$$

Constraint 3b: We can define the upper limit of the storage capacity of distribution centers. The difference between constraints 3a and 3b is that while in the case of the conventional distribution system the capacity of a distribution system depends on only the manufacturers and customers of the same distribution system, in the case of a cyber-physical distribution network all products produced by all manufacturers can be assigned to all distribution centers (warehouses):

$$\forall a: \ CW_a \geq \sum_{i=1}^{i_{max}} \sum_{\alpha=1}^{\alpha_{max}} q_{i\alpha} \in \Psi_\alpha \tag{24}$$

where CW_a is the storage capacity of the distribution center of distribution system a, $q_{i\alpha}$ is the customers' demands i assigned to route α of distribution system a.

Constraint 4b: We can define a time window for the potential manufacturing process for each demand of customers. It is not allowed to exceed this lower and upper limit while assigning customers' demands to manufacturers and scheduling them. In this cyber-physical network, the time windows can be defined for all manufacturers of the whole network, while in the case of conventional distributions networks, the time windows are focusing on the manufacturers of separated distribution systems:

$$\forall i, a: \ \tau_{ia}^{MINm} \leq \tau_{ia}^{m} \leq \tau_{ia}^{MAXm} \tag{25}$$

where τ_{ia}^{MINm} is the lower limit of the time window for the manufacturing process for customers' demand i at the manufacturer of the distribution system a, τ_{ia}^{MAXm} is the upper limit of the time window for the manufacturing process for customers' demand i at the manufacturer of the distribution system a, τ_{ia}^{m} is the scheduled manufacturing time for customers' demand i at the manufacturer of the distribution system a.

Constraint 5b: We can define a time window for the customers' demands. The manufactured products must be delivered within this predefined time window to the customers and it is not allowed to exceed this time window. In this cyber-physical network, the time windows can be defined for all customers of the whole network, while in the case of conventional distribution networks, the time windows are focusing on the customers of separated distribution systems:

$$\forall i, a: \ \tau_{ia}^{MINcd} \leq \tau_{ia}^{cd} \leq \tau_{ia}^{MAXcd} \tag{26}$$

where τ_{ia}^{MINcd} is the lower limit of the time window for delivering the manufactured product to customer i in the distribution system a, τ_{ia}^{MAXcd} is the upper limit of the time window for delivering the manufactured product to customer i in the distribution system a, τ_{ia}^{cd} is the scheduled delivery of manufactured product to customer i in the distribution system a.

Constraint 6b: The material handling operations can be performed by third-party logistics providers in the case of Tier1 and Tier 2. We can define an available time window of these 3PL providers and it is not allowed to exceed this time window while assigning and scheduling material-handling tasks performed by the 3PL providers. In this case, the 3PL providers can perform all logistics operations in the cyber-physical distribution network, while in the case of conventional distribution systems, the 3PL providers of separated distribution systems can work uncoordinated:

$$\forall i, a, \mu : \quad \tau_{ia\mu}^{MIN3PL} \le \tau_{ia\mu}^{3PL} \le \tau_{ia\mu}^{MAX3PL} \tag{27}$$

where $\tau_{ia\mu}^{MIN3PL}$ is the lower limit of the time window of availability of third-party logistics provider for customers' demand i in distribution system a in Tier μ, $\tau_{ia\mu}^{MAX3PL}$ is the upper limit of the time window of availability of third-party logistics provider for customers' demand i in distribution system a in Tier μ, $\tau_{ia\mu}^{3PL}$ is the scheduled logistics service for customers' demand i in distribution system a in Tier μ.

Constraint 7b: As a sustainability and energy efficiency-related constraint, we can define the available energy of transportation vehicles and other material handling equipment. For example, in the case of electric vehicles we can define the available capacity of batteries or the required reloading time:

$$\forall a, \alpha : \quad \varepsilon_{v_{\alpha a}} \left(q_{v_{\alpha a}} \in \Psi_{\alpha a} \right) \bullet l_{\alpha a}^{opt} \left(\Theta_{\alpha a} \right) \le E_{v_{\alpha a}}^{max} \tag{28}$$

where $E_{v_{\alpha a}}^{max}$ is the upper limit of available energy (capacity of a battery in the case of electric vehicles).

The decision variables of this NP-hard optimization problem are the followings:

- assignment of customers' demands to manufacturers (Tier 1),
- assignment of final products to 3PL providers in manufacturer–distribution center relation (Tier 1),
- assignment of customers' demands to distribution centers (Tier 2),
- scheduling of manufacturing of customers' demands (Tier 1),
- scheduling of logistics operations of 3PL provider in manufacturer – distribution center relation (Tier 1),
- assignment of 3PL providers to perform delivery operations from distribution centers to customers (Tier2),
- assignment of vehicles to routes and distribution networks (Tier1 and Tier2),

- scheduling of logistics operations of 3PL provider in distribution center – customer relation (Tier 2).

To solve this integrated assignment, scheduling and routing problem of the green distribution network and heuristic algorithms can be used. In the literature, we can find a wide range of heuristic solutions to integrated assignment, scheduling and routing problems [54–56].

4. Numerical example

This part of the chapter demonstrates a short numerical example of the application of the above-mentioned methodology from an assignment problems point of view. In our analyzed distribution system there are four suppliers, two distribution centers, and four customers, as **Figure 10** shows.

The input data of the scenario are shown in the Appendix, as follows:

- locations of suppliers, distribution centers, and suppliers of the scenario analysis (**Table A1** in Appendix A),

- the relative distances among suppliers and distribution centers (**Table A2** in Appendix A),

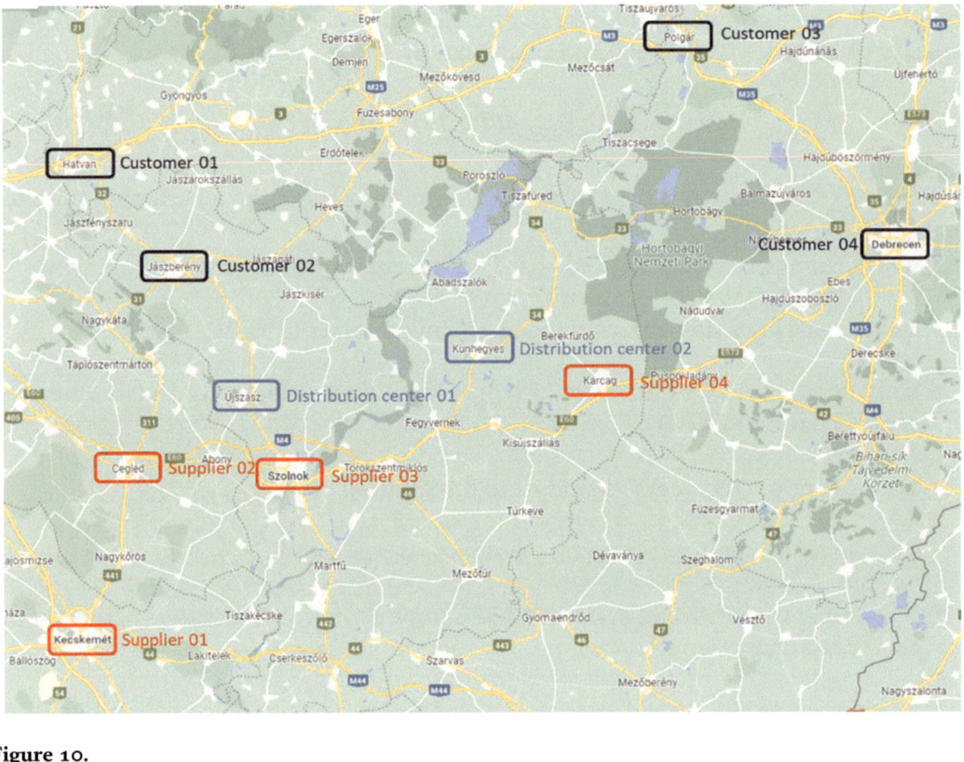

Figure 10.
Locations of suppliers, distribution centers, and suppliers of the scenario analysis (Source: GoogleMaps).

- the relative distances among distribution centers and customers (**Table A3** in Appendix A),
- the customers' demands (**Table A4** in Appendix A),
- the specific transportation cost among suppliers and distribution centers (**Table A5** in Appendix A). The specific transportation cost between distribution centers and customers is 1 EUR/TEU/km.

In the case of a conventional supply chain solution the optimized material handling (transportation) cost is 54,837 EUR, which can be divided into two main parts: the cost among suppliers and distribution centers is 15,537 EUR and the cost among distribution centers and customers is 39,300 EUR. In the case of a cyber-physical system, where all three levels of the supply chain are integrated through the Internet of Things technologies, the material-handling (transportation cost) is 51,929 EUR, which can be divided into two main parts: the cost among suppliers and distribution centers is 21,557 EUR and the cost among distribution centers and customers is 30,372 EUR. It means, that in the case of this simple scenario the total material handling cost can be decreased by 5.30%.

The optimal assignment of supplier and distribution centers with related material flow intensity is shown in **Table 1**, while the optimal assignment of distribution centers and customers is shown in **Table 2**.

	Kecskemét	Cegléd	Szolnok	Karcag
Újszász	30	25	25	0
Kunhegyes	55	65	25	165

Table 1.
The optimal assignment of suppliers and distribution centers with related material flow intensity [TEU/time window].

Distribution center	Customer	Demand 01	Demand 02	Demand 03	Demand 04
Újszász	Hatvan	10	0	15	0
	Jászberény	20	25	10	0
	Polgár	0	0	0	0
	Debrecen	0	0	0	0
Kunhegyes	Hatvan	0	0	0	25
	Jászberény	0	0	0	45
	Polgár	15	45	5	55
	Debrecen	40	20	20	40

Table 2.
The optimal assignment of distribution centers and customers with related material flow intensity in [TEU/time window].

The simplified numerical example shows, that the optimal solution of the integrated system does not lead to decreased costs at all levels of the supply chain, which means that the cyber-physical system focuses on the optimization of the whole system, while in the case of conventional supply chain solutions, the part systems of the supply chain are separately optimized.

5. Discussion and conclusions

The globalization of market processes requires the development of supply chains to meet the increasingly dynamic needs of individual customers with the efficiency of mass production. This means not only increasing the efficiency and flexibility of production processes but also improving related processes such as purchasing and distribution. In addition to increasing efficiency, there is a growing emphasis on the development of "green" systems and "green" solutions to reduce the environmental impact of processes related to meeting market needs.

In this chapter, a systematic literature review is carried out to identify the main lines of research, emphasizing the importance of product development, competitive distribution networks, risk evaluation, application of Industry 4.0 technologies, emission measuring and emission management, and optimization.

Based on the results of this systematic literature review, it is concluded, that using Industry 4.0 technologies, it is possible to transform conventional distribution systems into cyber-physical networks, where smart sensors, edge computing solutions, digital twinning, and discrete event simulation make it possible to coordinate the hyperconnected distribution network based on real-time data and perform a more sophisticated decision-making process. Within the frame of this chapter, a potential approach is described including both the functional model of a cyber-physical distribution network and the mathematical model to optimize the operation from environmental impact point of view.

The described method makes it possible to support managerial decisions, because depending on the results of the optimization different purchasing portfolios can be generated. The described methodology can be used to analyze the potentials of the potential transformation of conventional supply-chain solutions into a cyber-physical supply-chain.

The resources of manufacturing companies and third-party logistics providers are not taken into consideration and the parameters of the distribution network are given as deterministic parameters. These limitations show the directions for further research. In further studies, the model can be extended to a more complex model including resource optimization for manufacturing and logistics services. Second, this study only considered time, capacity, and energy consumption as deterministic parameters. Fuzzy models can be also suitable for the description of a stochastic environment, where capacities and time windows can be taken into consideration as uncertain parameters. This should be also considered in future research.

Conflict of interest

The authors declare no conflict of interest.

A. Input data of the scenario analysis

	Latitude	Longitude
Suppliers		
Kecskemét	46°53′15.9″N	19°40′17.4″E
Cegléd	47°10′15.2″N	19°47′36.7″E
Szolnok	47°09′54.7″N	20°10′32.7″E
Karcag	47°18′35.1″N	20°57′11.8″E
Distribution centers		
Újszász	47°16′17.5″N	20°05′33.2″E
Kunhegyes	47°22′01.7″N	20°39′54.6″E
Customers		
Hatvan	47°41′48.6″N	19°45′59.9″E
Jászberény	47°28′30.4″N	19°52′02.4″E
Polgár	47°52′33.6″N	21°08′46.5″E
Debrecen	47°32′00.7″N	21°38′54.7″E

Table A1.
Locations of suppliers, distribution centers, and suppliers of the scenario analysis.

	Kecskemét	Cegléd	Szolnok	Karcag
Újszász	62.2	29.4	31.7	82.2
Kunhegyes	102.0	81.5	48.8	31.0

Table A2.
The relative distances among suppliers and distribution centers in [km].

	Hatvan	Jászberény	Polgár	Debrecen
Újszász	80.1	35.0	153.0	183.0
Kunhegyes	108.0	82.4	89.4	96.1

Table A3.
The relative distances among distribution centers and customers in [km].

	Demand 01	Demand 02	Demand 03	Demand 04
Hatvan	10	24	9	25
Jászberény	20	25	10	45
Polgár	15	32	5	27
Debrecen	40	20	20	40

Table A4.
The customers' demands in [TEU].

	Kecskemét	Cegléd	Szolnok	Karcag
Újszász	1.100	1.085	1.120	1.150
Kunhegyes	1.200	1.160	0.950	1.050

Table A5.
The specific transportation cost among suppliers and distribution centers in [EUR/TEU/km].

Author details

Ágota Bányai
University of Miskolc, Miskolc, Hungary

*Address all correspondence to: altagota@uni-miskolc.hu

References

[1] Darnall N, Welch E, Cho S. Sustainable supply chains and regulation. In: Sarkis J, editor. Handbook on the Sustainable Supply Chain. Cheltenham, UK: Edward Elgar. Chapter 30. pp. 513-525. DOI: 10.4337/9781786434272

[2] Ala-Harja H, Helo P. Green supply chain decisions—Case-based performance analysis from the food industry. Transportation Research Part E: Logistics and Transportation Review. 2014;**69**:97-107. DOI: 10.1016/j.tre.2014.05.015

[3] Mohtashami Z, Aghsami A, Jolai F. A green closed loop supply chain design using queuing system for reducing environmental impact and energy consumption. Journal of Cleaner Production. 2020;**242**:118452. DOI: 10.1016/j.jclepro.2019.118452

[4] Kim I, Min H. Measuring supply chain efficiency from a green perspective. Management Research Review. 2011;**34**(11):1169-1189. DOI: 10.1108/01409171111178738

[5] Rahimi M, Baboli A, Rekik Y. Multi-objective inventory routing problem: A stochastic model to consider profit, service level and green criteria. Transportation Research Part E: Logistics and Transportation Review. 2017;**101**:59-83. DOI: 10.1016/j.tre.2017.03.001

[6] Khan SAR, Dong Q, Zhang Y, Khan SS. The impact of green supply chain on enterprise performance: In the perspective of China. Journal of Advanced Manufacturing Systems. 2017;**16**(3):263-273. DOI: 10.1142/S0219686717500160

[7] Huang Y, Wang K, Zhang T, Pang C. Green supply chain coordination with greenhouse gases emissions management: A game-theoretic approach. Journal of Cleaner Production. 2016;**112**:2004-2014. DOI: 10.1016/j.jclepro.2015.05.137

[8] Perotti S, Zorzini M, Cagno E, Micheli GJL. Green supply chain practices and company performance: The case of 3PLs in Italy. International Journal of Physical Distribution and Logistics Management. 2012;**42**(7):640-672. DOI: 10.1108/09600031211258138

[9] Wang HF, Hsu HW. A closed-loop logistic model with a spanning-tree based genetic algorithm. Computers and Operations Research. 2010;**37**(2):376-389. DOI: 10.1016/j.cor.2009.06.001

[10] Elhedhli S, Merrick R. Green supply chain network design to reduce carbon emissions. Transportation Research Part D: Transport and Environment. 2012;**17**(5):370-379. DOI: 10.1016/j.trd.2012.02.002

[11] Holt D, Ghobadian A. An empirical study of green supply chain management practices amongst UK manufacturers. Journal of Manufacturing Technology Management. 2009;**20**(7):933-956. DOI: 10.1108/17410380910984212

[12] Li J, Anser MK, Tabash MI, Nassani AA, Haffar M, Zaman K. Technology- and logistics-induced carbon emissions obstructing the Green supply chain management agenda: Evidence from 101 countries. International Journal of Logistics Research and Applications. 2021. DOI: 10.1080/13675567.2021.1985094

[13] Uemura Reche AY, Canciglieri Junior O, Szejka AL, Rudek M. Proposal for a preliminary model of integrated

product development process oriented by green supply chain management. Sustainability (Switzerland). 2022;**14**(4): 2190. DOI: 10.3390/su14042190

[14] Porkar S, Mahdavi I, Maleki Vishkaei B, Hematian M. Green supply chain flow analysis with multi-attribute demand in a multi-period product development environment. Operational Research. 2020;**20**(3):1405-1435. DOI: 10.1007/s12351-018-0382-5

[15] Kulshreshtha, K, Bajpai, N, Tripathi, V, Sharma, G. Consumer preference for eco-friendly appliances in trade-off: A conjoint analysis approach. International Journal of Product Development. 2019; **23**(2-3):212-243

[16] Ricardianto P, Kholdun AI, Fachrey KR, Nofrisel Agusinta L, Setiawan EB, Abidin Z, et al. Building green supply chain management in pharmaceutical companies in Indonesia. Uncertain Supply Chain Management. 2022;**10**(2):453-462

[17] Jolai H, Hafezalkotob A, Reza-Gharehbagh R. Pricing and greening decisions of competitive forward and reverse supply chains under government financial intervention: Iranian motorcycle industry case study. Computers and Industrial Engineering. 2021;**157**:107329. DOI: 10.1016/j.cie.2021.107329

[18] Trujillo-Gallego M, Sarache W, Sellitto MA. Identification of practices that facilitate manufacturing companies' environmental collaboration and their influence on sustainable production. Sustainable Production and Consumption. 2021;**27**:1372-1391. DOI: 10.1016/j.spc.2021.03.009

[19] Yachai K, Kongboon R, Gheewala SH, Sampattagul S. Carbon footprint adaptation on green supply chain and logistics of papaya in Yasothon Province using geographic information system. Journal of Cleaner Production. 2021;**281**:125214. DOI: 10.1016/j.jclepro.2020.125214

[20] Zhang D, Zou F, Li S, Zhou L. Green supply chain network design with economies of scale and environmental concerns. Journal of Advanced Transportation. 2017:6350562. DOI: 10.1155/2017/6350562

[21] Mutingi M. Developing green supply chain management strategies: A taxonomic approach. Journal of Industrial Engineering and Management. 2013;**6**(2):525-546. DOI: 10.3926/jiem.475

[22] Qihao H. Risk evaluation of green agricultural products cold chain logistics from the perspective of ecological economy. Journal of Environmental Protection and Ecology. 2021;**22**(5): 2232-2240

[23] Kazancoglu Y, Kazancoglu I, Sagnak M. Fuzzy DEMATEL-based green supply chain management performance: Application in cement industry. Industrial Management and Data Systems. 2018;**118**(2):412-431. DOI: 10.1108/IMDS-03-2017-0121

[24] Guan Y, Aamir M, Dayo ZA, Rahman Z, Abro WA, Ali I, et al. A coordinated optimization model of the complex system of the green supply chain distribution network. Discrete Dynamics in Nature and Society. 2021:4077151. DOI: 10.1155/2021/4077151

[25] Zhang X, Liu S. Action mechanism and model of cross-border e-commerce green supply chain based on customer behavior. Mathematical Problems in Engineering. 2021:6670308. DOI: 10.1155/2021/6670308

[26] Jandaghi H, Safaei AS, Divsalar A. A bi-objective green multi-period inventory-routing problem with multi-speed vehicles. International Journal of Applied Decision Sciences. 2021;**14**(3): 321-342

[27] Laguir I, Stekelorum R, El Baz J. Going green? Investigating the relationships between proactive environmental strategy, GSCM practices and performances of third-party logistics providers (TPLs). Production Planning and Control. 2021;**32**(13):1049-1062. DOI: 10.1080/09537287.2020.1784483

[28] Jemai J, Chung BD, Sarkar B. Environmental effect for a complex green supply-chain management to control waste: A sustainable approach. Journal of Cleaner Production. 2020;**277**: 122919

[29] Sallnäs U, Björklund M. Consumers' influence on the greening of distribution—Exploring the communication between logistics service providers, e-tailers and consumers. International Journal of Retail and Distribution Management. 2020; **48**(11):1177-1193. DOI: 10.1108/IJRDM-07-2019-0213

[30] Yu C, Sun X, Wang L. Research on mechanism of green supply chain coordination system. International Journal of Applied Environmental Sciences. 2013;**8**(7):841-849

[31] Eldien HH, Gazzeh K, Hammad E. Urban characterization by the green supply chain management concept: A review. International Journal of Supply Chain Management. 2020;**9**(4):962-971

[32] Rajabion L, Khorraminia M, Andjomshoaa A, Ghafouri-Azar M, Molavi H. A new model for assessing the impact of the urban intelligent transportation system, farmers' knowledge and business processes on the success of green supply chain management system for urban distribution of agricultural products. Journal of Retailing and Consumer Services. 2019;**50**:154-162. DOI: 10.1016/j.jretconser.2019.05.007

[33] Benotmane Z, Belalem G, Neki A. Green optimisation for LRP problem using a genetic algorithm and a dynamic island model. International Journal of Advanced Operations Management. 2019;**11**(1–2):46-68. DOI: 10.1504/IJAOM.2019.098523

[34] Rahmandoust A, Soltani R. Designing a location-routing model for cross docking in green supply chain. Uncertain Supply Chain Management. 2019;**7**(1):1-16. DOI: 10.5267/j.uscm.2018.7.001

[35] Tseng SH, Wee HM, Reong S, Wu CI. Considering JIT in assigning task for return vehicle in Green Supply Chain. Sustainability (Switzerland). 2019;**11**(22): 6464. DOI: 10.3390/su11226464

[36] Ismail LB, Alawamleh M, Aladwan K, Alragheb AA. The relationship between green SCM practices and organisational performance: Evidence from Jordanian pharmaceutical manufacturers. International Journal of Logistics Systems and Management. 2019;**34**(2): 172-192. DOI: 10.1504/IJLSM.2019.102209

[37] Bortolini M, Galizia FG, Gamberi M, Mora C, Pilati F. Enhancing stock efficiency and environmental sustainability goals in direct distribution logistic networks. International Journal of Advanced Operations Management. 2019;**11**(1–2):8-25. DOI: 10.1504/IJAOM.2019.098518

[38] Wu C, Barnes D. Partner selection for reverse logistics centres in green

supply chains: A fuzzy artificial immune optimisation approach. Production Planning and Control. 2016;**27**(16): 1356-1372. DOI: 10.1080/09537287.2016.1221159

[39] Lagoudis IN, Shakri AR. A framework for measuring carbon emissions for inbound transportation and distribution networks. Research in Transportation Business and Management. 2015;**17**:53-64. DOI: 10.1016/j.rtbm.2015.11.001

[40] Raghavendra TVS, Hema K, Omkar AMB, Manideep B, Sam Preetish G, Anudeep K. Estimation of carbon foot print in a transport network of supply chain. International Journal of Applied Engineering Research. 2015; **10**(8):19011-19032

[41] Coelho IM, Munhoz PLA, Ochi LS, Souza MJF, Bentes C, Farias R. An integrated CPU-GPU heuristic inspired on variable neighbourhood search for the single vehicle routing problem with deliveries and selective pickups. International Journal of Production Research. 2016;**54**(4):945-962. DOI: 10.1080/00207543.2015.1035811

[42] Xiao N, Rao YL. Multi-product multi-period inventory routing optimization with time window constrains. International Journal of Simulation Modelling. 2016;**15**(2): 352-364. DOI: 10.2507/IJSIMM15(2)CO8

[43] Wanke P, Correa H, Jacob J, Santos T. Including carbon emissions in the planning of logistic networks: A Brazilian case. International Journal of Shipping and Transport Logistics. 2015; **7**(6):655-675. DOI: 10.1504/IJSTL.2015.072681

[44] Jakhar SK. Designing the green supply chain performance optimisation model. Global Journal of Flexible Systems Management. 2014;**15**(3): 235-259. DOI: 10.1007/s40171-014-0069-6

[45] Falatoonitoosi E, Ahmed S, Sorooshian S. A multicriteria framework to evaluate supplier's greenness. Abstract and Applied Analysis. 2014:396923. DOI: 10.1155/2014/396923

[46] Mavi RK, Kazemi S, Najafabadi AF, Mousaabadi HB. Identification and assessment of logistical factors to evaluate a green supplier using the fuzzy logic DEMATEL method. Polish Journal of Environmental Studies. 2013;**22**(2): 445-455

[47] Wu D, Huo J, Zhang G, Zhang W. Minimization of logistics cost and carbon emissions based on quantum particle swarm optimization. Sustainability (Switzerland). 2018;**10**(10):3791. DOI: 10.3390/su10103791

[48] Srivastav S, Garg V, Tiwari P. The study to analyze the impact of green supply chain management in India. International Journal of Supply Chain Management. 2019;**8**(3):1033-1038

[49] Danloup N, Mirzabeiki V, Allaoui H, Goncalves G, Julien D, Mena C. Reducing transportation greenhouse gas emissions with collaborative distribution: A case study. Management Research Review. 2015;**38**(10): 1049-1067. DOI: 10.1108/MRR-11-2014-0262

[50] Sellitto MA, Bittencourt SA, Reckziegel BI. Evaluating the implementation of GSCM in industrial supply chains: Two cases in the automotive industry. Chemical Engineering Transactions. 2015;**43**: 1315-1320. DOI: 10.3303/CET1543220

[51] Opetuk T, Zolo I, Dukic G. Greening elements in the distribution networks.

Journal of Industrial Engineering and Management. 2010;**3**(2):353-369. DOI: 10.3926/jiem.2010.v3n2

[52] Tirkolaee EB, Dashtian Z, Weber GW, Tomaskova H, Soltani M, Mousavi NS. An integrated decision-making approach for green supplier selection in an agri-food supply chain: Threshold of robustness worthiness. Mathematics. 2021;**9**(11):1304. DOI: 10.3390/math9111304

[53] Tirkolaee EB, Goli A, Ghasemi P, Goodarzian F. Designing a sustainable closed-loop supply chain network of face masks during the COVID-19 pandemic: Pareto-based algorithms. Journal of Cleaner Production. 2022;**333**:130056. DOI: 10.1016/j.jclepro.2021.130056

[54] Matyi H, Veres P, Banyai T, Demin V, Tamas P. Digitalization in Industry 4.0: The role of mobile devices. Journal of Production Engineering. 2020; **23**(1):75-78. DOI: 10.24867/JPE-2020-01-075

[55] Veres P, Illés B, Bányai T. Integrated assignment and facility location approach based on black hole optimization. Academic Journal of Manufacturing Engineering. 2019;**17**(2): 66-71

[56] Veres P, Illés B, Landschützer C. Supply chain optimization in automotive industry: A comparative analysis of evolutionary and swarming heuristics. Lecture Notes in Mechanical Engineering. 2018:666-676. DOI: 10.1007/978-3-319-75677-6_57

Chapter 11

Sustainable and Efficient City Logistics

Shahrin Nasir

Abstract

This article is discussing the basic trend and challenges in city logistics operations. The role of each actor in city logistics has been highlighted. The actors have enabled city logistics to generates the main benefits for the city logistics operations need to focus. Critical trends and challenges that contributed towards city logistics development has shown that city logistics efficiency need to be addressed to ensure sustainable impact to the cities. Different approaches in making the city logistics operations were implemented to ensure that the customers get their possession according to the stipulated time. The usage of new technology has also assisted in enhancing the efficiency of city logistics deliveries. By providing the right strategies, the objective of achieving sustainable city logistics can be obtained.

Keywords: sustainability, trends, challenges, efficient, city logistics

1. Introduction

The city logistics has become an important development in urban freight development. With the numbers of trucks keep on increasing, the congestions become much worst and the environment also become deteriorate. City logistics enable to achieve the efficiency of delivery system in the city center. One of the main focus of city logistics is sustainability. Green logistics and reverse logistics are the main focus of the concept. City logistics need to serve varieties of customers which stays in different kind of environments. Other types of facilities available in the cities also need to serve. The complexity of city environment has made the logistics services much more complicated and difficult to arrange [1]. Delivering perishables item to the city center would require the delivery being done in a short period of time. Frequent and adequate delivery services must be made available to ensure that the citizen can be served properly. Logistics delivery in the cities need to adhere to the restriction of truck movement during a specified time. Even though such regulation may restrict the delivery process, but it needs to take into considerations for the logistics delivery to be much more efficient and effective. City logistics have to plan strategically in order to achieve the economic gain in sustaining the environmental aspects of the cities.

In 2020, the urban world populations are 56%. More than half of the world populations is residing in the city area. Almost 68% of the upper middle-income group is staying in the urban area. European Union enjoy among the highest population in the urban area with 81% of its populations. However, in developing countries, the populations that lives in the urban areas is around 35–45% of the populations are residing in the urban areas. The world bank data shown that many people are preferring to stay in the urban area hence the city logistics has become important to fulfill the needs of its residents [2]. The rapid growth of cities in the world has contributed towards the increase challenges in logistics operations. It was argued the big cities population has made the logistics operations much more difficult than other cities [3].

2. Actors in city logistics

Actors involve in city logistics can be categorized as follows: (a) shippers, (b) freight carriers, (c) receivers (d) residents, (e) other road users and (f) administrators [4]. The actors can be further divided into private and public sector. The public sector usually is the government administrators either the national or local government. The shippers, freight carries and residents can be considered as the private group [5]. Each of these actors has their own interest and responsibilities. There are differences between these actors and it need to be considered in planning for the city logistics activities. Shippers can be categorized as retailers, wholesalers and manufacturers. Shippers would require a high frequency of deliveries in order to meet the objectives of the company. In order to meet the objectives, shippers would require a quality service from the freight carriers. Shippers would inform the required delivery time however the service providers would determine the timing and routing for the delivery. The service providers need to consider many factors especially the delivery windows set by the receivers and also to adhere any restrictions imposed in the city center. It is a complex task for the service providers since they have to fulfill the needs of both suppliers and also the receivers [6]. The service provider would focus on reducing the operating costs while making any delivering and collecting of cargo in the city center. Even though obtaining a high profit might be the main objectives of services providers, they would not compromise with the service quality provided to their customers. The citizen who stays in the cities would definitely would like to experience less trucks operations in the city thus would be able to reduce the congestions and also the pollution in the cities. The citizen would love to control the externalities for a sustainable city. The receivers would set an agreement with the service providers in determining the time for delivery to their premises. The main determination of the receivers is to receive the goods on time, with reliable, cheap safe and door to door service. The government need to establish policies that not only acceptable to the citizen but also to the shippers and also service providers. The government have to consider all the actors before implementing those policies since it would have impact to the actors. On the hand, the actors and the government involve have to work together to ensure that the city logistics operations would be at the acceptable level of service and costs, so that it would remain competitive and also sustainable for the cities. Addressing the environmental impact such as congestions and pollution need to be the main concern of the actors in ensuring a sustainable city logistics operation.

The main focus for every actor in relation to the city logistics are totally different form one and another since every approach taken have contribute to the logistics activities [7]. The public sector main focus would to reduce the pollution, congestions and also to improve the road safety in the city centre since many freight vehicles moves in the city [8]. The shippers would focus on service efficiency and reliability [9]. As for the receivers in the city center mainly would like to have a comfortable and sustainable living environment with less hassle in moving in the city. The freight carriers need to reduce the cost of the deliveries and at the same time developing new distribution network for more efficient operations [10].

With the different stakeholders in the city logistics operations, it is important to discuss the objectives while planning for city logistics operations. The objectives can be divided into (a) public objectives and (b) private objectives [11]. The public objectives are concerned in ensuring the public needs are being taken care and the city logistics operations would affects their quality of life. The public objectives also looking into the economics sustainability. The private objectives which usually covers the need of the shipplers and service providers would be focusing on the operations efficiency and also ensuring the they would be albe to increase their profits. The different objectives have made it difficult to developed a policy which would fulfill the interests of all stakeholders [12]. To develop the right strategies, all the stakeholders have to work together in finding and implementing strategies that would benefits all stakeholders. They must be involved in every stage of strategies development so that whatever understanding and concern they have can be embedded in the strategies. By working together, the public and private objectives can be comprehended to ensure the urban mobility environmental sustainability and economic sustainability can be achieved. The stakeholders have an effect towards each other. Hence it is critical to ensure the balance between the different requirement of each actor.

3. Trends and conditions of city logistics

3.1 New platform in commercial business

The development of e-commerce has changed the supply chain than logistics design in the city. Before e-commerce, the turnover of inventory is longer and can easily be predicted. E-commerce has changed the expectation of the receivers in the city center. E-commerce has changed the way for the traditional retail business to increase their profit [13]. It has also urged the retail company to sought for a new and more dynamic business models in order to their business to be more sustainable. UNCTAD estimated e commerce sales at $25.6 trillion in 2018, increased by 8% compare to the year 2017. The development of digital business and solutions contributed towards these figures. The biggest countries with the highest sales in e commerce business are the United States of America, China and United Kingdom. From that figure the e commerce value for B2C e commerce sales was $4.4 trillion which representing 17% of the total e commerce sales. Compared to $1.9 trillion in 2014. It was estimated more than 1.4 billion people shopped online and it comes from all parts of the world [14]. With these numbers, it has become very much more critical for the citizen to be more involve in determining the city logistics concept in their respective cities. Price, quality of service time and other quality aspects need to be focus especially for the last mile delivery in the city center [15]. With the current trends, it is expected the last mile delivery to consumes residents will become very much more important comparing to the delivery process to the retail outlet in the city center. Small parcel delivery will be more significant with the need to have small trucks, van or motorcycle for deliveries and more frequent delivery would be the new trends in last mile deliveries.

3.2 Timely delivery

Quick and fast delivery has become critical and the service providers need to adapt to the changes of the supply chain, Many service providers need to offer 1 day delivery service in order to fulfill the customer requirements. Operational excellence has become important in supporting the ecommerce development. The logistics services need to be closer to citizen population. The traditional logistics services need to change to be more dynamic to service the citizen [16]. The traditional supply chain would deal with a longer inventory replenishment. With the younger generation dominating the cities, more online shopping has occurred and they really needed the quick and fact delivery from the service providers. With many cities has increase the speed of its internet connection, the online shopping also has increased gradually [15]. The last mile delivery is made either to the home of office of the receivers. This has made the service providers need to delivered the goods to different buildings and environments which has required them to change some of the traditional delivery methods.

3.3 Economic view

The development of technology and apps has made sharing economy become an important element in city logistics development. A shared economy model allows consumers to share creation, production, distribution, trade, and consumption of goods and services [17]. The main element in economic sharing is mutual cooperation. With the development of digital approaches especially with the introduction of apps, it has allowed everyone to be connected which enable them to share either service or products. E-hailing and p-hailing (parcel hailing) services are the examples of economic sharing model which has so successful for the past 5 years. The users use the platform to orders a service from a supplier or food provider and a third party perform the delivery which being chosen from the app's platform itself. In some occasion, the services can be share between different users for split the cost of using the services [16].

Two important differences in performing the sharing economy model are collaborative consumption and collaborative business [15]. Collaborative consumptions is a process where people share the access to products or services without having to own the product or services. This can be done by using the platform provided by the internet. In other perspective Collaborative consumption can be defined as the peer-to-peer-based activity of getting, providing, or sharing the accessibility to goods and services, through a coordinated community-based online services [18]. As for collaborative business, it focusing on sharing the same infrastructure and services with its competitors. Again, with the usage of technology, the logistics providers are able to share any available assets and capacities among the competitors in order to give more options to the customers [19]. Sharing of resources would need a greater requirement for consolidation of goods and this will enhance the percentage of capacity utilization. This sharing concept can reduce the number of cargo movements, number of fleets required and also to reduce the empty leg journey between the participating logistics providers. The new economic concept would base to the on-demand concept and efficient usage of internet will allow to match the demand and supplier in more effective manner. The concept of making the service to be available instantly can be achieved [20].

The firm involving with the total supply chain have to alert with the new trends that might be available in the near future. Since the Covid 19 pandemic in the beginning of 2020, many new trends have taken place. Pharmaceutical product such as self-test kit for detecting Covid 19 has become a critical product in many cities and countries. To ensure the sustainability of the city logistics operations, aggressive information collection on the new activities that has an impact towards the customer buying behavior have to be identified. The new buying behavior would be the new trend to ensure the sustainability of city logistics services. Failure to understand the new trend in purchasing power of the customers, would delay the improvement that city logistics operators need to implement. Hence it would affect the sustainability of the city logistics operations itself.

4. Challenges of city logistics

Cities all around the world needs to protect the sustainability of its cities. The logistics regulations and polices implemented usually would be looking into solving these challenges which are environmental sustainability, social sustainability and economical sustainability [6]. The environmental sustainability is on air pollution, social sustainability are the fatalities, noise road safety and economical sustainability is about unreliable services and delivery delays. Improving the efficiency for the goods movements has been the main focus of city logistics. City logistics has an affect towards the citizen living in the cities such as accidents and pollutions, the service providers which reducing their revenue because of the restrictions of movements and the world, based on the contribution of transport to global warming [21]. Restrictions on trucks in the city center has been one of the most effectives ways to reduce the challenges in the city. The restrictions are seen as the best way to reducing number of trucks during the peak period hence would help in alleviating the pollution. It has also avoided the trucks to compete with other modes in using the limited space available. However, this restriction has also impeded the trucks operations which would jeopardize the service level of the service providers hence would affect the delivery time to the citizen.

The last delivery to the receivers is known as the last mile delivery. Apart from the sustainable challenges, city logistics also need to deal with the last mile problems. The receivers might receive many deliveries per day. This would create a difficult delivery process. The receivers may receive its goods from several vendors, if consolidation between vendors can be done, it would reduce the number of deliveries to the respective receivers. Restrictions on deliveries has also created many challenges in city logistics operations. Many receivers would not approve if the deliveries to be made at night, thus this would increase the number of congestions during peak period during the day [22]. If the receivers are at home, the delivery might be inefficient since the delivery involve small parcels. However, with the development of ecommerce, small parcel deliveries have become very much critical.

The most crucial challenges in city logistics are the restrictions that have to be obeyed by the logistics service providers. The focus is to ensure the effective movement for the last and first mile delivery [23]. A lot of rules, regulations and restrictions need to be adhered by any service providers. Failure to fulfill these set of regulations will affect the city logistics deliveries. The regulations would different from one city to another [24]. However, the comments challenges are the window for making the deliveries, green zone area, predestination or active transport zone areas and much ore. This would make some destinations not accessible for the service providers. To ensure the last mile deliveries can be performed efficiently, the service providers need to consider the diversity of the receivers in the city centre. Different types of houses, office locations and industrial areas has enhanced the complexity of deliveries [11]. The last deliveries to the inner cities have become very much difficult due to the restrictions and it requires small parcels to be delivered more frequently in order to fulfill the demand.

The main challenges in providing city logistics deliveries are to ensure that the unsustainable impact can be minimize. However, transport and logistics has always been known has a negative impact on sustainability aspects. The negative impacts usually go the environmental issues. The environmental issues lie on people, profit and planet [11]. With many actors involves in the city logistics activities, many conflicting decisions on its operations may arises. Traffic congestions, pollutions and noise might have a severe effect on people in the cities. The restrictions on regulations for the deliveries will have an impact towards the efficiency of deliveries which will reduce the profitability of the service providers and the planet will be affected through the global warming and pollutions [25]. The diversity of actors in city logistics operations has indicated the differences on the needs of each actor in making the cities more sustainable. The administrators' main objective is to develop and maintain a livable city. Reducing the traffic congestions, reducing the air pollutions and reducing the noise level are the main target of the administrators. So, the regulations and restrictions implemented is to achieve the objectives. As for the carriers and logistics providers, their main objective to ensure the delivery of products can be done as efficiently as possible. They need to plan the deliveries according the regulations and restriction imposed by the administrators of the cities. With different regulations in different cities, the utilization of the capacity of the vehicles used may have an impact towards planning the delivery operations. Hence, the cost of delivery also may increase [26, 27]. The shippers would definitely need their product to be delivered on time since this will enhance the image of the shippers. The receivers of the city logistics service would require a reliable and efficient logistics service providers to delivery their products but with a minimum disruption to the environment. The other residents need to have a city with less pollutions and acceptable noise level from the transport that make the deliveries.

Another main challenge in city logistics is to understand the changes in consumer behavior. It is critical to understand consumer behavior since it consists of how the consumers choose and set priority on the products or services they consume. With the e-commerce has become an important trend in city logistics, it has increased the globalizations aspects of products that reach in any cities. Technology and the internet have changed the consumer behavior. Ordering process can be done at any time and any place [28]. The deliveries are expected to be done as quickly as possible. Thus, this has made the increase of demand which requires a flexibility in supply of the product. The e-commerce has demanded a new distribution channel and the last mile distribution has become very much complex and need to handle in effective manner. The number of parcel delivery logistics companies has been increasing since the rapid development of the usage of internet. This has also changed the type of product being delivery through this company. Food and groceries have been included in the last mile deliveries of city logistics which previously more focus on books, clothing and appliances.

With these challenges, the city logistics need to ensure that the policy that supports the operations of the trends need to be available. The administrator of the cities needs to carefully plan the type of policy that have to be updated. In certain situation, some new policies might need to be introduced to ensure that the city could support the new trend development. For the city to be sustainable, new logistics operations approaches have to be in place since the new trends might require a fresh type of logistics handling. The sustainability aspects are not only for the city logistics operators but also for the receivers benefits since the operations of city logistics would depends on the continuous buying from the receivers in the city center. The policy and regulations need to benefit not only the city logistics operators but also to the receivers. If the receivers are not satisfied with the services provided, repeat purchase might now happened and it would affect the sustainability of the city logistics operations.

5. Facilities in city logistics

Logistics facilities can be categorized as any buildings that is used for storage and warehousing activities. These facilities need to have a good accessibility infrastructure, in order words the buildings need to close to transport infrastructure. As for city logistics, it needs to be close with road network [29]. With the rapid development in city logistics operations, the density city of the warehouse is varying. It could be a huge building to a small office just to cater for a specific area for deliveries. The huge warehouse facilities usually located at the outskirt of the urban areas. This would enable the sorting and consolidating activities to be conducted. Then the service providers would establish a smaller office for the delivery of the specific locations. The hub for these areas has been developed in order to have a more effective delivery system [30]. The hub and spoke concept have been one of the concepts for the delivery process. **Figure 1** illustrate the hub and spoke concept for the delivery in the city center.

The main different these hubs facilities are the size of the hub. Since city logistics would require delivery to houses and offices, the last mile deliveries usually would focus on van or motorcycles. The deliveries from the hub and the city hub would be done by trucks. The city hubs would be located at the outskirt of the cities. It would help the hub to determine the right city hub to be delivered to [1]. Parcel hub need to be located as close as possible to the receivers. Since it is located in the city itself, the parcel hub usually would small in size due to the cost of land or owning the building.

Smaller local distribution centers like the parcel hub can ensure the receivers to get their cargo faster and efficiently. Based on the **Figure 1**, the last mile delivery from the parcel hub to the receivers would be the important link to complete the supply chain. The last mile delivery has become more varieties nowadays. The last deliveries are no longer to house of office premises, but there are also box facilities which can be located strategically. The box facilities or also known as parcel lockers could basically a short-term solution for the delivery to be made to places where the receivers are not available at a particular time The box facilities can be located at strategic places such as petrol stations or supermarket nearby by to the residents' houses. This would definitely reduce the problems in the last mile deliveries [31]. These boxes would enhance the contactless deliveries especially during the COVID 19 pandemic since its outbreak in end of 2019. However, the use the boxes facilities, the logistics service providers need to informed the receivers. The main communication tools would be through the mobile phones which and application (apps) can be developed for the communications between the relevant parties. Self-pickup points from e-commerce purchases have also become very much common nowadays. Even though it not a new

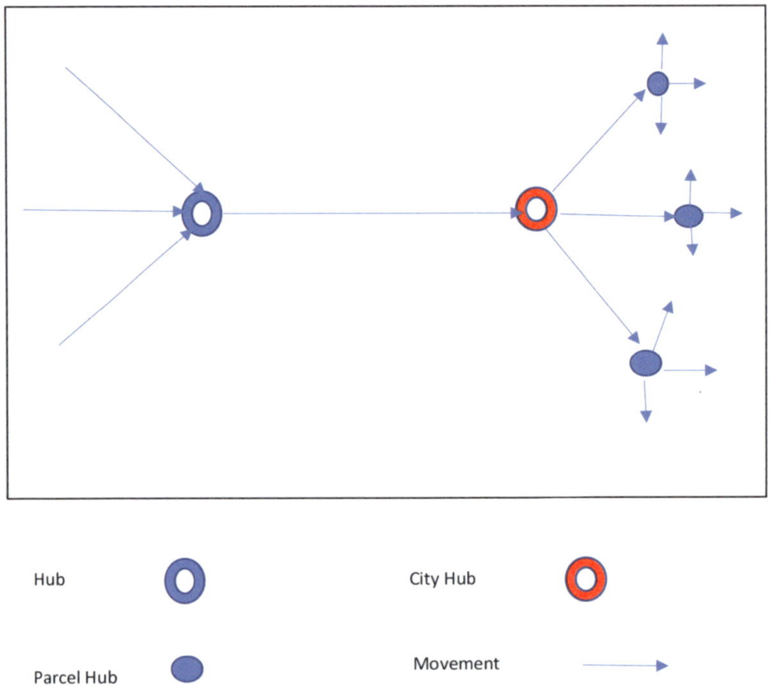

Figure 1.
Hub and spoke concept for city delivery.

trend in delivering products, this would reduce the number of products not being delivered. The self-pickup point also should be located near to residents' populations [32]. With the growing numbers of self-pickup points, the logistics service providers need to ensure that the mobility and accessibility of the self-pickup points so that the delivery can be done efficiently. In countries such as Germany and France, almost 20% of parcel deliveries, 91% of the populations have the access to the self-pickup points within 10 minutes of their houses [28].

6. City logistics: moving forward

The city logistics efficiency would highly be depending on the efficiency of the last mile delivery. The receivers in the city need to have quick, easy services and the service providers have to fulfill these requirements to remain competitive in the industry. The usage of the latest technology has been seen as one of the tools for the service providers to have competitive advantage in the business. The technology enables the service provider to obtain as much relevant data as possible and analyze the data in order to make improvements in their services. The big data concept has help service providers to understand the requirements of the customer much better. Technology would enable receivers to enjoy real time tracking information, monitoring the movements of cargo, can receive information if delay occurs and other relevant information which would make the receivers feels that the cargo is always with them all the time [16]. New services can be introduced by using technology for examples crowdsourcing from drivers can be done and this would assist small companies to compete with huge organization.

As the main objectives of city logistics is to remain the sustainability of the city, a few strategies can be implemented to help to sustain the environment. Introducing a specific requirement on type of trucks that can operate in the city center can be one of the approaches [21]. Trucks which fulfill the requirements will be given some identification so that they can operates in the city center. Apart from that developed specific regulations to manage urban freight movements should be in place. By managing the urban logistics, freight deliveries can be effectively rather than implementing strict restrictions for the deliveries. New zoning system can be incorporated to manage the freight deliveries. Locating the right locations for urban distribution center and also parking area can assists the effectiveness of the last mile deliveries. By having pick up and drop off boxes in strategic area, can reduce the number deliveries to houses and also office premises. This means the need of consolidating the cargo need to done and the concept of parcel hub before the last mile delivery process can be done successfully. Another difficult task to perform but will provide good result is encouraging deliveries during off peak period. This means the services providers need to change its operations time. However, this need to be agreed between the service providers and also the receivers. This approach can be effective if the government provide incentives not only to the service providers but also to the receivers as well.

The new strategies in the city logistics, could be more effective and efficient with the introduction of the new technologies to support the changes. The development of IR4.0 has made city logistics very much vulnerable to changes. City logistics need to embrace digital changes for the operations to be very much efficient. It is well known that big data, automation and digital connectivity has become the new crucial way in performing excellent city logistics operations [16]. The acceleration of cargo volume, velocity, the differences in real-time data which continuing very high important information has become the main focus. With this acceleration, the need to change all the data in meaningful decision making has become a reality and a critical technological enhancement to improve city logistics [33].

City logistics requires innovation in delivering and receiving of cargo if the new strategies implementation to be successful. A synchronous movement of cargo by separating the delivery time from the time cargo receive by customers. With development of IR4.0, automated and autonomous delivery system in the city logistics operations has been developed rapidly. The delivery by using drones, droids and automatic vehicles has been connected with automation efforts. Drones has been one of the latest approaches in making delivery in the city environments. It has been proven that drones are able to reduce the $C0_2$ emission in the city center [34]. However, to make drones delivery very much more practical, and integrated movement between road vehicles such as van and small trucks would enhance the efficiency of city logistics delivery since drones can be used for the definite last mile delivery. Even though drones can be seen as an interesting way of performing the very last mile delivery, there a few challenges that the drone's operators need to overcome. One of the problems, drones could be efficient for a very small package delivery. Ina research study, a number of 16 drones are needed to make a delivery for a van operation. Apart from that, a minimum space for landing and take-off must be available at the receivers' locations. If the receivers live in high rise apartment, this space might not be available. Other issues also need to adhere such as the security aspects, noise pollution, changing the current air space regulation and difficult to operation during bad weather could jeopardize the efficient operations of drones [35].

Apart from drones for the last mile delivery, many firms have the initiates to introduce road base autonomous vehicle deliveries or AVs. Many studies have been conducted to deliver different kind of product from pizza, grocery and medical supplies. Many types of AVs have been develop [36, 37]. These new delivery systems are estimated to reduce the delivery costs by 50% also and reduce congestions by 4% since the AVs are able to provide with better driving attitude with a good navigation system [38]. The usage of robot has also been another new technology alternatives in making deliveries. Is has also reduce the number of environmental issues, Congestions and also the delivery cost.

All the new digital technology implemented for making last mile delivery has shown that it will help to make the city center more sustainable. Air pollution, noise pollution, congestions and also cost of operations has been indicated can be reduced by using these new technologies. However, the initial cost of capital needs to plan so that the cost is not too expensive for the operators and firm to invest since it would attract more company to invest on the new digital system if the initial cost is not too high. This would be crucial for cities that are located in developing countries since capital investment will be one of the important criteria to make the investment decision, even though the system will benefit the firm operations in the long run. For the automation to successfully implemented in the city logistics operations, the development of internet of Things need to in place. IoT would enable cloud computing, artificial intelligent and data collection to assists the city logistics operations. These new technologies would ensure the real time information analysis can be further used in city logistics operations [39].

A new concept in introducing Interconnected City Logistics has the aim to improve economic, environmental and societal efficiency. The concept of Interconnected city logistics is supported by the physical internet. Physical Internet is aspired by the internet itself where information and communication technology help data to travel as quickly as possible. Physical internet is developed by redesigning the logistics activities which suites the efficiency and sustainability challenges [40]. Interconnected City logistics is focusing on nine core concepts. These concepts need to synthesize with the digitalization to make is more successful. The core concept is [41]:

a. cities as nodes of the world's logistics web

b. cities by system standardization

c. the multi-faceted activities of city logistics

d. city logistics networks in a city web architecture

e. the multiplicity of urban logistics centre

f. city logistics stakeholders into an open system

g. goods through modular logistics containers

h. people mobility and freight logistics in the city

i. city logistics with urban planning

One of the tools to ensure this concept is successful implemented is the usage of internet of things. Digital platforms need to be available to ensure that the connectivity is efficient which would assist in making better decision regarding city logistics delivery in the digitalization era.

7. Conclusion

Sustainable city logistics has become a global challenge. A good operations and management of city logistics has been a great important in many cities. Rapid growth of the population, increasing online business and more complex logistics demand had contributed to the enhancement of city logistics challenges. The development in social, environmental and economic has also contribute towards the city logistics activities. The new trend and challenges have challenged the capabilities of the city logistics providers to meet the new demand from the customers in the city center. Last mile delivery has undergone new changes and local parcel hub has become more desirable for deliveries since the receivers are not at home especially during weekdays delivery. The need to cater for the new demand has made the logistics operators to be more agile in making the last mile delivery.

With the new developments, new infrastructure and better utilization of space in the city center need to be upgraded. If this focus not been addressed, it would affect the efficiency of the logistics activities such as the, loading g and unloading activities for the last mile deliveries. The implemented of smart technology could assists in enhancing the efficiency of the city logistics operations. Internet of things (IoT) artificial intelligent, drone deliveries and other relevant technologies need to be the important investment for the logistics operators to operate efficiently in the city center. Apart from technology, the collaboration between the actors in the city logistics operators also be the main factors from the success of city logistics.

Author details

Shahrin Nasir
Faculty of Business and Management, Universiti Teknologi MARA, Puncak Alam Campus, Bandar Puncak Alam, Selangor, Malaysia

*Address all correspondence to: shahrin378@uitm.edu.my

References

[1] CBRE Research. Last Mile/City Logistics Global Industrial & Logistics. 2017

[2] Tadros W, Naguib S, Anna W, Das Maitreyi B, Nic P, Severine D'AO, et al. Demographic Trends and Urbanisation (English). Washington DC: World Bank Group; 2018

[3] Blanco E, Fransoo JC. Reaching 50 million nanostores: Retail distribution in emerging megacities. In: Beta Working Paper Series. Vol. 404. Eindhoven: Technische Universiteit; 2014

[4] Lindholm M, Behrends S. Challenges in urban freight transport planning a review in the Baltic sea region. Journal of Transport Geography. 2012;**22**:129-136

[5] Lindholm ME, Browne M. Freight quality partnerships around the world, 1st report on a survey. In: VREF Center of Excellence for Sustainable Urban Freight Systems. Sweden, UK: Chalmers University, University of Westminster; 2014

[6] Hussein S. Lidasan city logistics: Policy measures aimed at improving urban environment through organization and efficiency in urban logistics systems in Asia. Transport and Communications Bulletin for Asia and the Pacific. 2011;**80**:84-99

[7] Katsela K, Browne M. Importance of the stakeholders' interaction: Comparative, longitudinal study of two city logistics initiatives. Sustainability. 2019;**11**(20):5844. DOI: 10.3390/su11205844

[8] Pimentel C, Alvelos F. Integrated urban freight logistics combining passenger and freight flows – mathematical model proposal. Transportation Research Procedia. 2018;**30**:80-89. DOI: 10.1016/j.trpro.2018.09.010. ISSN 2352-1465

[9] Carbone V, Rouquet A, Roussat C. The rise of crowd logistics: A new way to co-create logistics value. The Journal of Business Logistics. 2017;**38**(4):238-252

[10] Quak HJ. Access restrictions and local authorities' city logistics regulation in urban areas. In: Taniguchi E, Thompson RG, editors. City Logistics: Mapping the Future. USA: CRC; 2014. pp. 177-199

[11] Macharis C, Melo S. City Distribution and Urban Freight Transport: Multiple Perspectives. UK: Edward Elgar Publishing—Business & Economics; 2011

[12] Hensher DA, Brewer AM. Developing a freight strategy: The use of a collaborative learning process to secure stakeholder input. Transport Policy. 2001;**8**:1, 1-10. ISSN 0967-070X. DOI: 10.1016/S0967-070X(00)00031-7

[13] Cap Gemini. Evolving E-Commerce Market Dynamics. Cap Gemini; 2013. Available from: https://www.capgemini.com/resource-file-access/resource/pdf/evolving_e-commerce_market_dynamics.pdf

[14] Available from: https://unctad.org/press-material/global-e-commerce-hits-256-trillion-latest-unctad-estimates

[15] Bensinger G. DHL. Logistics Trend Radar: Delivering insight today. Creating value tomorrow! UK: DHL; 2014

[16] Savelsbergh MWP, van Woensel T, Stewart HM. City logistics: Challenges and opportunities. Transportation Science. 2016;**50**(2):579-590

[17] Available from: https://onlinemba.wsu.edu/blog/yours-mine-and-ours-how-the-sharing-economy-is-transforming-business/

[18] Hamari J, Sjöklint M, Ukkonen A. The sharing economy: Why people participate in collaborative consumption. Journal of the Association for Information Science and Technology. 2016;**67**(9):2047-2059

[19] Matzler K, Veider V, Kathan W. Adapting to the sharing economy. MIT Sloan Management Review. 2015;**56**:71-77

[20] Arvianto A, Sopha BM, Asih AMS, Imron MA. City logistics challenges and innovative solutions in developed and developing economies: A systematic literature review. International Journal of Engineering Business Management. 2021;**13**:1-18

[21] Genevieve G, Thomas O'B, Laetitia D, Kevin H, National Academies of Sciences, Engineering, and Medicine. Synthesis of Freight Research in Urban Transportation Planning. Washington, DC: The National Academies Press; 2013. DOI: 10.17226/22573

[22] Xing Y, Grant D, McKinnon AC, Fernie J. Physical distribution service quality in online retailing. International Journal of Physical Distribution and Logistics Management. 2010;**40**(5):415-432

[23] European Commission. A call to action on urban logistics. SWD 524 final. Brussels: European Commission; 2013. pp. 1-10

[24] Dallasega P, Stecher T, Rauch E, Mat DT. Sustainable city logistics through shared resource concepts. In: Proceedings of the International Conference on Industrial Engineering and Operations Management Bandung; March 6-8; Indonesia; 2018

[25] Browne M, Allen J. The impact of sustainability policies on urban freight transport and logistics systems. In: Meermans H, Van de Voorde E, Winkelmans W. 8th World Conference on Transport Research (WCTR). Volume 1-Transport Modes and Systems. Antwerp: Elsevier; 1999. pp. 505-518

[26] Quak HJ, De Koster MBM. Delivering in urban areas – how to deal with urban p olicy restrictions and the environment. Transportation Science. 2009;**43**(2):211-227

[27] Quak HJ, Van Duin JHR, Visser J. City logistics over the years... lessons learned, research directions and interests. In: Taniguchi E, Thompson RG, editors. Innovations in City Logistics. New York: Nova Science Publisher; 2008. pp. 37-54

[28] Kaufa S. City logistics—a strategic element of sustainable urban development. Transportation Research Procedia. 2016;**16**:158-164

[29] Heitz A, Launay P, Beziat A. Heterogeneity of logistics facilities: An issue for a better understanding and planning of the location of logistics facilities. European Transport Research Review. 2019;**11**:5. DOI: 10.1186/s12544-018-0341-5

[30] Merenne-Schoumaker B. La localisation des industries. In: Enjeux et dynamiques. Rennes: Presse Universitaire de Rennes; 2011

[31] Klauenberg J, Elsner L-A, Knischewski C. Dynamics in the Spatial Distribution of Hubs in Groupage Networks—The Case of Berlin. Shanghai: World Conference on Transport Research—WCTR; 2016

[32] Morganti E, Seidel S, Blanquart C, Dablanc L, Lenz B. The impact of E-commerce on final deliveries:

Alternative parcel delivery services in France and Germany. Transportation Research Procedia. 2014;**4**:178-190

[33] OECD. Data-Driven Innovation: Big Data for Growth and Well-Being. Paris: OECD Publishing; 2015

[34] Goodchild A, Toy J. Delivery by drone: An evaluation of unmanned aerial vehicle technology in reducing CO_2 emissions in the delivery service industry. Transportation Research Part D: Transport and Environment. 2018;**61**:58-67. DOI: 10.1016/j.trd.2017.02.017

[35] Paddeu D, Calvert T, Clark B, Parkhurst G. New Technology and Automation in Freight Transport and Handling Systems. Bristol: University of the West of England; 2019

[36] Paddeu D, Parkhurst G. The potential for automation to transform urban deliveries: Drivers, barriers and policy priorities. In: Advances in Transport Policy and Planning. 1st ed. Vol. 5. UK: Elsevier Inc.; 2020. DOI: 10.1016/bs.atpp.2020.01.003

[37] Bouton S, Hannon E, Haydamous L, Heid B, Knupfer S, Naucler T, et al. An Integrated Perspective on the Future of Mobility, Part 2: Transforming Urban Delivery. Chicago: McKinsey & Company; 2017. p. 48

[38] World Economic Forum. The Future of the Last-Mile Ecosystem. 2020

[39] DHL. Shortening the Last Mile: Winning Logistics Strategies in the Race to the Urban Consumer. Deutsche Post DHL Group; 2018. pp. 1-24. Available from: https://www.logistics.dhl/content/dam/dhl/local/global/core/documents/pdf/g0-core-wp-shortening-thelast-mile-en.pdf

[40] Bektas T, Crainic TG, Woensel TV. From Managing Urban Freight to Smart City Logistics Network. Canada: CIRRELT; 2015

[41] Crainic TG, Montreuil B. Physical Internet Enabled Interconnected City Logistics. Canada: CIRRELT; 2015